The Social Construction of International News

THE SOCIAL CONSTRUCTION OF INTERNATIONAL NEWS

We're Talking about Them, They're Talking about Us

PHILO C. WASBURN

Praeger Series in Political Communication

Westport, Connecticut
London

Library of Congress Cataloging-in-Publication Data

Wasburn, Philo C.
    The social construction of international news : we're talking about them,
they're talking about us / Philo C. Wasburn.
        p. cm. — (Praeger series in political communication, ISSN 1062-5623)
    Includes bibliographical references and indexes.
    ISBN 0-275-97810-9 (alk. paper)
        1. Foreign news. I. Title. II. Series.

    PN4784.F6 W35 2002
    070.4′332—dc21   2002067934

British Library Cataloguing in Publication Data is available.

Library of Congress Catalog Card Number: 2002067934
ISBN: 0-275-97810-9
ISSN: 1062-5623

First published in 2002

Praeger Publishers, 88 Post Road West, Westport, CT 06881
An imprint of Greenwood Publishing Group, Inc.
www.praeger.com

Printed in the United States of America

The paper used in this book complies with the
Permanent Paper Standard issued by the National
Information Standards Organization (Z39.48-1984).

10 9 8 7 6 5 4 3 2 1

Copyright Acknowledgments

The author and publisher gratefully acknowledge permission to reprint from the following:

Philo C. Wasburn and Arie S. Soesilo, "Constructing a Political Spectacle: American and Indonesian Media Accounts of the Crisis in the Gulf." *The Sociological Quarterly*, vol. 35, no. 2 (Spring 1994): 367–381. Copyright © 1994 by JAI Press. Reprinted with permission of the University of California Press.

Philo C. Wasburn and Barbara R. Burke, "The Symbolic Construction of Russia and the United States on Russian National Television." *The Sociological Quarterly*, vol. 38, no. 4 (Fall 1997): 669–686. Copyright © 1997 by the Midwest Sociological Society. Reprinted with permission of the University of California Press.

Philo C. Wasburn, "The Symbolic Construction of Rival Nations: Radio Japan's Coverage of U.S.–Japanese Trade Disputes." *Political Communication*, vol. 14, no. 2 (April–June 1997): 191–206. Copyright © 1997. Reprinted with permission of Taylor & Francis, Inc., http://www.routledge-ny.com.

Dean Rusk, then Secretary of State, in response to a question that he considered unhelpful from ABC's diplomatic correspondent, John Scali, answered, "Whose side are you on?" Thus, the very loyalty of a reporter who asked a critical question was challenged.

Meg Greenfield

To Mara, Aaron, Hope, Leah, Jered, and Adam

Contents

Tables

Series Foreword

Those of us from the discipline of communication studies have long believed that communication is prior to all other fields of inquiry. In several other forums I have argued that the essence of politics is "talk" or human interaction.[1] Such interaction may be formal or informal, verbal or nonverbal, public or private, but it is always persuasive, forcing us consciously or subconsciously to interpret, to evaluate, and to act. Communication is the vehicle for human action.

From this perspective, it is not surprising that Aristotle recognized the natural kinship of politics and communication in his writings *Politics* and *Rhetoric*. In the former, he establishes that humans are "political beings [who] alone of the animals [are] furnished with the faculty of language."[2] In the latter, he begins his systematic analysis of discourse by proclaiming that "rhetorical study, in its strict sense, is concerned with the modes of persuasion."[3] Thus, it was recognized more than 2,300 years ago that politics and communication go hand in hand because they are essential parts of human nature.

Back in 1981, Dan Nimmo and Keith Sanders proclaimed that political communication was an emerging field.[4] Although its origin, as noted, dates back centuries, a "self-consciously cross-disciplinary" focus began in the late 1950s. Thousands of books and articles later, colleges and universities offer a variety of graduate and undergraduate coursework in the area in such diverse departments as communication, mass communication, journalism, political science, and sociology.[5] In Nimmo and Sanders's early assessment, the "key areas of Inquiry" included rhetorical analysis, propaganda analysis, attitude-change studies, voting studies, government and the news media, functional and systems analysis, technological changes, media technologies, campaign techniques, and research techniques.[6] In a survey of the state of the field in 1983, the same authors and Lynda Kaid found additional, more-specific areas of concern, such as the presidency, political polls, public opinion, debates and advertising to name a few.[7] Since the first study, they also noted a shift away from the rather strict behavioral approach.

A decade later, Dan Nimmo and David Swanson argued that "political communication has developed some identity as a more or less distinct domain of scholarly work."[8] The scope and concerns of the area have further expanded to include critical theories and cultural studies. While there is no precise definition, method, or disciplinary home of the area of inquiry, its primary domain is the role, processes, and effects of communication within the context of politics broadly defined.

In 1985, the editors of *Political Communication Yearbook: 1984* noted that "more things are happening in the study, teaching, and practice of political communication than can be captured within the space limitations of the relatively few publications available."[9] In addition, they argued that the backgrounds of "those involved in the field [are] so varied and pluralist in outlook and approach . . . it [is] a mistake to adhere slavishly to any set format in shaping the content."[10] More recently, Nimmo and Swanson called for "ways of overcoming the unhappy consequences of fragmentation within a framework that respects, encourages, and benefits from diverse scholarly commitments, agendas, and approaches."[11]

In agreement with these assessments of the area and with gentle encouragement, Praeger established the Praeger Series in Political Communication. The series is open to all qualitative and quantitative methodologies as well as to contemporary and historical studies. The key to characterizing the studies in the series is to focus on communication variables or activities within a political context or dimension. As of this writing, nearly seventy volumes have been published, and there are numerous impressive works forthcoming. Scholars from the disciplines of communication, history, journalism, political science, and sociology have participated in the series.

I am, without shame or modesty, a fan of the series. The joy of serving as its editor is in participating in the dialogue of the field of political communication and in reading the contributor's works. I invite you to join me.

Robert E. Denton, Jr.

NOTES

1. See Robert E. Denton, Jr., *The Symbolic Dimensions of the American Presidency* (Prospect Heights, Ill.: Waveland Press. 1982); Robert E. Denton, Jr., and Gary Woodward, *Political Communication in America* (New York: Praeger, 1985; 2nd ed., 1990); Robert E. Denton, Jr., and Dan Han, *Presidential Communication* (New York:

Praeger, 1986); and Robert E. Denton, Jr., *The Primetime Presidency of Ronald Reagan* (New York; Praeger, 1988).

2. Aristotle, *The Politics of Aristotle,* trans. Ernest Barker (New York: Oxford University Press, 1970), p. 5.

3. Aristotle, *Rhetoric,* trans. Rhys Roberts (New York: The Modern Library, 1954), p. 22.

4. Dan Nimmo and Keith Sanders, "Introduction: The Emergence of Political Communication as a Field." In *Handbook of Political Communication,* ed. Dan Nimmo and Keith Sanders (Beverly Hills, Calif.: Sage, 1981), pp. 11–36.

5. Ibid., p. 15

6. Ibid., pp. 17–27.

7. Keith Sanders, Lynda Kaid, and Dan Nimmo, eds., *Political Communication Yearbook: 1984* (Carbondale: Southern Illinois University, 1985), pp. 283–308.

8. Dan Nimmo and David Swanson, "The Field of Political Communication: Beyond the Voter Persuasion Paradigm." In *New Directions in Political Communication,* ed. David Swanson and Dan Nimmo (Beverly Hills, Calif.: Sage, 1990), p. 8.

9. Sanders, Kaid, and Nimmo, *Political Communication Yearbook: 1984,* p. xiv.

10. Ibid.

11. Nimmo and Swanson, "The Field of Political Communication," p. 11.

Introduction

Ever since Herbert Gans (1979) asked how media organizations decide "what's news," communication researchers, political scientists, and sociologists have been conducting extensive research on news content and the political, economic, and cultural forces that shape it. Most of their studies have concerned the products of American commercial news media. The analyses have focused on news dealing with events occurring in the United States, or with events in other countries in which the United States is directly involved. Such research can be seen as inquiring into what we (American commercial news media) say about ourselves.

Although American commercial news media talk about many apparently different subjects that constitute news, studies indicate that our commercial news media have created a rather consistent and enduring image of ourselves (American society, culture, and the location of the United States in the structure of global political, economic, and military competition). The first chapter considers a theoretical approach that explains how media construct political reality. The chapter then summarizes some of the major research findings on what we say that has become part of our shared and taken-for-granted understanding of our nation.

There are, of course, numerous occasions when we (American commercial news media) talk about them (foreign countries). Analyses of what we say about them (foreign news) are not as common as studies of domestic news. Research has tended to focus on how we treat other nations as allies, competitors, or enemies in various political, ideological, economic, and military conflicts. The second chapter reviews media coverage of two wars: the Falklands War between Great Britain and Argentina (1982) and the war between Iran and Iraq (1980–1988). Each of the cases suggests that

1

we talk about ourselves in a consistent way, even when we are reporting international conflicts in which the United States is not a direct participant. Chapter 3 extends this analysis by considering both U.S. and foreign reporting of two internal wars: clashes between Israel and the Palestinians (1987–1993) and the Tiananmen Square uprising (1989), and three assassinations: Israel's Yitzhak Rabin (1995), Egypt's Anwar el-Sadat (1981), and India's Indira Gandhi (1984).

Most of what social scientists know about the relationship between media and society are generalizations based upon the predominant relations in the United States and Britain (Downing 1996: x-xxi). However, European media scholars are now producing a significant body of work on the way in which news is constructed in their own countries. Like the efforts of their American counterparts, their research has tended to deal primarily with media construction of events occurring at home, or with events in other nations that directly involve their country. Also, like their American counterparts, their findings identify the ways in which news content creates a socially shared and taken-for-granted national self-image that generally supports the dominant groups, organizations, and institutions of their society. From the standpoint of Americans, such research can be seen as investigating what they (foreign news media) say about themselves.

Comparative studies indicating differences between what they say about themselves and what we say about them reveal the constructed nature of news and suggest the interests being served by the alternative accounts—ours as well as theirs. Such studies have tended to be limited to analyses of alternative accounts of events offered by nations that are enemies (see Edelman 1988, 66–89). Such differences are clear and sometimes are discussed by the media of the nations themselves. However, such discussion tends to take the form of a contrast between their efforts to spread *propaganda* and our commitment to report the *Truth*. An analytic rather than a partisan response to the differences would suggest that the distinction between *propaganda* and *news* is often very fine.

With the exception of wartime and Cold War propaganda analyses, there have been very few studies of what they say about us. This is the subject of Chapters 4 through 7. Informed by the theory and research reviewed in the first three chapters, each is a case study of what the news media of one nation or a group of nations has said about American military, economic, or political affairs.

During the Cold War, Russian media had a great deal to say about the United States. In international affairs, America was depicted as the world's leading imperialist power driven by military–industrial interests. Discussions of America's domestic life emphasized racial conflict, crime, homelessness, inequality, and social injustice. Much of what Russian media said about their own country, to both domestic and international audiences, was offered by way of contrast to the United States. Internationally, the nation was portrayed as the world's leading opponent of capitalist imperialism. Domestically, while certainly not described as a worker's paradise, Russia was depicted by its media as a nation comparatively free from the social ills that it claimed plagued the United States. Chapter 4 examines what Russia was saying about the United States, and, in a related way, about itself, during the post–Cold War era (1990–2001). The case study examines how what they say about us changed when they no longer had available their long-used and serviceable explanatory framework for making sense of daily happenings in domestic and international political and economic affairs.

Given the vast amount of its media coverage throughout the world, reports on the "Gulf Crisis" provide considerable material for analyzing alternative ways in which military actions of the United States are reported by the media of other nations. Chapter 5 presents a comparative study of how a leading American newspaper, *The New York Times*, and a leading Indonesian newspaper, *Kompas*, reported on the situation in the Persian Gulf between August 2, 1990, when Iraqi tanks and infantry entered Kuwait, and January 16, 1991, when a military assault was initiated by forces of the United States and a coalition of other nations with the explicitly stated objective of driving Iraqi forces out of Kuwait. Differences in the accounts are discussed in terms of differences in domestic political and economic interests at play within the United States and Indonesia, differences in the interests of the two countries in the structure of global political, economic, and military competition, and differences in the norms of the media systems of the two countries.

Although there is research literature on what national media say about their country and its enemies during times of war, there has been little investigation of how media construct news about their nation and its adversaries in international *economic* conflicts. Such research was called for in the post–Cold War era in which "it appear[ed] to be economic interests, rather than ideological antagonism, that play[ed] the central role in determining news about other nations" (Wu 2000, 127).

Chapter 6 presents an analysis of the newscasts of Radio Japan, one of Japan's official media of international political communication, which were broadcast during a period of major trade disputes between Japan and the United States. The case study identifies the way in which a clear and serviceable image of the United States as an international trade rival was created as a cumulative product over an extended period of newscasts.

American commercial television coverage of national presidential nominating conventions and presidential inaugurations tends to serve the interests of the dominant political parties and, in a sense, the nation as a

4 THE SOCIAL CONSTRUCTION OF INTERNATIONAL NEWS

whole; foreign media reports of these events are less likely to do so. There is evidence of some resentment of the present predominant position of the United States in the world political economy, even on the part of our closest allies. Chapter 7 explores the way in which such sentiment finds expression in British, Canadian, and French coverage of the 1996 presidential nominating conventions and the 1997 presidential inauguration. Their accounts subverted American political party and national ideological interests by reporting these as news rather than as *media events* (see Dayan and Katz 1992). Analysis suggests how the media of one nation construct images of their country's "friends-at-a-distance" during times of peace.

The four case studies, based on the outputs of Indonesian newspapers, Japanese radio, and Russian, British, Canadian, and French television, all show that what they say about us is not always what our mainstream commercial news media routinely tell us about American military, political, and economic affairs. In so far as our understanding of these matters is based on material provided by our news media, the empirical studies suggest that we should reassess some of our shared and largely unquestioned beliefs about our country. Specifying the theoretical and empirical reasons supporting such a reassessment is the task of the final chapter. Chapter 8 also discusses issues for future research on the social construction of international news raised by the 2001 attacks on the United States.

Part I

What Our News Media Say

Chapter 1

We're Talking about Us: The Social Construction of the United States by America's Commercial News Media

In May, 1998, *The Cincinnati Enquirer* published an eighteen-page special section alleging, among other things, that Chiquita Brands International, a powerful transnational corporation headquartered in Cincinnati, sprayed Costa Rican workers with dangerous pesticides, that it set up land trusts to disguise its ownership of various plantations to circumvent Honduran law, and that its executives bribed Colombian officials. Items quoted corporate voice mails to support many of the allegations. The newspaper described the voice mails as obtained from a "high-level source who was one of the Chiquita executives with authority over the company's voice mail system."

Chiquita sued the reporter in federal court charging defamation and wiretapping violations. The corporation demanded that he reveal his sources and not disclose any confidential material he had obtained. Facing the possibility of a huge libel case, *The Cincinnati Enquirer* signed a deal with the corporation. On June 28, 1998, the newspaper published a front-page apology stating that the conclusions of its report were untrue and that it had created a false and misleading impression of Chiquita Brands International. However, the newspaper never specified exactly which of its claims were untrue.

On June 17, 1998, CNN broadcast the premiere of its television news-magazine program, *NewStand: CNN & Time*. The program featured an item, "Valley of Death," which claimed that, during the Vietnam War, American Special Forces on a secret mission in Laos used lethal sarin gas to kill U.S. defectors. The report was challenged by several national news organizations shortly after it was aired.

In a fifty-four-page report commissioned by CNN, outside investigators found that CNN reporters and producers had not fabricated the story. However, they had overlooked or discarded contrary evidence, and they had subtly encouraged sources to confirm the report by asking hypothetical questions. A month later, CNN's chief executive officer issued a formal retraction and apologized for the network's mistakes. Two CNN producers were fired and one resigned. One of the producers continued to insist that the story was true but that her sources had folded under pressure from the military.

Which, if any, claims made in the two stories are true, and which, if any, are false, has never been established conclusively. If both stories are entirely false, questions are raised about the professionalism of American news journalists. If any claim made in the report concerning the operations of Chiquita Brands International is true, because the entire story was formally retracted by the newspaper, questions are raised about the integrity of American news media, and specifically about the ways in which corporate interests shape news content. If any claim made in the report concerning the operation of the American military in Laos is true, because the entire story was formally retracted by the television network, questions are raised about the integrity of American news media, and specifically about the ways in which interests of the U.S. military shape news content.

The topic of the influence of America's corporate, military, and political bureaucracies in the process of constructing the news will be considered later in this chapter. The point being emphasized here is that *The Cincinnati Enquirer* and *CNN–Time* items illustrate dramatically the kind of subjects that American commercial news media are not likely to talk about. The stories are disconcerting. Although the American public is not so naive as social scientists tend to assume (see Gamson 1992), we are not accustomed to news accounts alleging that one of our corporate giants engaged in such illegal and morally outrageous acts. (This is not, after all, a story about matters such as monopolistic practices.) Nor are we accustomed to reports alleging that our military violated the human rights of its own members.

Each of the stories may well have been doubted by most members of the media audience who attended to it—including media professionals themselves. Claims in the accounts violated shared understandings of the way things usually are, that is, our assumptions about reality. The nature of these assumptions, and the role America's commercial mass media play in creating and perpetuating them, is the subject of this chapter.

THE SOCIAL CONSTRUCTION OF POLITICAL REALITY

All of us carry in our minds a "stock knowledge of physical things and fellow citizens, of social collections and artifacts, including cultural objects" (Schutz 1932/1967, 81). For Schutz, this stock of knowledge provides a frame of reference or orientation with which we can interpret objects and events as we conduct our everyday lives. Moreover, the objects and events of the world have no inherent or universal meaning apart from this imposed framework.

For Schutz, our stock of knowledge *is* our reality. It is experienced as the objective world existing "out there," independent of our will and confronting us as fact. This stock of knowledge has a taken-for-granted character and is seldom the object of conscious reflection. It is understood by us in a commonsense fashion as reality itself. Although we can doubt this reality, we very seldom do so, and we cannot do so when we are engaged in our routine activities. The perspective suggests that most of us might feel too busy to attend seriously to seemingly outrageous stories about the acts of important organizations of our legitimated social order.

Schutz contends that we assume other members of our society generally share our stock of knowledge and will experience the world in the same way we do. We assume that others will see the world as being made up of the same types of objects and events, that these objects and events will have the same meaning for them, and that they will respond to them in ways they themselves have learned are appropriate. After all, what reasonable citizen would believe that one of our huge corporations would act in ways that, if discovered, would destroy its image worldwide? Who could believe that our military would convict and sentence to death any of its members without due process, and would impose the death sentence using universally condemned weapons?

According to Schutz, we rely on *typifications*, or "recipes," for action that exist in our culture. These typifications, which are part of our stock knowledge, provide us with ready-made courses of action, solutions to problems, and interpretations of the social world. Although the typifications constitute a cultural framework that is experienced as requiring no further analysis, problematic situations can arise that call the typifications into question. If successful efforts at discrediting them had not been made, each of the two stories could have presented such a situation. We might have asked some critical questions about our corporations and about our military establishment.

Some inferences about social discourse can be drawn from Schutz's perspective. The approach suggests that in everyday conversations we use typifications about objects and events. Our statements are meaningful to others who have learned the same stock of knowledge of which the typifications are a part. To the extent that listeners share the speaker's interpretation of the world and the speaker avoids using typifications in idiosyncratic or unconventional ways, listeners will assume that the speaker is telling the truth. This is the routinely unquestioned assumption that speakers themselves also make about their own statements. The assumption of truth is likely to be made by an audience, unless one or the other of two related conditions prevail: claims made by the speaker are challenged directly by a source seen by the audience as credible, or the claims contradict typifications. In the cases of the stories about Chiquita Brands International and about the U.S. military, both conditions were present.

Schutz's analysis also suggests that we are more likely to believe what mainstream American commercial media tell us about military, economic, and political affairs, both domestic and international, than we are to believe comparable claims of foreign media. We are particularly likely to be skeptical of foreign media when they're talking about us. "Credibility in the mind of the audience is the *sine qua non* of news. All else is either *propaganda* or *entertainment*" (Smith 1973, 109).

Recognition of the observable differences among societies, in terms of what is taken for granted as knowledge in them, is the point of departure for Peter Berger and Thomas Luckmann's analysis of

the processes by which any body of "knowledge" comes to be established as "reality." Sociological interest in questions of "reality" and "knowledge" is initially justified by the fact of their social relativity. What is "real" to the Tibetan Monk may not be "real" to an American businessman. . . . It follows that specific agglomerations of "reality" and "knowledge" pertain to specific social contexts. (Berger and Luckmann 1966, 3)

In addition to discussing, in a manner similar to that of Schutz, processes by which we create the realities of our everyday lives, Berger and Luckmann consider the construction of symbolic realities. Although language, with its typifications, has primary reference to objects and events that we routinely experience and share with others in a taken-for-granted manner, it can be used to transcend the here and now. Language can bring to life the entire world beyond our everyday experience, such as political, economic, and military events in our country and in foreign nations. It can tell us about our shared past or project occurrences into the future (e.g., America's role in the global political economy of the twenty-first century). Language also is capable of constructing symbols that are highly abstracted from everyday experience (e.g., the national interests of the United States). It can create symbol systems (such as religion, philosophy, ideology, and science) that become essential constituents of everyday life and the conscious expression of this reality (1966, 38–42; also see Adoni and Mane 1987).

Berger and Luckmann observed that social institutions appear to have an objective reality of their own as given, self-evident aspects of the world. The social world, which is a human product, confronts its producer as an external reality—as something other than a human product. New generations learn about this reality through the process of socialization, just as they learn about the other things that make up the world they encounter daily.

New generations also learn meaning of the social order, which bestows on that order not only cognitive validity but normative legitimacy as well. Socialization involves the simultaneous transmission of knowledge and values. All understandings of the social world carry with them evaluations. Berger and Luckmann's position thus eschews the traditional distinction between the explanation and evaluation of the social world. This position is developed in their discussion of "levels of legitimation" (1966, 94–104).

Incipient legitimation involves assigning labels to objects of experience. As an example, Berger and Luckmann noted that the transmission of a kinship vocabulary *pro facto* legitimates the kinship structure. The second level of legitimation contains practical explanatory schemes such as proverbs, adages, moral maxims, legends, folk tales, and so on. The third level of legitimation contains explicit and relatively complex theories that explain the structure and operation of the given social order. The theories provide a frame of reference for understanding institutionalized patterns of conduct. Because of their complexity, they are often transmitted by specialized personnel in formal socialization contexts.

Symbolic universes constitute Berger and Luckmann's fourth and most comprehensive level of legitimation. These abstract symbol systems are social products whose history must be understood in order to have a full grasp of their meaning. A symbolic universe provides meaning for realities other than those of everyday experience and "puts everything in its right place." Because the "right place" is the reality of everyday life, and because the social order is part of it, "the symbolic universe provides the ultimate legitimation of the institutional order by bestowing upon it the primacy in the hierarchy of human experience" (1966, 98).

VALUES INHERENT IN THE NEWS

Studies of values inherent in U.S. commercial media news content and research on America's stock of knowledge about domestic politics serve to illustrate the involvement of our national news media in the social construction and legitimation processes identified by Berger and Luckmann. The works identify what our media say about us and, consequently, what we take for granted as given features of both our everyday world of experience and of the world beyond. Despite a vast theoretical and empirically grounded literature specifying and documenting bases for rejecting it, most of us make the assumption of a generally nonproblematic correspondence between objects and events in the world (including political, military, and economic events) and their symbolic representations constructed by the mass media and transmitted by them as news (see Bennett 1996; Edelman 1988; Epstein 1973; Fishman 1980; Herman and Chomsky 1988; Lee and Solomon 1991; Negrine 1996; Parenti 1986/1993; Qualter 1985; Real 1989; Schudson 1978; Sigal 1973; Smith 1973; Sproule 1997; Tuchman 1978).

Gans's (1979) classic study of *The CBS Evening News, NBC Nightly News, Newsweek,* and *Time* will serve as the point of departure for discussing the values that structure American commercial news. Though his research was conducted more than twenty-five years ago, more recent analyses, cited in the following discussion, suggest the enduring nature of the news value Gans identified. To the extent that we depend on commercial news media to provide meaning for public events, the values shape our shared understanding of our nation and its role in the international community. According to Gans, the enduring values in American commercial news "can be grouped into eight clusters: *ethnocentrism, altruistic democracy, responsible capitalism, small-town pastoralism, individualism, moderatism, social order,* and *national leadership*" (1979, 42).

Ethnocentrism is expressed in media treatment of the United States as the world's most important and most valued nation. "The U.S. orientation of world coverage is so pervasive and routine that the possibility of any broader coverage can be difficult even to contemplate" (Croteau and Hoynes 1994, 50). When we're talking about ourselves, we tend to tell stories that support official policies and actions, and to avoid telling stories that are critical of our military, economic, and political institutions. For example, throughout most of the Vietnam War,

[American domestic] media coverage and interpretation of the war took for granted that the United States intervened in the service of generous ideals, with the goal of defending South Vietnam from aggression and terrorism and in the interest of democracy and self-determination. (Herman and Chomsky 1988, 169)

"Left out of this view was any thought that the United States had waged a horrific war in support of a dictatorship and against a largely civilian population to prevent a popularly supported but noncapitalist alternative social order from gaining power" (Parenti 1986/1993, 176). America's commercial media, relying largely on material provided by the Pentagon, also validated U.S. military action during the Gulf War in terms of helping enforce the principle of the sovereignty of nations and the protection of human rights (MacArthur 1992). Media trivialized opposition to the war (Cohen 1992).

Another manifestation of ethnocentrism is seen in American commercial media's relative inattention to foreign news. We don't talk about them nearly as often as we talk about ourselves. As correspondent Christiane Amanpour put it, "Unless American soldiers are there, American television is not there" (quoted in Aluetta 1997, 82). In general, American media cover countries in which the United States has its most significant diplomatic contacts (Graber 1993, 374). The amount of international news presented by American commercial media fluctuates over time. During the Cold War period, about one-third of news stories could be classified as international. During the late 1980s and early 1990s, the number of international news stories grew sharply, reflecting the dramatic events of these years, such as the fall of the Berlin Wall; the breakup of the Soviet Union; the first free elections in Eastern and Central Europe; developments in the Middle East, China, and Panama; and the Gulf War. This was followed by a sharp fall between 1992 and 1995, when foreign coverage accounted for only twenty-nine percent of the news stories. News turned back again toward the predominant domestic agenda, returning to a position similar to or slightly lower than that during the Cold War period (Norris 1995, 363). Although data are not yet available, it seems highly likely that following the 2001 attacks on the United States, the proportion of news items presented by our commercial media dealing with international events vastly increased. However, most of these items certainly concern the role of other nations in America's "war on terrorism."

Altruistic democracy refers to the value, implicit in the news, that "politics should follow a course based on the public interest and public service" (Gans 1979, 43). Some violations of this norm make them newsworthy. These include reports of corruption, political decisions based on either self-interest or partisan concerns, and many of the activities of corporate lobbyists. The highly successful and critically acclaimed news magazine *60 Minutes* largely deals with revelations of such matters (Himmelstein 1994, 254). However, there are other violations that typically go unreported. These include nondramatic but unrelenting acts of racism in America (see Campbell 1995) and coverage of poverty that focuses on images of poor people but omits discussion of social policy (Iyengar 1990).

Media also construct the image of the United States as a society committed to altruistic democracy by portraying ordinary citizens as politically passive and generally naive individuals who will, without serious questioning, respond to public figures as heroes if they can be understood as embodying unselfish commitment to the common good. This perspective was illustrated in media accounts of enormous popular support for the presidency of Ronald Reagan. During the 1987 Iran–Contra hearings, the view was seen again in media depictions of public reaction to Oliver North, a key figure in the hearings. The term "Olliemania" commonly appeared in the media to depict the extraordinary enthusiasm that the public supposedly expressed toward North. Such reporting occurs despite substantial reasons to doubt this characterization of the American public (Schudson 1995, 124–141; Thelen 1996). However, an impressive example of continuing public support for a political leader widely believed to be promoting the common good (defined primarily in terms of maintaining a robust economy) is provided by public approval given Bill Clinton in 1998, despite his involvement in the most frequently reported sex scandal in recent American history and his subsequent impeachment by the U.S. Senate on grounds of perjury and obstruction of justice. A study by the Center for Media and Public Affairs, reported in many major newspapers, found that, in 1998, the ABC, CBS, and NBC television networks had carried more news items on the Lewinsky scandal than on all the other major news topics of the year combined. These included economic crises in Asia and Russia, America's standoff with Iraq, bombings of the U.S. embassies in Africa, a major strike by the United Auto Workers, the Middle East peace process, nuclear testing in India and Pakistan, and John Glenn's return to space. The networks also frequently noted that Clinton's positive public evaluation had not diminished.

The theme of *responsible capitalism* is expressed in news items suggesting that America's free-market system promotes democracy and increasing economic prosperity for all. ("Capitalism became reconciled to democracy once it felt confident that the many could not use their power to make any too dangerous an assault upon the privileges of property" [Qualter 1991, 10].) American corporations are assumed to refrain from unreasonable profits and gross exploitation of workers and customers.

Media coverage of poverty in the context of American corporate capitalism emphasizes that our welfare state will protect America's "deserving poor," who cannot participate in the market. Socialist alternatives to corporate capitalism get little play in the news.

Our commercial news media support corporate America by omitting items that seriously discredit a product or an industry. For example,

the Tylenol poisoning of several people by a deranged individual was treated as big news but the far more sensational story of the industrial brown-lung poisoning of thousands of factory workers by large manufacturing interests (who themselves own or advertise in the major media) has remained suppressed for decades despite the best efforts of worker safety groups to bring the issue before the public. (Jensen 1997, 28)

In an era of headlines on cutting welfare to the poor, there has been no counterpoint emphasis on the $86 billion a year in taxpayers' subsidies (welfare) to American corporations, some of which help support the relocation of their operations to other countries, resulting in massive employee layoffs within the United States. To its credit, *The New York Times* has become more cognizant of social dislocations of

this kind than the average daily paper or newscast seen by most Americans. (Bagdikian 1997, xx)

America's commercial media do not question the rightness of the basic
features of U.S. corporate capitalism. They evoke a consensual image
when domestic or international events impact on the operation of "our"
economy. Media have both commercial and political interests in fostering
agreement on a range of consumer-oriented values and conveying approval of a stable, familiar ideology (Fowler 1991, 48–54). Insofar as corporate or government economic decisions are debated in the media, discussions tend to be carried on by people who share similar social locations
and political interests. Coverage is aimed at an audience seen as investors
rather than as workers, consumers, or citizens (Croteau and Hoynes 2001).
Our news media are capitalist enterprises in a capitalist economy and
prosper by legitimating the capitalist system. Our news media promote an
assumption that the uncritical attitudes of the public toward a modified
capitalism in a mixed economy are the norms of all sensible and responsible people the world over, and that American capitalism itself is fair
minded, public spirited, and benign (Qualter 1985).

Commercial media deliver this message in such a way that it goes virtually unnoticed by domestic audiences. It merely expresses a view that
most Americans incorporate as a part of our stock of knowledge.

The problem facing the victims and critics of the global corporate order is not that
alternative courses are *technically impossible* as much as they are *unthinkable....*
Those who question its postulate of benevolence may still not escape its assumptions of naturalness and inevitability, which induce quiescence and passivity. (Herman and McChesney 1997, 35)

The "corporate voice" states our view that seldom sees as problematic
the relationship between corporate financial health and citizen well-being;
the "corporate view" largely is the American view (Schiller 1989). "The executive of the large corporation is, on many counts, the contemporary of
the landed gentry of an earlier era, his voice amplified by the technology
of mass communication" (Lindblom 1977, 356).

It certainly is not true that our media never present material that is
clearly antibusiness. *The Cincinnati Enquirer*'s articles on the operation of
Chiquita Brands International, described at the beginning of this chapter,
were remarkably critical. However, corporate reaction to the published
material and the newspaper's subsequent response is suggestive. Even in
cases in which the option of initiating lawsuits may not be available,

[business has] privileged access to media executives through common corporate
associations and lobbies, and it [can] produce large-scale advertisements to

counter antibusiness news and, increasingly, to use threats of withdrawal against hostile media. And corporate leaders [can] invoke against the media that peculiar American belief [ironically created more by the media than by any other source] that to criticize big business is to attack American democracy. (Bagdikian 1997, 54)

Small-town pastoralism, the fourth media theme identified by Gans (1979, 48–50), appears in news items depicting urban centers as sites of racial conflicts, crime, and fiscal insolvency (to which now should be added poverty, homelessness, drug problems, inadequate mass transportation, failing schools, ethnic conflict, political corruption, and even the threat of terrorist attack) and in news items depicting small towns as sites of the good life in America: cohesive, friendly, slow paced, predictable, and orderly. According to Gans, the theme reflects the fear of bigness (big labor, big business, big government) and its threat to the autonomy and freedom of the individual.

A more recent expression of small-town pastoralism can be found in media discussions of the social consequences of widespread computer use in America. Among other things, news items commonly point out that electronic communication can have the desirable consequence of making geographic location irrelevant to the conduct of work. Many people no longer find it necessary to endure the difficulties of working in the city but can work in the much friendlier confines of suburban or rural home offices. Similarly, new information technologies such as computer networks and bulletin boards, electronic mail and faxes are valued, in part, for their ability to create virtual communities sharing various kinds of interests—including those that are political and ideological.

There is, of course, irony in American commercial media's continuing celebration of the small and the local. Increasingly, individual media corporations are becoming parts of giant international telecommunications conglomerates. A consequence of this absorption is the loss of any democratic control over the media that might effectively serve noncorporate interests (Herman and McChesney 1997).

In part, the value of *individualism* is expressed in the news in its focus on individual actors, rather than on groups or on social policies or social structures or processes. Gans (1979) found that about ninety percent of news items concern people and what they say and do. The news most commonly focuses on individual public officials, business leaders, well-known personalities and scientists, as well as on the heroic acts of ordinary people, such as police and firefighters during disasters. Similarly, Bennett notes that news is *personalized* in the sense that it "gives preference to human interest angles in events while downplaying institutional and political considerations that establish their social contexts" (1996, 48). He argues that the political consequences of such *personalization* include failure to inform the public well enough so that they can detect or correct mistakes in government policies and failure to provide the news audience with an adequate view of power and its political consequences.

Without a grasp of power structures, it is virtually impossible to understand how the political system really works. As a result, the political world becomes a mystical realm populated by actors who either have the political "force" on their side or do not. The absence of attention to power further encourages the audience to abandon political analysis in favor of casting their political fates with the hero of the moment. (1996, 51)

Gans also sees the expression of individualism in media treatment of communism and socialism. (His study was published a decade before the end of the Cold War. Nevertheless, it seems that even today, to the extent that these subjects are discussed, either as abstract political ideologies or as concrete political economies, his characterization remains valid.) He argues that "communism and socialism are feared because they emasculate the individual, and capitalism is valued less for itself than for the freedom it offers at least some individuals" (Gans 1979, 51). He adds that individualism also is presented as a source of economic, social, and cultural productivity. These points are extensions of the responsible capitalism theme noted above.

The discussion of *moderatism* presents the claim that "insofar as the news has an ideology of its own, it is moderate" (1979, 52). The news, Gans found, is critical of individuals, groups, or ideas that can be seen as extreme: atheists or religious fanatics, those engaged in conspicuous consumption or members of the counterculture, ideologues or the narrowly self-seeking, and so on.

Media coverage of the 1993 confrontation in Waco, Texas, provides a dramatic illustration of Gans's claim. The Branch Davidians, a religious sect led by a controversial messiah, David Koresh, was suspected by federal agents of caching automatic weapons, abusing children, and other illegal acts. Law enforcement officers went to the sect's compound and demanded that members come out. The members refused and subsequently exchanged gunfire with officials. After a standoff that lasted fifty-one days, government agents brought in armored vehicles to attack the compound by inserting tear gas to force out sect members. A fire started and quickly destroyed the structure, killing all eighty-five of its inhabitants, including twenty-four children. Media did not question the official government position that, while the assault may have been ill advised in retrospect, it was the leader, David Koresh, who bore responsibility for the deaths; the government had acted responsibly in its efforts to conclude the standoff (Altheide 1995, 20–21). Reporting revealed little sympathy for those who were generally characterized as zealots. It was not until late in 1999 that media began carrying reports questioning the details of the government's actions.

A study of *Nightline*, once advertised as perhaps the best program in the history of broadcast journalism, provides a less graphic but more politically substantive example of the enduring news value of moderatism. Croteau and Hoynes (1994) found that the program did not offer its audience exposure to a wide range of political views. Rather, *Nightline* limited discussions to those along a narrow spectrum of people who shared more-or-less centrist political interests. It failed to inform the public because it did not present debates between those at the center of power and those challenging that power.

Much of the news, Gans notes (1979, 52–64) concerns either social order (the routine activities of leading public officials and the periodic selection of new officials) or disorder (natural, technological, social, or moral events that threaten to disturb the public peace). Such items, he observes, suggest two additional news values: the desirability of a certain type of social order, and the need for national leadership in maintaining that order.

News items that focus on political, military, or corporate officials routinely are based on material transmitted through formal channels—press releases, press conferences, and official proceedings. One study found that nearly half of the sources for national and foreign news stories on page one of *The New York Times* and *The Washington Post* were officials of the United States government (Sigal 1986, 25). "News gathering is normally a matter of representatives of one bureaucracy picking up prefabricated news items from members of another bureaucracy" (Schudson 1986, 81). This process has several related consequences. First, those lacking access to effectively functioning formal channels are not likely to have their views represented in the media. Second, the perspectives of those in high administrative positions within large bureaucracies are privileged. Their perspectives tend to support the institutionalized social order: the government, its agencies, private enterprise, and the prestigious professions. What American commercial news media say about public affairs generally reflects this distinctive viewpoint. The range of opinion on a topic reported in the news rarely extends beyond the range expressed in mainstream government debate. Media legitimate officials as the primary interpreters of events (Bennett 1990; Croteau and Hoynes 1994; Paletz and Entman 1981; Soley 1992; Woodward 1997). Political and economic elites play a major role in the construction of the symbolic universe we routinely encounter as our daily news.

News items dealing with a variety of disorders contribute to the media's portrait of the United States. *Natural disorder news*, concerned with events such as floods, tornadoes, and earthquakes, routinely suggests that Americans and their government are compassionate. Stories about heroic rescue efforts, generous contributions of ordinary citizens and voluntary organizations, and responses of government relief agencies serve as examples.

Even when media present interviews with disaster victims who criticize government response as being too slow or inadequate, such interviews are often accompanied by images of officials visiting disaster sites, expressing their deep personal concern, and stressing the magnitude of government aid efforts.

Technological disorder news concerns accidents that cannot be ascribed to nature, such as airplane crashes and nuclear power plant accidents. Reports of such events invariably contain references to the efforts of government agencies, such as the National Transportation Safety Board or the Nuclear Regulatory Commission, to investigate and correct any technical causes of the disasters. Media advertisements for airlines are certainly more common than are news items questioning airline safety. Media advertisements promoting nuclear energy, sponsored by the U.S. Council for Energy Awareness, are far more prevalent than are news items reporting criticism of the nuclear power industry expressed by the Union of Concerned Scientists. American news media depict the United States as a nation greatly benefiting from its commercial industries' employing high technology and kept safe by effective government oversight and regulation.

The final news value identified by Gans is evident in U.S. commercial news media's focus on *national leadership* and upon the president as the ultimate protector of the institutionalized social and political order. The presence of the value helps explain the extraordinary amount of media attention devoted to the 1998 Lewinsky scandal noted earlier.

[The president] is the final backstop for domestic tranquility and the principal guardian of international security. . . . Through his own behavior and the concern he shows for the behavior of others, the president also becomes the nation's moral leader. He sets an example that might be followed by others. . . . Finally, he is the person who states and represents the national values and he is the agent of the national will. (Gans 1979, 63)

American media tend to be deferential to the president when he participates in activities that involve his role as a symbol of the nation's identity. Such occasions include delivering his inaugural address, giving the state of the union message, welcoming foreign dignitaries, and representing the country at an international conference. (Chapter 7 will discuss how foreign media can depict the president on such ceremonial occasions.) However, in other contexts, since the late 1960s media often have been skeptical of presidential action and have discussed policy inadequacies and failures (see Paletz 1999, 244–256).

OUR MEDIA-CONSTRUCTED NATIONAL SELF-IMAGE

The media values identified by Gans have encouraged the production and incessant reproduction of a rather consistent image of the United

States. That image constitutes the symbolic universe in terms of which most Americans understand our nation and its place in the structure of international political, economic, and military relations. It is an image carried around the world by the products of American media corporations.

In the symbolic universe, the United States is the world's most important nation; an essential part of grasping global events involves recognizing their bearing on U.S. business and/or political and/or military interests as defined by institutional elites, such as corporate executives, leading political figures, and Pentagon officials. Events in which such interests are not clearly involved tend to receive little, if any, coverage in U.S. commercial media, even though they may dramatically affect the lives of vast numbers of people. For example, in 1991, famine in Africa resulted in more deaths that year than did worldwide natural disasters and the Persian Gulf War combined, but it received little media attention (Moeller 1999).

Typically, we don't talk about global events unless it involves talking about ourselves. This tendency helps explain the deep concern expressed by numerous media analysts during the 1970s and 1980s over "media imperialism." Their claim was that although our media espouse commitment to doctrines of impartiality, accuracy, and objectivity, their products routinely define social reality in ways that support U.S. domination of the developing nations of Asia, Africa, and Latin America (see Cherry 1978; McPhail 1987; Schiller 1976; Smith 1980; Tunstall 1977). The tendency also helps account for the overall decline in U.S. media coverage of international events during the post–Cold War period noted earlier (see Norris 1995; Salwen and Matera 1992; Shoemaker, Danielian, and Brendlinger 1991).

In the symbolic universe constructed by our commercial news media, not only is the United States at the center of all major world events, but our altruistic democratic polity and our capitalist economy, while no longer presented as the only alternative to "communist totalitarianism" as it was from the end of World War II until 1989, are still understood as the "natural" order within which people can best conduct their routine lives as citizens and consumers. In the post–Cold War period, this view did not appear profoundly ideological to news makers (see Qualter 1991, 51–55).

Although the "natural" order is socially constructed and legitimated by the media, the media sometimes do identify problems occurring within that order. Discussions of conditions defined as problems tend to be accompanied by specifications of ready-made courses of action to deal with them (Berger and Luckmann's "typifications"). These solutions generally do not seriously call into question the operation of *altruistic democracy* or *responsible capitalism* in America. They often express the values of *individualism* and *moderatism* but seldom stress the need for *national leadership*.

In the domestic media-created image of the United States, those conditions acknowledged as America's social problems are amenable to solution either at the level of individual behavior or through the intervention of various professions. Media presentation of material suggesting that social problems can be dealt with effectively through policy initiatives, particularly those that require some significant reallocation of scarce social resources, are rare. Hence, as features of the media-constructed symbolic universe, public service announcements proclaim that the economic problems of higher education largely can be solved by "giving to the college of your choice"; environmental degradation can be reduced through individual attention: "People start pollution, people can stop it"; and personal carelessness is the prime source of the country's loss of forest land: "Only you can prevent forest fires" (Paletz 1999, 163–165). Significantly increasing state funding of education, more strictly regulating industrial pollution, and expanding government conservation programs are not commonly presented as courses of action for serious public consideration.

Media are most likely to express the need for national leadership in the context of international news. This pattern is generally consistent with the interests of political leaders, the concerns of news audiences, and the news media's constant need to reaffirm its objectivity. Sometimes we talk about them to avoid talking about ourselves. "Leaders have often maintained a supportive following by focusing attention on foreign threats that divert concern from unresolved domestic troubles" (Edelman 1988, 28). In conducting international relations, America's political leaders can manipulate symbols of political community and myths of "us and them" to present their policy initiatives as pragmatic approaches with bipartisan support (see Elder and Cobb 1983; Nimmo and Combs 1980).

Media reassure audiences that the nation is following military policies that ensure national security and trade policies that further the global economic interests of the country. Conforming to the values discussed above, the policies are interpreted as supporting a broad consensus concerning freedom, democracy, and human rights, and doing so within acceptable limits of costs and risks. Domestic commercial news media sometimes are critical of U.S. foreign policy, but only after the fact. In each of the historical cases of Kennedy and the Bay of Pigs, Johnson and Vietnam, Nixon and Cambodia, Carter and the hostages in Iran, and Reagan and Lebanon, journalists initially adopted the perspective of the government (Berry 1990).

Protest is now central to politics in Western democracies, but it is known to citizens mainly through portrayals in the media. Yet, news media cover only a small fraction of public protests, raising the possibility of media bias (McCarthy, McPhail, and Smith 1996). Furthermore, media have marginalized and ridiculed challenge groups protesting major military and economic policies. Such was the fate of those protesting U.S. involvement in Vietnam (Gitlin 1980; Hallin 1986), the Gulf War (Kellner 1992; MacArthur 1992), and U.S. participation in World Trade Organization meetings in Seattle in December 1999, "a coalition that this week united tree huggers and steel workers, chicken farmers and vegetarians" (Pearlstein 1999).

Understanding the image of the United States constructed by our commercial news media is central to understanding what these media say about other nations. This discourse is the subject of Chapters 2 and 3. Due to new information technologies and the development of giant media monopolies, the content of U.S. commercial news media is now instantly available throughout most of the world and certainly influences what they say about us. The impact of American news media is further amplified by the fact that correspondents for foreign news agencies working in the United States are often forced by staff restrictions and limited mobility to rely on domestic media as a secondary and sometimes primary source of news (Ghorpade 1984).

Chapter 2

We're Talking about Them: U.S. News Media Construction of Wars between Other Nations

In a 1990 lecture at Harvard University, CBS anchor Dan Rather told students:

Don't kid yourselves; the trend in American journalism is away from, not toward, increased foreign coverage. Foreign coverage is the most expensive. It requires the most space and the most time because you're dealing with complicated situations which you have to explain a lot. And then there's always somebody around you who says people really don't give a damn about this stuff anyway. . . . If you have to do something foreign, Dan, for heaven's sake, keep it short, will you? (Quoted in Hess 1996, 6)

Data generally confirm Rather's prediction that the amount of foreign news produced by U.S. commercial media would decline after 1990; it would continue to decline until 2001. A content analysis of network news in the Cold War and post–Cold War period (1973–1995) found a dramatic increase in the amount of international news during the transition period (1989–1990), reflecting the momentous events of the years, followed by a sharp fall between 1991 and 1993, then only a slight recovery in 1994 (Norris 1995). A subsequent study indicated that between 1985 and 1995 space devoted to international news in *Newsweek*, *U.S. News*, and *Time* fell from about twenty percent to about fourteen percent while the ABC, CBS, and NBS television networks reduced the amount of time devoted to foreign news from forty-five percent of their newscasts in the 1970s to about thirteen percent by 1995 (Hodge 1997, 49).

From the mid-1990s to 2001, international news coverage by our commercial news media largely was limited to (crises) in those places too big or too combustible to overlook (China and the former Yugoslavia); dramatic events in smaller countries that had historical relations with the United States (Panama, the Philippines, Haiti); social movements too powerful to ignore (market capitalism comes to Eastern Europe, notably Poland, Czechoslovakia, and Hungary); and direct U.S. involvement overseas (the Gulf War Trio of Iraq, Kuwait, and Saudi Arabia; Panama; Somalia). (Hess 1996, 30)

A comparative study of international news reported by the media of thirty-eight nations indicates that the United States is the most covered country in the world (Wu 2000). The amount of attention American commercial news media pay to our nation's domestic and foreign affairs far outweighs their attention to conditions and events in other nations. However, the extent of this inequality has varied over time. Domestic events such as presidential campaigns and major scandals reduce time and space allocated to foreign news. On the other hand, wars, crises, and dramatic events in other nations, such as those noted above, can increase the relative frequency with which our media discuss other nations. Less obviously, new information technologies, such as transmission via the cable networks or the World Wide Web, might influence the amount of time and space traditional commercial news media can devote to other nations. For example, ABC, CBS, and NBC television news programs reduced the amount of coverage given the 2000 presidential campaign in recognition of the fact that interested audiences had extensive coverage available to them on the CNN, MSNBC, and FOX cable networks (Bauder 2000).

Although the amount of foreign news offered by American commercial media may be relatively small (*CNN Headline News* may have established the benchmark in early 2001 by introducing "The Global Minute" as part of its half-hour programs), ethnocentrism is not in short supply. The focus of items about other nations is sharply on their relationships with the United States. Furthermore, media stay closer to the State Department line on foreign news than to the White House line on domestic news (van Ginneken 1998, 28). Even the view of public opinion in other countries reported in American media often comes from U.S. political leaders who have interpreted the opinion in a way that legitimates a policy they are proposing (Barton 1997). Stories about foreign countries per se, their institutions and policies are uncommon (*Times Mirror* 1995, 1–2). Wallis and Baran (1990, 179) estimated that British and Swedish news media offer about twice as much foreign news as some of their U.S. counterparts, but show about half as much ethnocentrism. American audiences encounter international news that places foreign events against the background of a world they silently take for granted (see Berger and Luckmann 1981, 172).

Wars, violent internal conflicts, and assassinations are foreign events likely to attract the attention of U.S. commercial news media. Representations of these events are symbolic realities constructed by the media through a number of processes which, as will be illustrated below, produce coverage that reflects U.S. political, economic, and military interests of the period. These processes include deciding how much attention to give an event, choosing a vocabulary to describe the event, selecting particular occurrences to characterize broad features of the event, and deciding how to represent U.S. and international public opinion on the event.

This chapter will consider American media coverage of two wars in which the United States military was not directly involved: the brief battle in the South Atlantic between Great Britain and Argentina over the Falkland Islands (April-May 1982) and the long war between Iran and Iraq (1980–1988). The concluding pages of Chapter 3 will identify recurring patterns in the accounts American commercial news media constructed of these historical events.

THE FALKLANDS WAR

The Falkland Islands lie three hundred miles east of the coast of Argentina and eight thousand miles away from Great Britain. Argentina had claimed sovereignty over the islands and its associated island dependencies, including South Georgia and the South Sandwich Islands one thousand miles east of the Falklands, since the early nineteenth century, but Britain had occupied and administered the islands since 1833 and had consistently rejected Argentina's claims. Falklanders themselves had repeatedly affirmed their wish to remain British.

On January 4, 1982, Great Britain protests the visit of an Argentine businessman to South Georgia aboard a navy ice breaker as a violation of British sovereignty, warning that if any further landings were made without proper authorization, the British government reserved the right to take whatever action it might deem necessary. Subsequently, Argentina and Britain reach an agreement, in talks at the United Nations, to establish a permanent negotiation commission. However, on March 18, 1982, Argentine workers associated with the businessman land in South Georgia. On March 23, the British government under Prime Minister Margaret Thatcher sends a warship to expel the Argentines from the island.

Argentina, reluctant to comply with the British demand to remove its citizens under threat of force, launches a military invasion of the Falklands on April 2. Argentine troops easily overcome the small garrison of British military there. By late April 1982 Argentina has more than ten thousand troops stationed on the Falklands.

In response, the British government declares a Total Exclusion Zone for two hundred miles around the Falklands with the purpose of sealing off the Argentine garrison from further reinforcement. Britain asserts that any Argentine warships and naval auxiliaries found within this zone will be treated as hostile and are liable to be attacked by British forces. Britain sends a naval tasks force to the war zone via the British-held Ascension Island. Meanwhile, Britain also initiates air operations, attacking the airport at Stanley and destroying several Argentine planes.

On May 2, 1982, Fernando Belaunde Terry, President of Peru, presents a peace proposal to Argentine President Leopoldo Galtieri, who gives a preliminary acceptance and proposes some modifications. Before the Argentine junta ratifies the acceptance, a British submarine sinks the Argentine cruiser *General Belgrano* as it approaches the war zone, resulting in a loss of 321 lives. The junta rejects the proposal on the table. Two days later, Argentina sinks the HMS *Sheffield*, using Exocet missiles. Twenty officers and enlisted men are dead or missing. Further battles ensue between the land-based Argentine air force and the British naval force. Attempts by both the United Nations and the United States to mediate the crisis at this point prove unsuccessful. Argentine air attacks sink two British destroyers and two frigates. Again using Exocet missiles, the Argentines hit the container ship *Atlantic Conveyor*, which sinks with valuable logistic cargo. However, the Argentines fail to prevent the British from making an amphibious landing near Port San Carlos on the northern coast of East Falkland on May 21, 1982.

From their beachhead, the British infantry advances southward to capture several settlements after which they turn eastward to surround the Falklands capital of Stanley on May 31. The large Argentine garrison there surrenders on June 14, 1982, effectively ending the conflict. The British reoccupy the South Sandwich Islands on June 20, 1982, and formally declare an end to the hostilities.

The British capture about ten thousand Argentine prisoners during the war, all of whom are later released. Argentina sustains about 700 fatalities, while Britain loses about 250. Argentina's humiliating defeat severely discredits the military government and leads to the restoration of civilian rule in that country in 1983.

British Media Report the Falklands War

British as well as American scholars produced a substantial body of research on how British media constructed the Falklands War. A brief review of some of this research will provide a rare comparative basis for discussing how our media reported the conflict. In the process of comparing British and U.S. media accounts of the Falklands War, some general points can be made about alternative media construction of news and the political, economic, and military interests that differing reports reflect.

In Great Britain during the Falklands War,

the right to the free flow of information in a democratic society was set against the need for censorship in the interest of the war effort. The right to present different points of view about the issue was set against a call to speak for the "national interest." (Glasgow University Media Group [GUMG] 1985, Introduction)

This is to be expected because all governments will, to some extent, attempt to control the media of their society, and never more so than at a time of crisis.

Limits are directly imposed by the Ministry of Defense. Only British journalists are permitted to go with the task force. No television coverage is allowed except for the military's own cameramen. Reporters have no facilities for sending satellite pictures and experience extreme difficulties in sending back copy. Copy from journalists is censored first by Ministry of Defense officials on the Falklands and then again by public relations staff at the Ministry in London.

One of the chief concerns in both British government and military circles is that television is a potentially dangerous weapon in lowering morale. It is understood to have contributed to the U.S. public's increasing disillusionment with Vietnam (GUMG 1985, 8, 19; Cumings 1992, 100). This occurs despite the lack of historical evidence to support the belief (Morrison and Tumber 1988, 345).

Such direct censorship is only one factor shaping the way in which British media talk about their nation's war in the South Atlantic. The government also has recourse to Britain's Official Secrets Act according to which all government information is secret unless an "official" statement is made about it. In addition, a structural feature of the British media system encourages media reliance on official sources. Known as the "Lobby System," a core group of 140 journalists based at Westminster has access to white papers and government documents before they are released to the general public. Lobby members, who provide a great deal of what becomes news in Britain, are also briefed by the government on important affairs of the day. A book of rules governs lobby briefings. Anyone who breaks the rules may have his/her lobby privileges withdrawn. Journalists come to rely on senior civil servants and ministers to provide prepackaged information. This process of information gathering comes to be seen as natural by lobby members. It is the origin of phrases in British journalism, such as "Whitehall sources have revealed tonight." It allows political elites to assume that a limited number of people expressing a limited range of views will be featured in the media. It permits journalists to question the activities or competence of particular ministers, but not to explore major sensitive issues, such as those concerned with national defense (GUMG 1985, 1–7).

The political socialization of British journalists also must be considered in accounting for the way in which they talk about the international affairs of their country. The symbolic universe most have encountered from their early school days onward is likely to have encouraged the understanding and internalization of an ethnocentrically British perspective. This set of understandings or body of common knowledge is likely to have been dominant in the schools of journalism they attended and in the newsrooms in which they have worked. It is likely to be reflected in the views of the political, military, and economic elites on whom they often depend for information. More than their American counterparts, the British historically have expected fair treatment from their government and have expressed this in deference to the independent authority of government (Almond and Verba 1965).

External pressure on the British media to have their news presentations support government policy was considerable during the Falklands War, particularly that directed toward the BBC. The application of such pressure indicates that even among deferential British journalists there were some doubts about the legitimacy of their nation's military engagement.

The task of reporting independently on the Falklands conflict was almost impossible. . . . Any mention on the BBC of dissident opinion was noisily declared to be treachery. The BBC and the rest of the media were often caught between the conflicting interests of the government (keen to announce victories) and the military (keen to retain military secrets). At the same time, the traditional civil service spokesman (often of the same reportorial breed as the BBC staff) who gave correct but limited information, was being replaced by a new type of public relations spokesman whose prime duty it was to exercise news management. A statement by Mrs. Thatcher in Parliament that "the case for our country is not being put with sufficient vigour on certain programmes of the BBC" might seem fairly innocuous to an American network news producer (considering what Washington was saying about U.S. television news during the Vietnam War). But in the British system, it was seen as signaling what former head of News and Current Affairs, Alan Protheroe, called on Granada TV a "concerted attack to discredit and damage the BBC." (Wallis and Baran 1990, 47)

The attacks on the BBC, and *The Guardian* as well, may have represented more than assaults on these entities as news organizations. According to Morrison and Tumber (1988), they could be understood as cultural attacks on the "intelligentsia," seen as the primary producers and consumers of the products of these media, for failing to support responsibly the Conservative government which had come to power in 1979.

There was some material in the British media that was sharply critical of British policy in the Falklands. For example, *The Guardian* (April 7, 1982) published this political commentary by Peter Jenkins:

By what gigantic lack of proportion was the loss of the Falkland Islands to be seen as a major national humiliation? How could it be seriously said that this was the gravest international crisis since the War? By what weird calculus was it reckoned that the fate of all free peoples might hinge upon the fate of these 1800 Islanders and their 600,000 sheep? (Quoted in Femenia 1996,153)

Such materials were rare. The vast preponderance of what British media had to say about their nation's war supported Britain's political and military action. Beyond this, it bolstered the fading self-image of Britain as a leading member of the international community. These results largely were achieved though processes illustrated in their presentations of the Falklands War's two most controversial events: the sinking of the *General Belgrano* and the development of the peace talks. In each of these, language use, direction of attention, and representation of British public opinion played key roles.

Controversy surrounding the May 2, 1982, sinking of the *General Belgrano* results from the location of the ship outside the two hundred-mile Total Exclusion Zone at the time of the attack; the British had violated their own rules of engagement. Furthermore, the attack occurs on the very day Argentina gives preliminary acceptance of a peace proposal suggested by Peru. Nevertheless, the predominant theme on (British) television news was that the sinking was justified (GUMG 1985, 55).

With some exceptions, British media discussion of the *Belgrano*'s sinking centered around the word *threat*. Accounts emphasized that, because of the cruiser's weapon capacity, sinking was justified as a necessity for the safety of British men and ships (1985, 337–343). News reports concerned the military decision to sink the *Belgrano* and did so as if the decision had occurred in a political vacuum without an independent figure to account for it. The language of *threat* and *defense* avoided the issue of whether the British were intentionally escalating the military conflict, rather than simply using the minimum of force necessary to back up diplomacy as the Thatcher government claimed (1985, 61).

Media reports on the consequences of the attack focused attention on British efforts to rescue survivors rather than the number of Argentine sailors killed. This contrasted sharply with accounts of the Argentine attack on the *Sheffield*, which stressed casualties and the human tragedy involved (1985, 316–322).

Portrayals of the home front during the war were deployed to create a sense of unity and patriotism in a time of crisis. Characterization of public attitudes toward military engagement is illustrated by this quotation appearing in the April 6, 1982, *London Times*:

For older watchers the sight of British ships going to war was an evocation of times past; for their children and grandchildren the stuff of fireside yarns. "We've been kicked out of so many places in the world and now the Falklands," said one man to a neighbor. "I'd like to see the Navy do what it's paid for." (Quoted in Femenia 1996, 189)

A content analysis of BBC and ITN television newscasts covering the period of April 2 (the day of the Argentine invasion of the Falklands) to June

15 (the day Argentine forces surrendered) revealed that diplomacy is the most frequent theme appearing in news items about the war; the theme was present in sixty-five percent of the items (Morrison and Tumber 1988, 274). However, references to diplomacy in the British media use language expressing the view of the British government. Argentina is described as "intransigent" and "unlikely to compromise" and in negotiations is said to be "obstructive" and "playing for time." Britain, on the other hand, is often described as "flexible" and working "urgently" and "constructively" with the United Nations for a peaceful resolution of the conflict (GUMG 1985, 145–153).

When peace talks fail to advance, attention is directed to the actions of Argentina rather than to British escalation of the use of military force. There is little suggestion that British policy is to seek a military victory rather than a negotiated settlement. Discussion of military operations is divorced from consideration of diplomacy "so that it was easy for journalists to concentrate on military advances without having to consider whether they had to be made" (1985, 171).

Media can influence public opinion by telling the public what public opinion is. The representations of British public opinion on the Falklands War by the British media support the policy of the Thatcher government.

The issue of public opinion on the war was rarely analyzed in television news coverage. . . . Public opinion was not treated as controversial or particularly newsworthy, on the grounds that it was taken to be largely in support of the military campaign. As Patricia Holland writes about the press: "The popular papers, indeed, construct 'public opinion' as one of the characters in their drama. It becomes a kind of alternative Greek chorus, a crowd which occasionally troops onto stage to offer patriotic support to 'the nation' and 'our boys.'" (1985, 136)

Features of the British media system, military censorship, reliance on official sources, the political socialization of British journalists, and Britain's location in the structure of world political, economic, and military affairs at the time of its occurrence together shaped the way in which the British media reported the Falklands War. The results were illustrated by the ways in which the media used language, directed attention, and characterized public opinion with regard to two of the most controversial events of the war: the sinking of the *General Belgrano* and the progress of the peace talks. The results are not surprising. Constructing a symbolic universe for the British public in which Britain engages in armed aggression and frustrates the course of international peace would be as unlikely for British media as the U.S. media's constructing a symbolic universe for the American public in which major U.S. corporations engage in international bribery and endanger the health of their workers, and the U.S. military violates the human rights of its own soldiers. We now turn to consider how our media talked about their conflict.

Our Media Report the Falklands War

The U.S. military do not fight in the Falklands War. American media are not involved in reporting the fortunes of "our side" in the war, nor in the legitimating functions performed by such coverage. However, the United States is not a disinterested observer of the conflict. The amount of attention our media devote to the war, the language they use to discuss the war, aspects of the conflict to which they attend, and their representation of public opinion in the United States and elsewhere in the world reflect U.S. political, economic, and military interests of the period. United States media discussions of the sinking of the *General Belgrano* and the peace talks can be contrasted with British media accounts to suggest some systematic differences between the ways in which media talk about their own nation's conflicts and the ways in which those conflicts are discussed by the media of other nations not directly involved in the events.

For months following the outbreak of the crisis, the United States, caught between two allies, tries to restrict its role to shuttle diplomacy and attempts to show evenhandedness. In early April 1982, U.S. Secretary of State Alexander Haig attempts to mediate the dispute, but, at the end of the month, Haig announces his mission has been terminated and President Ronald Reagan declares U.S. support for Britain. The U.S. provides British forces with satellite communications links and weather forecasting from satellite observations; supplies weapons, such as new varieties of Sidewinder missiles; and makes Ascension Island usable for the British by repairing roads, building fuel pipelines, and supplying water purification facilities. The government suspends loan guarantees of the U.S. Commodity Credit Corporation to Argentina. The United States joins fourteen other nations on the British side by imposing other economic sanctions, including suspending all military exports to Argentina. However, the United States does not sever trade ties with Argentina, and lively trade continues. (In 1981 the United States had sold $2.4 billion worth of goods to Argentina and had imported $1.12 billion worth of goods; Ganley and Granley 1984, 79–90.)

Even though the conflict is over remarkably small, obscure, and sparsely populated islands in the distant South Atlantic, U.S. commercial news media pay considerable attention to the war between two of America's "friends." According to the Associated Press, the war in the Falklands is the third "top news story" of 1982, receiving more coverage than all topics other than the U.S. economy and seven deaths linked to cyanide-laced Extra-Strength Tylenol. Other major events of the year include the death of

Leonid Brezhnev, Israel's invasion of Lebanon, a massacre in Palestinian camps in Lebanon, and the first artificial heart transplant. The event's newsworthiness is enhanced by the fact that it involves elite, culturally proximate nations in an unexpected, intense, large-scale and continuing conflict (see van Ginneken 1998, 22–40).

The reaction of the British government to the coverage of the war by the media of its own country is of considerable concern to America's news organizations. Although, as noted above, British commercial news media generally discuss the war in ways that support government policy, the level of support provided by Britain's prestigious public broadcasting organization, the BBC, apparently falls short of that desired (if not expected) by British officials.

In early May, Prime Minister Margaret Thatcher encourages public protest against the BBC, and calls upon listeners/viewers to complain about the network's war coverage. Subsequently, in a May 15 editorial, *The New York Times* characterizes Thatcher's statements as abetting "deplorable attacks on the BBC for its failure to wave the Union Jack roughly enough."

On May 27, *The Washington Post* gives the British government the opportunity to speak for itself by publishing a commentary by Alan Clark, a Conservative member of Parliament and a member of its Defense Committee. Clark notes that although most British citizens expect the BBC to provide objective news reports, many are offended by the BBC's avoiding references to "us" and "them" when discussing the war and referring to "British claims" in a manner that raises doubts as to their accuracy. Clark goes on to assert that the BBC was promoting a dovish/left-wing position on the war with remarks in their newscasts, such as "the widow in Buenos Aires is no different from the widow in Portsmouth."

Some British authorities are distressed not only by what their own media have to say about the Falklands War, they are also angry at some news items reported by U.S. news organizations. For example, on May 7, 1982, *The Chicago Tribune* notes that the British Defense Ministry denies the occurrence of a major sea battle reported in some U.S. newspapers and that British officials object to items appearing in U.S. newspapers claiming Pentagon officials doubt the accuracy of some British accounts of the fighting.

Language used by U.S. media in reporting the sinking of the *General Belgrano* did not include conspicuous use of descriptors, such *as threatening*, when discussing the cruiser's relation to the British task force, nor *defensive*, when characterizing the reasons for Britain's attack on the Argentine ship. Rather, news items virtually ruled out use of such adjectives. For example, the front page of the May 5, 1982, *New York Times* reports that British allies "react with shock and dismay to the sinking of the *General Belgrano* with the presumed loss of many lives." The newspaper also notes that several

European governments, including France, Ireland, Sweden, and West Germany, were calling for a cease-fire and negotiations. A Swedish official is quoted as saying, "This violent British action is out of all proportion to the situation." Such reactions, writes *The New York Times* columnist William Borders, suggests a widely held view that "Britain was no longer blameless in the crisis." On May 9, 1982, U.S. media call attention to the facts that the *General Belgrano* was a forty-three-year-old cruiser that had been overhauled frequently and was no longer capable of her original speed, that the ship was located outside the blockade zone, and that its sinking had taken the lives of an estimated 248 of the warship's crew members.

British media frequently use words such as *intransigent, uncooperative,* and *obstructive* to characterize Argentine reactions to the peace process. Seldom do they use these same terms to describe the behavior of the British government. United States media coverage suggests that these words could be applied to the behaviors of both nations. For example, a May 5, 1982, editorial in *The New York Times* by James Reston accuses Britain of "trying to settle a political dispute by force." On May 7, *The New York Times* reports consensus of diplomats and American officials in the United States that, despite a flurry of diplomatic activity, neither side has made significant movement toward resolving the crisis. Rather, there is the assumption that Argentina and Great Britain are trying to position themselves to lessen international and domestic criticism if major fighting were to continue. On May 16, 1982, *The New York Times* reports what Argentina had been claiming: Great Britain is responsible for delaying United Nations negotiations.

The historical context of the Falklands War has three features that influence the focus of attention of U.S. commercial news media. First, it occurs during a stressful period in the Cold War. International conflicts of the time are discussed largely in terms of any perceived relationship they might have to the global struggle between the United States and its allies and the Soviet Union. Second, and related, it occurs during the launch phase of the largest peacetime military buildup in American history. Political, military, and business leaders undoubtedly have considerable interest in learning about the successes and failures of various costly weapons systems under conditions of actual warfare. Third, it occurs shortly after Congress passes most of President Reagan's supply-side economic policies. United States corporations are looking toward further expansion of international business and have concern with conditions that might affect the stability of global trade patterns.

Cold War themes are expressed in reports on official Soviet reactions to the Falklands War, in accounts of Soviet involvement in the conflict, in speculations about the consequences of the crisis for future East–West relations, and in editorials about the "lessons learned" from the war. Media interest in official Soviet responses is illustrated by these items. The May 4, 1982, *Washington Post* discusses a Russian news agency *Tass* claim that U.S. support of Great Britain in the Falklands is "promoting British aggression." On May 5, *The New York Times* notes that Soviet President Leonid Brezhnev has denounced what he terms "a return to colonial brigandage in Latin America" and is urging negotiated settlements for conflicts in Central America and the Falklands. The June 5, 1982, *Chicago Tribune* discusses Brezhnev's accusation that the British are guilty of "foreign oppression" for attempting to regain the Falkland Islands. After the fighting has ended, *The New York Times* cites Soviet press claims that the military outcome of the Falklands War has produced a "new flare up of jingoism in Great Britain" and has obscured the fact that the problem of sovereignty is far from over.

Cold War themes also are present in accounts of Soviet facilitation of Argentina's war effort. For example, on April 18, 1982, *The Chicago Tribune* reports that the USSR is supplying intelligence to Argentina. On May 1, a *Chicago Tribune* item claims that U.S. intelligence has obtained evidence indicating Soviet-made antisubmarine equipment and other electronic gear have been flown to Argentina from Cuba. On May 3, 1982, *The New York Times* notes that the USSR reportedly has been using between six and eight intelligence-gathering satellites to watch Argentine and British military movements in the Falklands. On June 4, *The Washington Post* reports a disclosure by Argentine officials that Soviet technicians have been working to link Argentine radar systems into a nationwide network to guard against possible British attack.

Columnists address the question of the long-term consequences of the Falklands conflict for the Cold War. For example, James Reston's May 9, 1982, article in *The New York Times* concerns the impact the war may have on U.S.–USSR strategic conflict for influence in the South Atlantic. Similarly, a May 20 *Chicago Tribune* item by John MacLean holds that the Falkland Islands crisis has offered the USSR a chance to enlarge its growing commercial and military ties with Latin America at the expense of the United States. Other articles deal with the impact of the Falklands War on international organizations that are major players in Cold War relations. For example, the May 30, 1982, *New York Times* notes strained relations between the Organization of American States (OAS) and the United States as a result of U.S. aid to Great Britain. A June 16 *New York Times* item reports expression of concern by the British government that resources scheduled for the island's defense are likely to weaken Great Britain's contributions to the North Atlantic Treaty Organization (NATO) unless there is a significant increase in military spending.

United States commercial news media also offer observations on the lessons learned from the Falklands War. In addition to the military lessons noted below, the war is seen as a warning that a minor territorial dispute can quickly blow up into an episode that puts the reputations and interests of superpowers at risk (*The Chicago Tribune*, June 20, 1982). More specifically, a June 23 *New York Times* article by Jiri Valenta, an international affairs fellow at the Council on Foreign Relations, contends that the Falklands War demonstrates the falsity of the Cold War notion that the aim of Russia and Cuba is to establish Marxist–Leninist states in the Western Hemisphere. Both countries had supported Argentina's right-wing junta, just as they had supported the anti-American left in Nicaragua and in El Salvador. Their objective is not narrowly ideological but rather quite general: weaken U.S. hegemony in Latin America by whatever means.

The Reagan administration's decision to increase military spending significantly generated considerable debate about the best ways to invest the new resources to meet purported U.S. security needs. The May 6, 1982, *New York Times* observes: "Naval engagements between Great Britain and Argentina add urgency to U.S. debate over the future of naval forces in an era of advanced weaponry. . . . " The May 6 *Chicago Tribune* cites the argument of U.S. Navy officials that Great Britain's loss of the destroyer *Sheffield* demonstrates that the United States should build large ships instead of smaller, less-costly vessels. More specifically, Navy officials argue for the purchase of more super aircraft carriers, one of the most expensive items in the military budget (*The New York Times*, June 20, 1982). In a series of articles appearing throughout the period of the war, *The New York Times* military analyst Drew Middleton considers the value of helicopters, air cover, and guided weaponry demonstrated in Falklands battles. All of this is of considerable interest, not only to the military, but also to U.S. defense contractors and the politicians who represent the districts in which their corporate headquarters and plants are located.

Throughout the Falklands crisis, commercial U.S. news media report on the economic concerns that have been raised for those engaged in international business. *The New York Times* (April 28) points out that American corporations had doubled their investment in Argentina since the mid-1970s and that outstanding loans are a particular worry. Individual companies with international business interests have their own problems. For example, on July 3, a *New York Times* article notes that Reynolds Aluminum is disputing news reports that destroyers *Sheffield* and *Coventry* had aluminum superstructures, which led to sinking after being hit by missiles. On July 28, 1982, the newspaper reports that IBM is filing suit to prove it lost a contract because a British firm, Severn-Trent Water, thought the United States was not pro-British enough over the Falklands crisis.

During the Falklands War, U.S. Secretary of State Alexander Haig referred to Britain as "our closest ally" (*The Chicago Tribune*, May 1, 1982). However, U.S. media did not provide the Thatcher government with language choice, topic selection, and characterizations of domestic and international opinion in reporting the war that generally characterized the supportive coverage by British commercial media. On April 22, 1982, *The Chicago Tribune* asserts that "an Anglo–Argentine war over the Falkland Islands would be ridiculous." A month later, the newspaper refers to the conflict as "stupid and unnecessary." In light of the threat to U.S. diplomatic, strategic, and economic interests in Latin America caused by U.S. support of its ally, the expression of such opinion is not surprising.

THE IRAN–IRAQ WAR

On September 22, 1980, Iraqi military forces invade Iran at several points along the 850-mile border between the two countries. The existing border, and rights to the Shatt-al-Arab waterway, which was historically the border between the two countries, had been established by the 1975 Algiers Treaty. The treaty had been drafted at the height of the power of the shah of Iran, Mohammad Reza Pahlavi, and Iraq had always viewed its provisions as antithetical to Iraqi political and economic interests. Iraqi President Saddam Hussein was seeking to reassert his country's sovereignty over both banks of the waterway, Iraq's best access route to the Persian Gulf. Iraq also was attempting to gain control over the oil-rich Iranian province of Khuzistan.

A successful preemptive strike against Iran would achieve additional, broader goals for Iraq and its leader. Saddam Hussein was concerned about attempts by Iran's new Islamic revolutionary government to incite rebellion among Iraq's Shiite majority. A military victory over Iran would eliminate the increasing threat of Iran's fundamentalist, religion-based regime to his personal leadership, to his secular government, and to the political stability of other Gulf states in which Muslim, particularly Shiite, sentiment was strong (Hourani 1991, 432). A military victory also would address the humiliating Algiers agreement, gain for Iraq a position of preeminence in the Arab world, and greatly enhance Saddam's personal prestige and influence at home, both among Arabs and among the nonaligned nations.

Iraq's invasion is timed to take advantage of conditions in Iran. The Islamic Revolution is only in its second year and Iran's political leadership is in disarray. Several political factions in the government had been unable to agree on the disposition of fifty-two hostages taken by Iranian militants who had seized the American Embassy in November 1979. (The related Iran–Contra Affair will be discussed below.) Iran's once-prosperous oil economy is faltering. Its regular armed forces, which had been large and well equipped under the shah, is demoralized by purges and defections. Iraq expects a quick and easy victory.

The advantage of surprise enables Iraqi troops to advance into Iran's Khuzistan province and capture the port of Khorramshahr. However, after some successes, Iraqi troops soon encounter unusually difficult terrain and unexpectedly strong resistance, and they fail to capture the oil-refining center of Abadan. Three months after their initiation of the war, the Iraqi military bogs down about seventy-five miles inside Iran.

Iran launches counterattacks, using its revolutionary militia to bolster its regular armed forces. In May 1982, Iranians recapture Khorramshahr. Later that year, Iraq voluntarily withdraws its troops from captured Iranian territory and begins seeking peace agreements with Iran. Now, however, Iran has little interest in peace initiatives and continues the war in an effort to overthrow Saddam Hussein. The Iranians launch numerous infantry attacks at a tremendous cost of lives on both sides, but like Iraqi forces, those of Iran fail to achieve their military objectives when confronted by difficult logistics and an impassioned military defending its own soil.

As early as 1983, reports of extraordinary events in the war begin to appear. Iran is said to be launching infantry attacks using human assault waves composed partly of young, untrained conscripts; they are repelled by the superior firepower and airpower of the Iraqis. Iraq is said to be using lethal chemical weapons against Iranian troops. In 1983, cumulative battle losses for the two countries reach an estimated three hundred thousand fatalities; approximately sixty thousand prisoners are held by the two sides (Brown and Snyder 1985, 124). Despite such human cost, the war continues. Both nations initiate periodic air and missile attacks against each other's cities and military and oil installations.

In April 1984, Iran and Iraq expand the war to the Persian Gulf, increasing concerns that the conflict will provoke a worldwide oil crisis. In anticipation of this possibility, the Carter administration had sent Airborne Warning and Control System (AWACS) aircraft to Saudi Arabia in September 1980. Subsequently, the United States deploys additional warships to patrol the Persian Gulf (Levy and Froelich 1985). Concern over the consequences of the war are not limited to the West. Although Syria supports Iran because of its own disagreements with Iraq, most other Arab states give financial or military support to Iraq, because an Iranian victory would destabilize the political system in the Gulf and might spark Shiite militancy throughout the region.

In 1985, the United States becomes more directly involved in the Iran–Iraq conflict. Senior officials of the United States National Security Council (NSC) secretly visit Iran and negotiate the sale of antitank and antiaircraft missiles to Iran in exchange for the help of its government in obtaining the release of U.S. hostages being held in Lebanon by Shiite groups loyal to

Iran. This and additional weapons sales to Iran later in 1986 directly contradict the Reagan administration's publicly stated policy of refusing either to bargain with terrorists or to aid Iran in its war with Iraq, a policy based on the belief that Iran was a sponsor of international terrorism. A portion of the $48 million that Iran paid for the arms is diverted by the NSC and given to U.S.-backed rebels fighting to overthrow the Sandinista government of Nicaragua. These activities violate the Boland amendment, a law passed by Congress in 1984 that bans direct or indirect military aid to the rebels. The NSC's illegal actions come to light in November 1986, and congressional hearings are held on the so-called Iran–Contra Affair. (The role of U.S. commercial news media, particularly television, in shaping public opinion by its coverage of these hearings is discussed in detail in Thelen 1996.)

Two additional events bring the United States into deadly contact with Iraq and Iran. On May 17, 1987, an Iraqi warplane launches a missile attack on the U.S.S. *Stark*, a navy frigate on patrol in the Persian Gulf, killing thirty-seven U.S. sailors. Iraq apologizes for the attack, claiming it was inadvertent. A U.S. warship shoots down an Iranian commercial airliner on July 3, 1988, after mistaking it for an F-14 fighter jet, killing all 290 aboard the plane.

The war, which had been a military stalemate since the mid-1980s, continues until August 1988. Then, Iran's deteriorating economy, a result of its severely reduced oil-exporting capacity, and recent Iraqi gains on the battlefield compel Iran's government to accept a United Nations cease-fire it had rejected previously. Neither side had won territory, and, as detailed below, both had lost heavily in human lives and economic resources. However, the war had not triggered a worldwide oil crisis, neither regime had collapsed under the stress of war, and the Iranian revolution had not spread to Iraq or the Persian Gulf.

Casualty estimates for the Iran–Iraq War range from 420,000 to one million or more dead and 900,000 to 1.7 million wounded. The number of refugees created is estimated at more than 1.5 million. Neither side issued its own account of casualties or economic damages. As for the overall cost, estimates range from $200 billion to $400 billion.

Estimates indicate that war damage to petroleum installations amount to $28 billion for Iran and $85 billion for Iraq. Loss in oil revenues over the course of the war are set at $23 billion for Iran and $65 billion for Iraq. Lloyd's of London said 546 ships had been attacked during the conflict, of which 90 were sunk or destroyed, and announced that its underwriters paid more than $1 billion in shipping claims, with other insurers having paid a similar amount. In light of these statistics, American commercial media news coverage of the Iran–Iraq War is particularly interesting.

Iranian and Iraqi Media Report the Iran–Iraq War

The state-controlled media of Iran and Iraq dutifully present the official views of their governments on the causes of the war and its various developments over time. Each locates events of the war within a different symbolic universe. The media system of neither Iran nor Iraq is explicitly committed to the idea of objectivity as it is generally understood in the United States and Western Europe. However, as Schudson (1978) points out, commercial media in the West emerged and succeeded by catering to diverse audiences at the same time. To do so, they had to focus their news reports on those aspects of perceived reality that all relevant audiences would be able to agree upon, and largely ignore those aspects about which the relevant audiences might differ. In this context, objectivity is purely an economic device.

As noted in Chapter 1, the notion of objectivity is always implicitly related to the notion of an agreement between relevant audiences. What might appear as objectivity to Western audiences (all relevant groups agreeing about that point of view) might appear as politically or ideologically biased to non-Western audiences, and vice versa. Even in the West, the question remains about the extent to which news is collected and presented by news organizations and the extent to which it consists of representing official statements, proposals, decisions, and perspectives.

The use of language to mediate reality is considerably more apparent in Iranian and Iraqi news reports than in their Western counterparts. By U.S. standards, their war coverage appears as little more than examples of crude propaganda. Much of Iranian and Iraqi war coverage focuses not on their direct military adversaries, but on the United States and its regional ally, Israel.

World-devouring America, by imposing the destructive war on the two Iranian and Iraqi nations who could have played a great role in the struggle against Israel's occupying regime, inflicted losses of 250 billion dollars on them. In addition to the 250 billion dollars, countless human losses have been inflicted on the two nations. This is precisely what world-devouring America and Zionist Israel wished and continue to wish. (*The Teheran Times*, August 14, 1982)

Our Media Report the Iran–Iraq War

During the midst of the conflict, Levy and Froelich observe:

the Iran–Iraq War is one of the most destructive conflicts since World War II. It has potentially profound implications for the stability of the region, the Arab-Israeli conflict, the West's petroleum lifeline, and for other interests of the superpowers. It is also of considerable theoretical interest as a model of conflict in an era of declining superpower influence, emerging regional powers, and revolutionary change. Yet in spite of its importance, the Iran–Iraq War has received surprisingly little attention in the United States. While the media have provided a running account of the course of the war, there have been few attempts at a more interpretative analysis. Drawing particularly little attention is the question of the causes of the war. This is critical, not only for understanding how the war might be resolved, but also for anticipating whether similar wars are likely to occur in the future and knowing how they might be avoided. (1985, 127)

Particularly in light of the 1991 Gulf War and renewed U.S. concerns with the region following the 2001 terrorist attacks, our commercial news media do appear to have given the Iran–Iraq War remarkably little attention. According to the Associated Press, the war was a top story only in 1980, when it began; in 1987, when it was discussed largely in terms of the Iran–Contra Affair; and in 1988, when the war ended and its implications for U.S. military and political–economic interests could be assessed. In the intervening years, the following topics appear to have been considered "more newsworthy" according to the Associated Press ratings: an attempt on the life of Pope John Paul II (1981); a professional football players' strike (1982); domestic weather (1983); the Los Angeles Summer Olympic Games (1984); a volcano eruption in Colombia (1985); and the ouster of Ferdinand Marcos from the Philippines (1986).

It is not the actual onset of the Iran–Iraq War itself that attracts U.S. media attention in late September 1980. Rather, it is the implications of the conflict for the fate of U.S. hostages held in Iran since November 4, 1979, that is the focus of initial media reports, as well as those reports about the war that follow until the hostages are released on January 20, 1981.

The overthrow of the shah of Iran by an Islamic revolutionary government earlier in 1979 had led to a steady deterioration of Iran–U.S. relations. In response to the exiled shah's admission to the United States for medical treatment in September 1979, a crowd of several hundred seize the U.S. embassy in Iran. Fifty-two U.S. citizens remain captive in the embassy until the end of the crisis. President Jimmy Carter applies economic pressure by halting oil imports from Iran and freezing Iranian assets in the United States. At the same time, he begins several diplomatic initiatives to free the hostages; all of these fail. On April 24, 1980, the United States attempts a military rescue mission that also fails. In the United States, inability to resolve the crisis contributes to Carter's defeat in the presidential election. After the elections, with the assistance of Algeria, successful negotiations begin. On January 20, 1981, the day of President Ronald Reagan's inauguration, the United States releases Iranian assets, and the hostages are freed after 444 days of Iranian detention.

Throughout its course, the hostage crisis, as much as any major feature of the war itself, is a focal point of U.S. media coverage of the Iran–Iraq conflict. Two additional media concerns also are apparent in media reports from the first days of battle to the war's conclusion: the Cold War interests of the United States and the impact of fighting about access to oil supplies important to the operation of the American economy.

All of these central concerns are apparent in the September 23, 1980, front-page article in *The New York Times* appearing under the headline, "Iraqi Planes Strike 10 Airfields in Iran: Oil Area Imperiled." A *Washington Post* editorial appearing on the same day (September 23, 1980) also emphasizes both the bearing of the war on U.S. interests in the region, a potential venue for Cold War confrontation with the Soviet Union, and the consequences of the outbreak of the war for the American hostages in Iran.

At the beginning of 1984, the United States and the Soviet Union continue their Cold War verbal assaults, labeling one another a threat to world peace. On January 10, the Soviet Union calls for a ban on chemical weapons in Europe. Western diplomats, responding cautiously, note that previous negotiations on the subject had failed because of Soviet reluctance to agree to verification procedures. On January 23, 1984, President Ronald Reagan sends a report to Congress alleging seven probable Soviet violations of arms control agreements. They include Soviet use of chemical weapons in Afghanistan and Southeast Asia. Whether the United States itself should pursue development of chemical weapons is a topic of congressional debate.

Against this background, the Iran–Iraq War becomes considerably more newsworthy on March 6, 1984, when U.S. accusations that Iraq is employing chemical weapons against Iran are reported. Throughout March, April, and May, 1984, U.S. newspapers frequently publish articles and editorials on this aspect of the war. Without this contextualization, reports on the war, even with the presence of such weapons, might well have remained on the back pages of newspapers and been largely omitted from nightly commercial television newscasts.

Two other events prompt American media to remind the public of Iran and Iraq. On May 17, 1987, an Iraqi Mirage F-1 jet mistakenly attacks the U.S. frigate *Stark,* killing thirty-seven sailors. The ship was on patrol in the Persian Gulf in international waters. Iraqi President Saddam Hussein admits that Iraq was responsible and terms the event an "unintended accident" that should not affect relations between Iraq and the United States. The event is given extensive coverage from May 18, 1987, through early June. News items focus on U.S. casualties, reasons why the ship's advanced electronic equipment failed to detect the launching of the missile against the vessel, the U.S. mission in the Gulf, and memorial services.

Newspaper editorials discuss the event in terms of U.S. military policy. For example, *The New York Times* notes that the attack "has once again raised the question that has bedeviled U.S. foreign policy for a quarter-century: does Washington think through with sufficient rigor commitment of U.S. forces and prestige to trouble spots around the globe?" (May 22, 1987). A *Washington Post* editorial says that the "Iran arms initiative and the *Stark* tragedy raise the question of who has authority to commit the U.S. to military deployment?" (May 22, 1987). In all of this, there is little, if any, mention of the context in which the accident occurred—the Iran–Iraq War.

On July 3, 1988, the U.S. cruiser *Vincennes* shoots down an Iranian commercial airliner, after apparently mistaking it for an attacking F-14 fighter jet. All 290 aboard the plane die. President Ronald Reagan expresses deep regret for the loss of life. American media, treating the event as major news, describe it as a "tragedy" and raise numerous questions about the conditions under which it occurred. They also raise more general questions about U.S. policy in the Persian Gulf. Other topics discussed in conjunction with the incident include new threats to airline and airport security in Europe and the United States, and possible consequences for the treatment of the U.S. hostages, being held at that time in Lebanon.

U.S. commercial news coverage of the Iran Airlines plane contrasts sharply with their reporting of a comparable incident occurring five years earlier (Entman 1991). On September 1, 1983, a Soviet fighter plane shoots down Korean Airlines (KAL) flight 007, killing its 269 passengers and crew. As in the case of the Iran Airline destruction, military officials identified a passenger plane as a possibly hostile target and claimed the shooting was justified under the circumstances. However, when the Soviet Union is the perpetrating nation, U.S. media emphasize its moral bankruptcy and guilt. In reporting U.S. action, they de-emphasize guilt and focus on the complex problems of operating military high technology. American media (specifically *Time*, *Newsweek*, CBS Television, *The New York Times*, and *The Washington Post*) provide about twice as much coverage of the KAL matter as that of the Iranian Airlines. More often, they tend to refer to the Soviet action as an "attack" and the U.S. action as a "tragedy," more often use humanizing words, such as "innocent human beings" and "loved ones," in referring to victims of the Soviet attack, while selecting words such as "civilians," "passengers," and "travelers" to refer to the victims of the U.S. attack. On July 7, 1983, *The Washington Post* reports the results of a poll indicating that seventy-one percent of Americans support the *Vincennes* action in the Persian Gulf. Here again, commercial news media by focusing attention, selecting language, and representing public opinion, socially construct events in ways supporting existing U.S. government interests. Despite the extent of its coverage, the Iranian Airline incident does not produce discussion of the incessant Iran–Iraq War and its devastating consequences for the Iranian and Iraqi people, including loss of life, property destruction, interruption or termination of needed social programs, inflation, and so on. Apparently all of this does not so clearly merit application of the term *tragedy* by U.S. commercial news media. Their focus and language use is consistent with the following reported observation:

The daily flux of television coverage is remarkably isolationist, as David Halberstam has pointed out; TV moguls think ordinary foreign news doesn't sell because ordinary folks aren't interested in it. The eight year Iran-Iraq War, for example, was a "non-event" for American TV. (Cumings 1992, 107)

HOW WE TALK ABOUT THEIR WARS

A review of U.S. commercial news coverage of the Falklands War and the Iran–Iraq War reveals that, when reporting such foreign news, our media not only construct images of other nations, but also define the legitimate interests of our country and provide rationales for its various actions. As in all discourse, when we talk about them, we simultaneously talk about ourselves. In the process of reporting international news, our media employ typifications and reveal the artificiality of the distinction between explanation and evaluation of the social world, while offering its items as reports on the natural order of things.

The ethnocentrism of American news media reports is more easily identified by foreign than by domestic audiences (see Wasburn 1992, 79–83). Like most media presentations of purportedly factual material, our accounts of the two wars were likely to have been understood as *news* by American audiences. The reports were less likely to have been assigned such credibility by the Argentinians, British, Iranians, and Iraqis who read or viewed them. Certainly there were those in the warring nations who were critical of their government's actions and skeptical of war reporting presented by their own domestic media. However, it seems unlikely that most Argentinians understood their war effort, in which hundreds of their countrymen lost their lives, as having been manipulated by the Soviet Union in its attempt to enlarge its commercial and military ties with Latin America. Certainly many British would reject characterization of the decision to send their fleet to the Falkland Islands, with all its attendant risks, as trying to settle a political dispute by force. Sustaining huge losses of life and economic resources, Iranians were unlikely to view their fighting with Iraq as having been driven by Ayatollah Khomeini's taste for tension and martyrdom. Similarly, Iranians, particularly members of the Shiite majority, would seem unlikely to have understood their sacrifices as having been incurred in the interests of an autocratic, secular government.

Should they have encountered them, American commercial news constructions of the two wars would likely have been dismissed as U.S. propaganda by citizens of the involved nations. (Historical ties and cultural similarities made this reaction much less likely for members of British audiences than for readers/viewers in Argentina, Iran, and Iraq.) However, domestic U.S. audiences would have little reason to question the media reports. They employed the typifications on which our public relies to make sense of the world and our country's place in it.

In covering the Falklands War, Britain is presented as inappropriately aggressive in dealing with a Third World nation—an extension, perhaps, of its history as a colonial power. By way of contrast, American media reporting of U.S. involvements in Vietnam, Laos, Cambodia, El Salvador, Guatemala, Nicaragua, and Granada seldom suggested the existence of U.S. imperialism. Rather, this country's actions were characterized as supporting those struggling for "freedom" and "democracy" throughout the world (Herman and Chomsky 1988; Parenti 1986/1993). When we talked about British imperialism, we were suggesting a lack of such in our own Third World engagements.

In the context of the Cold War, when we talked about Argentina being manipulated by the Soviet Union, we were suggesting that the United States did not engage in such covert activity in Latin America. U.S. commercial news media paid little attention to U.S. involvement in the 1973 military coup in Chile, had used euphemistic phraseology in describing the acts of the Chilean military, and had characterized the event as a move to restore domestic order to the nation (Lee and Solomon 1991, 49).

Whatever its merits, the suggestion by U.S. news media that Argentina was being influenced by the Soviet Union was unlikely to be accepted by the citizens of Argentina. Argentine citizens had greater reason to reject the claim, made by foreign news media, than U.S. audiences had for rejecting the assertions carried by their own domestic media, namely, that a major U.S.-based corporation knowingly endangered the lives of its workers in a Third World country, and that the U.S. military summarily executed some of its defectors.

Discussion of U.S. Cold War interests are as prominent in commercial news coverage of the Iran–Iraq War as they are in their reports of the Falklands conflict. Media repeat the government's concern that politically unstable Iran will encourage Soviet incursion into a region of strategic political, economic, and military importance to the United States. Ethnocentrism is apparent again, this time in the focus of attention on the fate of American hostages, to the near exclusion of expressing any concern for the impact of the war on the people of Iran and Iraq. This is seen again in discussions of the mistaken Iraqi attack on a U.S. naval vessel and the unintended destruction of an Iranian civilian airliner by a U.S. warship. In both cases, the primary issue raised was that of clearly defining the role of the U.S. military in international trouble spots, rather than the loss of life.

In the United States, the downing of the Iranian passenger plane is presented by the media to the public as a tragedy. Such a characterization promotes the idea that the United States would never intentionally engage in such an act (see Entman 1991). The assumption is not so easily made by those in countries whose media construct the United States as "world devouring."

Chapter 3

We're Talking about Them: U.S. News Media Construction of Other Nations' Internal Wars and Assassinations

The term "internal war" was originally proposed by Harry Eckstein (1966) to denote any resort to violence within a political system to change its constitution, rulers, or policies. It is conducted practically without mutually observed normative rules and involves serious disruptions of settled institutional patterns. All species of internal wars have in common the use of force to achieve purposes that can also be achieved without violence. All indicate a breakdown in the legitimate political order and the existence of collective frustration and aggression in the population. All presuppose certain capabilities for violence by those who make the internal war and a certain incapacity for preventing violence among those on whom it is made. All tend to scar societies deeply and prevent the formation of consensus indefinitely.

This chapter reviews U.S. and foreign media reporting of two internal wars that received extensive news coverage throughout the world. Each conflict has had lasting impact. Hostilities between Israel and the Palestinians (1987–1993) re-ignited in 2000. Questions about China's political future raised by the Tiananmen Square uprising (1989) remain; previously classified Chinese government documents concerning the government's response to the event became public in 2001 and cast doubt as to the legitimacy and stability of the regime. Chapter 3 also considers U.S. commercial news media accounts of three political assassinations—a form of internal war. Analysis of the way in which each assassination was reported suggests how we construct political reality and how we talk about ourselves, even when we report their domestic conflicts and their state rituals.

THE PALESTINIAN REBELLION

A series of actions directed by Palestinians against the rule of Israel in the Gaza Strip and the West Bank erupt in Winter 1987, and continue until late 1993. Known as the *Intifada* (Arabic word for "shaking"), over time they include strikes, boycotts of Israeli goods, demonstrations in support of Palestinian nationhood, blocking roads, tire burning, Molotov cocktail attacks, physical assaults against Israeli civilians and settlers, and rock throwing by young men and boys against Israeli soldiers. The *Intifada* differs from earlier Palestinian protests in its wide support, duration, and involvement of Islamic groups including the Palestine Liberation Organization (PLO) and Hamas.

The particular event precipitating the uprising occurs on December 8, 1987, when an Israeli army truck runs into a group of Palestinians near the Jabalya Refugee Camp in the Gaza Strip, killing four and injuring seven. Rumors spread that the four had been killed by Israelis as a deliberate act of revenge for the stabbing death of a Jewish salesman that had occurred in Gaza. Also, Palestinians are already aroused by a recent increase in pressure by Jewish militants to take over Islam's third holiest site, the Havam al Sharif, the revered Temple Mount to Jews, in Arab East Jerusalem.

Daily, the riots escalate throughout the territories, and are particularly severe in the Gaza Strip, a 5-by-28 mile area packed with about 550,000 people, mostly refugees. Israel reacts with efforts at armed suppression, including use of live ammunition. Its riot-control methods produced strong criticism from the United Nations (UN) Security Council, as well as from human rights organizations throughout the world, such as American Friends Service Committee and Amnesty International. Constant rumors of human rights violations on the part of both Palestinians and Israelis contribute to the continuation and increasing intensity of the conflict.

The UN Security Council also is critical of Israel's response to the uprising, voting 14–0–1 on December 22, 1987, to support a resolution deploring Israel's "policies and practices which violate the human rights of the Palestinian people in the occupied territories." The United States, the lone abstainer, nevertheless reproaches Israel for its harsh security measures and the excessive use of live ammunition (*The New York Times*, December 23, 1987).

Despite White House criticism of Israel, Congress subsequently passes provisions that expanded its aid by agreeing to refinance Israel's $9-billion debt to reduce its interest rates. In addition, Israel is granted $3 billion in economic and military aid, allowed to use $150 million of its military aid on an advanced aircraft research and development program in the United States, and permitted to use another $400 million of its military aid for defense procurement in Israel (Mark 1991).

The continuation of U.S. financial aid does not mean that Israel is unconcerned about the potential effects of U.S. media coverage of the *Intifada* with its almost nightly visual depictions of rock-throwing adolescents confronting heavily armed Israeli troops, and its seemingly endless discussions of closing Palestinian schools, deportation, demolition of the homes of suspected "terrorists," and restriction of the work life of ordinary Palestinians, not to mention statistics reporting the number of Palestinians killed and wounded. Nevertheless, Israeli Defense Minister Yitzhak Rabin comments that while international news coverage of the *Intifada* has produced a negative image of Israel, this is a temporary cost Israel must pay in order to eliminate violence in the territories (*The New York Times*, January 25, 1987).

Despite the human, political, and economic costs incurred by both Palestinians and Israelis, the *Intifada*, like the Iran–Iraq War, goes on month after month, year after year. In late 1991, a new round of peace talks is set in motion. After an initial general meeting, which included the United States, Israel, and several Arab nations, Israel and the Palestinians meet for bilateral talks, but negotiations seem to be ending in deadlock. However, in early 1993, without informing Washington, Israel and the Palestinians begin meeting in secret in Oslo, with Norway acting as moderator. By late August 1993, the two sides come to an agreement, and the Clinton Administration is finally notified. On September 13, 1993, amid great ceremony on the south lawn of the White House, Israel and the Palestine Liberation Organization sign "The Declaration of Principles of Interim Self-Government Arrangements," generally referred to as the "Oslo Accords." The document includes a schedule for Israel's disengagement from the occupied territories and for a transitional period of Palestinian self-rule leading to a permanent settlement based on United Nations Security Council resolutions.

The signing of the Oslo Accords signals mutual recognition of the PLO and Israel, and produces some expectation of peace in the Middle East. With this, the *Intifada* essentially ends. However, after the Israeli elections of 1996, relations between the Palestinians and Israel deteriorate, and violent confrontation between the two parties has erupted periodically to the present time.

Israeli and Palestinian Media Report the *Intifada*

It is hardly surprising that the Palestinian newspaper *Al-Fajr Jerusalem* and the Israeli newspaper *The Jerusalem Post* talk about the *Intifada* in vastly different ways. A content analysis of the newspapers by Collins and Clark (1993) found that *Al-Fajr* labels the uprising a "rebellion" and describes events as a natural result of Israeli persecution of Palestinians—of the strong oppressing the weak. In the symbolic universe constructed by

Al-Fajr, the Palestinian people are victims who are exercising constraint in the face of unrelenting oppression; the Palestinian people are a David waging a war for international public opinion against the Israeli Goliath. The *Intifada* is a quest story for justice and equality.

The narrative structure employed by *Al-Fajr* supports its construction of political reality. The newspaper lists each act of the Palestinians and each response of the Israelis, producing the cumulative image of a widespread, organized uprising with unity and purpose. In addition, "the accounts separate the Palestinian protest from the Israeli response so that the soldiers' violence stands alone as Israeli repression. In this fashion the injustice and inequality experienced by the occupied peoples are highlighted" (Collins and Clark 1993, 194).

Unlike the single, consistent, official Palestinian version of the *Intifada* presented in *Al-Fajr*, *The Jerusalem Post* sometimes challenges the Israeli government's account, reflecting, to some extent, the division of opinion among Israel's public. Occasionally, in *The Jerusalem Post*, events are referred to as acts of *rebellion*, rather than acts of *terrorism*. Occasionally, there is an expression of support for a peaceful settlement of the conflict, rather than the use of repressive measures. Nevertheless, the narrative structure of *The Jerusalem Post* clearly favors an Israeli perspective. In the newspaper, Israel's police and military actions are defensive responses to unwarranted violence on the part of Palestinian "extremists." Attention is focused on Israel's "historic land rights." Readers are not exposed to the injustice and victimization story that dominates *Al-Fajr*'s account of the *Intifada*.

Instead of separating the accounts of school closures and each use of a petrol bomb, *The Jerusalem Post* is more likely to mention rebellion generally. "Demonstrations occurred throughout the territories" replaces a list of each site. When closures, deportations, or the like are mentioned, they are seldom detailed as in the Palestinian coverage. The iterative style minimizes both the scope of the disruption and the military response. (Collins and Clark 1993, 194–195)

For *The Jerusalem Post*, the *Intifada* is a continuation of powerful Arab terrorism against tiny, peace-loving Israel. The account is in keeping with Israelis' shared understanding of both Palestinians and their fellow countrymen. What reasonable Israeli citizens could believe that their soldiers would intentionally kill Palestinians teenagers without a real and direct threat to their own lives? What sensible Israeli citizens could not treat *Al-Fajr*'s reports on the *Intifada* as little more than propaganda? While there was some division of opinion among Israeli elites as well as among the general public, the symbolic universe of Israelis and Palestinians simply did not coincide.

Our Media Report the *Intifada*

American commercial news media provided extensive coverage of the *Intifada* throughout 1988, exceeding that given events occurring closer to the United States, such as power struggles in Panama and Sandinista–Contra warfare in Nicaragua. The amount of attention is of concern to the Israeli government because of our media's largely critical view of Israel's policy and response (Gilboa 1993, 95–96). However, Israel's claim that the *Intifada* draws "exaggerated" coverage in the United States does not appear to find support (Cohen, Adoni, and Nossek 1993, 128). The newsworthiness of the *Intifada*, like that of the Falklands War, is related to the fact that it involves a close U.S. ally in an intense, large-scale and continuing conflict.

American media play a central role in the *Intifada* as part of the Palestinians' "force-policy" strategy. The Palestinian goal is to generate favorable coverage of the uprising that will influence public opinion in America and convince Washington to adopt policies they desire. Chief among these policies is putting pressure on Israel to establish a Palestinian state (Gilboa 1993, 112). The strategy is partially successful. American media news reports do talk about them in the ways they desire. Coverage is favorable to the Palestinian cause to the point that Avi Pazner, the Israeli prime minister's press adviser, refers to it as intentionally distorted and one-sided and accuses television reporting in particular as exhibiting blatant bias (Lederman 1992).

According to Lederman, the pro-Palestinian disposition of American commercial news media sometimes goes so far as to involve making inaccurate and misleading statements, thereby providing highly unequal coverage of the two sides. Lederman provides the following examples, among numerous others:

On March 12, NBC's Connie Chung introduced a piece by Jim Bitterman by saying, "More Arab policemen who work for Israel in the occupied territories resigned today to protest Israel's treatment of the Palestinians." But what Jim Bitterman said less than a minute later in his report was that the policemen had resigned "apparently [following] threats from the PLO." (1992, 266)

The Palestinian side was covered in considerable depth, with a strong emphasis on the human side of the story. [*New York Times* correspondent John] Kifner's dispatches included eyewitness accounts, interviews with a broad spectrum of Palestinians, and investigative reporting—including one of the very first interviews with a leader of the Palestinian underground. But the *Times*' reporting on the Israeli side was restricted to official public statements, speeches, and comments by Israeli journalists and a relatively small number of interviewees. (1992, 227)

At least during the initial phase of the *Intifada*, U.S. commercial news media coverage is so favorable to the Palestinians that "many went so far as to suggest that Israel was engaging in a holocaust against the Palestinians. Some compared Israel's alleged treatment of the Palestinians to South Africa's apartheid policy and treatment of blacks" (Gilboa 1993, 96). The construction of the *Intifada* favorable to the Palestinians is particularly interesting in light of its inconsistency with the perspective of the U.S. government. Washington's view is reflected in the policy of continuing substantial military aid to Israel during the period. The pattern of reporting is also interesting because it is inconsistent with public opinion in the United States. Since the establishment of Israel in 1948, Americans have always sympathized more with Israel than with the Arab states (1993, 100). This reflects U.S. difficulties with Libya and Iraq; the public's identification of the PLO as a "terrorist organization," rather than as a "national liberation movement"; the public's negative opinion of PLO leader Yasir Arafat; widespread perception of common values and interests shared with Israel; and negative stereotypes of Arabs present in American culture of the time (1993, 100–110).

Several factors contribute to the unusual situation in which U.S. commercial media discourse about other nations is inconsistent with both official government policy and American public opinion. According to Wolfsfeld (1997, 131), three conditions provided the Palestinians with the opportunity to make their case to the world. First, Israel lacked the ability to initiate or to control events of the *Intifada*. Second, Israel also was unable to regulate the flow of information to the news media. Third, Israeli elites themselves were divided on how to respond to the Palestinian uprising; smaller parties from the left and the right formed a vocal opposition to government policy in the territories (also see Cohen, Adoni, and Bantz 1990).

United States commercial media, particularly television, presented images of the *Intifada* that supported the Palestinian narrative. Generally favoring the most dramatic, attention-grabbing pictures to tell a story about conflict, American media feature pictures of young Palestinian men and boys throwing rocks and shooting slingshots at their adversaries—regular Israeli military armed with weapons ranging from tear gas grenades to tanks and attack helicopters. Although any given picture is open to a number of interpretations (as will be illustrated below in a discussion of a now legendary photograph taken during China's Tiananmen Square conflict), the repetitious presentation of "soldier versus child" pictures—particularly those graphically showing Palestinian casualties over a period of weeks and months—is considerably less open to a variety of readings. Given Israel's inability to control news coverage of the *Intifada*, American media's images dictated its message more than did the constant repetition of an argument.

As the *Intifada* continues, its repeated images lose some of their emotional impact, and media interest shifts to events more directly linked to major international interests of the United States—events with their own drama. Chief among these are Mikhail Gorbachev's campaign for reform in the Soviet Union; revolutionary changes throughout Eastern Europe; tearing down the Berlin Wall; and, above all else, ending the Cold War that had dominated international news for more than four decades. The *Intifada* becomes a minor disturbance in world affairs (Gilboa 1993, 112). It remains as such until 2000, when there is a dramatic escalation of Palestinian–Israeli conflict.

THE TIANANMEN SQUARE UPRISING

After the announcements of the death of former General Secretary of the Chinese Communist party Hu Yaobang on April 15, 1989, hundreds gather in Beijing's Tiananmen Square to pay tribute to his memory. In 1987, Hu had been forced from his leadership position by party conservatives who disapproved of his reformist sympathies and "bourgeois liberalism."

Students sympathetic to the political perspective Hu had come to represent immediately stream to Tiananmen Square, and within a week, their numbers reach approximately two hundred thousand. In the aftermath of the Cultural Revolution, and in the wake of ten years of slow-moving political change, they come to demand a variety of specific reforms within China under the leadership of the Communist party. Such reforms include better treatment for intellectuals (such as more money for education, better salaries, and job assignments after graduation); an end to corruption (existing in many forms, including a dual-pricing system and preferential treatment given party officials and their relatives, such as access to lucrative jobs, better housing arrangements, increased ration coupons, access to foreign goods, and better college placement for their children); greater government accountability and responsiveness to citizens' input into government policy; and respect for freedoms that are guaranteed in China's constitution but not realized in practice (specifically, freedom to demonstrate, freedom of speech, and freedom of the press). Such demands, particularly those focusing on ending corruption, are widely supported by socially diverse groups throughout China (He 1996; Shorenstein Center 1992).

By the third week in April 1989, unrest has spread to other cities, notably Chanqsha and Xi'an. On April 24, students at universities in Beijing boycott classes. Student leaders meet with several officials, but subsequently claim that their complaints would not be addressed.

On April 26, 1989, *The People's Daily* publishes an editorial entitled, "Resolutely Oppose Turmoil." The editorial claims that the student movement was instigated by a handful of "bad elements" who had "ulterior motives" and that it is a planned conspiracy against the leadership of the

Chinese Communist party and against China's socialist system (He 1996, 50). The editorial escalates tensions, galvanizes opposition to the government, and prompts a major demonstration the day after it appears (Mark 1991b, 264).

Demonstrations continue for weeks and spread to Shanghai, Zhejiang, Hubei, Hainan, Jainqsu, and Sichuan. On May 15, 1989, Soviet President Mikhail Gorbachev arrives in Beijing in the midst of protests in Tiananmen Square that now include a hunger strike involving about two thousand students. Gorbachev's long-planned visit is the first of a Soviet leader to China since 1959, and is a symbol of the rapprochement of the world's two largest Communist nations after thirty years of bitter antagonism. (The countries are still engaged in disputes. At the time, they are backing different factions in a military conflict in Cambodia.) Hosting the summit meetings between the two countries had tremendous potential for enhancing international credibility for the Chinese government and its leading figure, Deng Xiaoping. However, to the students, Gorbachev personified the ideal of political reform within the socialist framework, while Deng represented the very source of the problems to which the demonstrations were a response.

On May 17, 1989, an estimated crowd of one million persons, including many workers, pack Tiananmen Square. Demonstrations also occur in at least twenty other cities throughout China. After Gorbachev's departure, top officials, including Premier Li Peng and Communist party head Zhao Ziyang visit Tiananmen Square and say that the demonstrators have "good intentions" but that they must be patient. Zhao issues a written statement on behalf of the Politburo, affirming the students' "patriotic spirit" and calling on them to stop the hunger strike.

Despite such statements, on May 20, 1989, Premier Li Peng announces the imposition of martial law in Beijing. Troops with armored vehicles and tanks move toward the capital. In response, thousands of workers and students block military convoys. Large demonstrations are held, not only throughout China, but throughout the world to protest Li's action. (Some 500,000 people march in Hong King.) Within the following week, hundreds of thousands march in Beijing to show their defiance of martial law and to demand the resignation of Li Peng and other hard-line leaders. However, the number of troops around Beijing is increased to an estimated 200,000 by May 26, 1989. Subsequently, the number of students in Tiananmen Square begins to decline. Engaging in "image politics," on May 30, Chinese art students erect a thirty-foot-high statue called Goddess of Liberty in the square, suggestive of the Statue of Liberty (see DeLuca 1999).

The Chinese government abandons restraint on June 3, 1989, and orders the People's Liberation Army to put an end to the demonstrations. Shooting at crowds and using armored vehicles and tanks, the army kills hundreds and wounds thousands. The army suffers hundreds of wounded as well. The government then begins rounding up dissident leaders. Some of the student organizers flee abroad. Party officials who had shown some conciliation toward the students, from Zhao to local level bureaucrats, are removed from office. Zhao himself is accused of fostering "counterrevolutionary rebellion."

By the end of June 1989, public protest has ended, but the movement has not been without consequence. In July, the Politburo adopts reforms aimed at combating official corruption. In September, Deng reaffirms that China would adhere to the tenets of Communism, but also that the regime would keep its doors open to the West and preserve the economic policies of the past decades.

Chinese Media Report the Tiananmen Square Uprising

Throughout most of the history of Communist China, news media serve the interests of the state. However, state control has varied over time. The news media serve as a kind of political barometer for citizens to gauge the extent to which dissent could be voiced. In the late 1980s, the government establishes a climate that seems to encourage open expression of political discontent, at least in discussing official corruption. Such coverage is in line with a government campaign to root out official profiteering and other forms of misconduct (Mark 1991b, 261).

By the time of the Tiananmen Square uprising, Chinese journalists had been waging a lengthy struggle for greater press freedom. The uprising provides journalists with a significant opportunity to explore the limits of their independence and their ability to establish a set of professional norms that are contrary to those imposed on the media by the party (He 1996, 184–188).

Following the death of Hu Yaobang, there is an outpouring of articles in his memory. However, a few days later, when students begin marching in support of the former leader and the ideals he had come to represent for them, their activities are largely ignored. Politburo member Hu Qili orders newspapers not to cover demonstrations on grounds that publicizing them will provoke further unrest and contribute to political instability. However, in spite of this order, less tightly controlled Chinese newspapers, such as *Science and Technology Daily* and *The World Economic Herald*, publish extensive accounts of an April 22, 1989, march involving about six thousand students.

Four days after this exercise of media autonomy, *The People's Daily* is ordered to publish an editorial based on a secret speech of Deng Xiaoping. Its description of the protests as "counter-revolutionary rebellion" justifies government efforts to halt them. Available methods include tightening control over all domestic news media to create a uniform view of the turmoil that supports the regime.

Freedom of the press now becomes a major issue and directly involves journalists in the conflict. While largely avoiding the issue of the legitimacy of China's government, many journalists are already sympathetic to the demonstrators because of their attack on rampant corruption and their call for better treatment for intellectuals (a category that includes their profession). Some turn to American media as an outlet for their own accounts of some events.

The degree to which Chinese journalists were frustrated can be measured by how much information the Western news media was able to obtain from them. "We saw more than you did, but you published more than we did," one Chinese journalist told *The New York Times* regarding student clashes with police. (Mark 1991b, 282–283)

The relationships among Chinese media, Western media, and the demonstrators becomes increasingly complex throughout May 1989, significantly affecting Chinese media output. Western journalists had been devoting considerable coverage to the demonstrations since the third week in April when students clashed with police in Tiananmen Square. Their coverage focused on the dramatic demonstrations and the government's ill-conceived attempts to quell them.

As students and the government appear to reach a stalemate in early May, Western media refocus their attention on Gorbachev's visit. This change is welcomed by the party leadership, who wish not only to divert international attention from the demonstrations, but also to disseminate worldwide images promoting recognition of China as a major player in world politics at the beginning of a new decade. To this end, the government grants permission for more than one thousand foreign journalists to join the regular Beijing press corps, gives them extra satellite privileges, and permits them to cover the demonstrations. However, Western media subvert the party's interest. "[The] journalists were greeted by thousands of workers and intellectuals and other citizens protesting the government's response to the student movement. The images of Gorbachev and Deng Xiaoping were overwhelmed by marching youths" (Mark 1991b, 268).

Students see the presence of international media as an opportunity to get attention and sympathy in the West, particularly in the United States. Many signs carried by the protesters are in English; "We Shall Overcome" is sung and the papier-mâché Goddess of Liberty is paraded before Western television cameras (Hachten 1999, 76). In addition, student leaders are convinced that the presence of the large international press corps will help restrain hardliners in the government who want to use the police and the military to restore order, whatever the cost (Mark 1991b, 270).

Although protesters do receive the desired coverage, they do not get the protection they assumed they would have. "On May 19, 1989, on the eve of the imposition of martial law, U.S. audiences experienced government censorship firsthand when CBS and CNN interrupted their broadcasts to cover themselves being thrown off the air" (1991b, 270). Under martial law, the flow of uncensored information from Chinese media organizations is shut off. Newspapers continue to operate, but under tight controls imposed by a newly formed Special Propaganda Committee that dictates publishing the official government perspective and orders discrediting Western media as "rumor mongers" (Cheng 1990, 143).

Government control of domestic media is in place when, on June 3, 1989, troops are ordered into Tiananmen Square to end the uprising by military force. However, the violence and its aftermath are so dramatic that a newscaster with the English Language Service of Radio Beijing, China's official international radio broadcasting organization, is moved to comment:

Radio Beijing's English Department deeply mourns those who died in the tragic incident and appeals to its listeners to join our protest for this gross violation of human rights and the most barbarous suppression of the people. Because of the abnormal situation here in Beijing, there is no other news we could bring you. We sincerely ask for your understanding and thank you for joining us at this most tragic moment. (Quoted in Mark 1991b, 259)

The newscaster, Li Dan, is subsequently summoned to a meeting with government officials; the limit of China's tolerance of media independence had been surpassed. Following the suppression of the Tiananmen Square uprising, Chinese media rarely speak with other than an official voice.

Our Media Report the Tiananmen Square Uprising

We have seen that U.S. political, economic, and military interests are reflected in the symbolic realities constructed by our commercial news media as representations of foreign wars and internal conflicts, even those in which the United States is not directly involved. However, the extent to which such interests structure news content in different historical cases varies with the apparent clarity of those interests to political elites and to various segments of the American public.

Reporters on the West Bank were as emotionally involved with the Palestinian children and youths who challenged armed Israeli troops . . . as they were later with the Chinese students who engaged in a hunger strike. But there was one aspect of the Middle East story that checked any tendency toward emotional writing and loss of objectivity. (As one journalist commented): "We knew that there was an audience back home, the Jewish community, that would blow us out of the water if we showed our bias. We also knew that there was no equivalent audience to keep us honest on the Chinese story." (Shorenstein Center 1992, 99)

During the spring of 1989, the Tiananmen Square uprising dominates the foreign news content not only of U.S. commercial media, but also that of media throughout the West. Events in Tiananmen Square are dramatic, involving conflict between socially constructed forces of good and evil. Sometimes the conflict is violent. New satellite technology is in place to provide the West with its first live view of political turmoil in a communist nation. More important than this, however, in accounting for the vast amount of attention paid by U.S. commercial news media, is the amenability of reports to incorporation as essential parts of the most important political news story told by Western commercial news media since the end of World War II: the "collapse of Communism." According to this narrative, people throughout the world, particularly young people, are struggling for the cause of American-style freedom and democracy. Now their goals appear close to being realized.

From the beginning of its coverage of the demonstrations, U.S. news media characterize students as participants in a "prodemocracy" movement (Mark 1991b, 283–284). More than most descriptors used to characterize a political movement, *prodemocracy* is vague, ambiguous, and emotion laden. As AP correspondent Tom Kent observes,

I can recall the word democracy appearing on the lips of Afghan guerrillas, Ethiopian revolutionaries, Yeltsin, Kuwaiti students, Kurdish tribesmen and an announcer from North Korean radio. Something here suggests that definition is necessary when the word is used and I think that's something that we will carry forward from this [Chinese experience]. (Quoted in Shorenstein Center 1992, 45)

Commercial news media's use of the simplifying label "prodemocracy" to characterize the uprising refers to a core value of American society that is likely to generate a high level of audience interest. Use of the term immediately makes the Cold War frame available to news producers to tell the overall story of Tiananmen Square. The frame facilitates the selection of particular events to report and suggests the vocabulary to use in describing them. However, as noted above, the term *prodemocracy* is notoriously vague. Furthermore, its use is misleading, for protesters are pursuing a wide range of goals, but one that does not include establishing American-style political democracy in China. As ABC correspondent Jackie Judd comments in retrospect, "I believe we tried to put a 'made in the U.S.A.' democracy stamp on it" (quoted in Shorenstein Center 1992, 40).

Media use of "prodemocracy" creates a symbolic universe featuring typifications of protesters as heroes and Chinese officials as villains. The language encourages media to select information sources who conform to its assumptions and who, in turn, further facilitate the creation of thematically consistent accounts of events.

Reporters tend over time to adopt the outlook of the news sources with whom they are associated; they ask questions appropriate to their sources' world. In as much as questions contain their own answers, guiding where one may look for an answer and thus what one may find, the questions may be said to reconstitute not only a topic but a world. (Tuchman 1978, 152)

Among the major sources of information about events are Chinese students—not only those directly involved in the events unfolding in Tiananmen Square but even students who are far away studying at American universities. "These students became in many ways surrogates for their peers in China. They became instant experts, although many had been away from China for years. They were looked upon as sources even though many of them only had second hand information" (Shorenstein Center 1992, 75). Even when those interviewed are in Beijing, "some of the press tended to accept the statements of any stray student in the street at face value, while reporting official government statements in ways that indicated to readers and viewers that they should be taken with a grain of salt" (1992, 68).

When the media do seek expressions of opinion from individual government officials, those most likely to respond are liberal, cosmopolitan, and generally sympathetic to the activists. Reliance on such sources, coupled with a remarkably unquestioning approach to the use of information provided by Chinese students, produces a pattern of reporting in which our media abandon their usual criteria for "objective" reporting. Their usually maintained distinction between *news* and *propaganda* in international reporting, however vague and misleading, simply is disregarded.

Perhaps the most interesting aspect of the way in which our media talk about the 1989 Tiananmen Square uprising is the fact that not only is media bias recognized, it is actually celebrated. This is no more clear than in the introductory pages of *Turmoil at Tiananmen: A Study of U.S. Press Coverage of the Beijing Spring of 1989* (Shorenstein Center 1992), a study on which much of this section is based. Despite its overall critical analysis, the report presents an heroic image of the media performance that brought the violent and oppressive acts of the Chinese government to worldwide attention.

Our news media's obvious willingness to abandon its conventional practices of "objective" reporting when such action promotes our government's most frequently expressed ideological perspective has at least two major potential consequences. First, the U.S. government is further encouraged to manipulate the media in support of its interests. Second, activists in other nations are encouraged to seek support and cooperation from U.S. news media, and they do so in ways that can obfuscate their real objectives.

When Chinese media talk about political turmoil in their own country, they often are exploring the limits of their independence from government control. When our commercial news media talk about political turmoil in the antagonistic state, they are guided by media values such as ethnocentrism, altruistic democracy, and responsible capitalism, the use of which legitimates our government.

POLITICAL ASSASSINATIONS

Political assassinations are dramatic and violent events unlikely to escape the attention of U.S. commercial news media, even when they occur in nations they otherwise tend to ignore. As noted in the coverage of the wars and internal conflicts previously discussed, the amount of attention paid by the media to a political assassination, the vocabulary they use to describe it, the sources they consult, the overall characterization of the event, and representation of U.S. and international public opinion are all shaped by media understanding of American political, economic, and military interests as defined by the U.S. political, economic, and military elites at the time of its occurrence. This structuring of news will be illustrated in the analysis of each of three political assassinations.

The following discussion draws on the research of Susan Moeller (1999, 157–219). Her study reveals not only how our media socially construct the internal wars of other nations, but also the remarkable way in which our news media Americanize those nations' political rituals. The assassinations will be discussed in order of the amount of attention they received from U.S. commercial news media and the American public.

The 1995 Assassination of Israeli Prime Minister Yitzhak Rabin

Yitzhak Rabin is a soldier turned statesman, who plays leading roles in virtually all of Israel's major historical events—from its founding to its efforts at establishing peaceful relations with its Arab neighbors. Given Israel's history, it is inevitable that he becomes a controversial figure on the world scene.

Rabin was a member of the Palmach, an elite group in the Jewish underground army that fought to drive the British out of Palestine. In 1948, he commands the Harel Brigades that defend Jerusalem during Israel's War of Independence. (When Rabin discloses in his 1979 memoir that during the war he was involved in forcing fifty thousand Arab civilians from their homes, there is furor in Israel, where officials had long denied that Arab civilians were pushed out of their lands.)

After the war, Rabin remains in the military, and becomes Chief of Staff of the Israeli army in 1964. Three years later, in this role, he helps lead Israel to military success in the Six Days War. Israel's victory triples Israeli territory, taking the West Bank and East Jerusalem from Jordan, the Gaza Strip from Egypt, and the Golan Heights from Syria. Rabin becomes a national hero.

Rabin leaves the military and is appointed ambassador to the United States, a position he holds until 1973. Though a political novice, Israel's ruling Labor party names Rabin its leader and Prime Minister. He quickly establishes strong ties with the United States, hosting U.S. Secretary of State Henry Kissinger, who conducts shuttle diplomacy to achieve an interim peace agreement between Egypt and Israel. However, in 1977, Rabin is forced from office when it becomes public that his wife maintains bank accounts in the United States in direct violation of Israel's currency laws. Foreign Minister Shimon Peres assumes leadership of the Labor party, but the party soon loses its parliamentary majority to the right-wing Likud party.

In 1979, Israel signs a peace treaty with Egypt, the first Arab state with which it reaches such an agreement. The treaty returns the Sinai Peninsula to Egypt and promotes hope that this will lead to greater peace throughout the region. However, in the 1980s, tensions only increase.

Rabin returns to government in 1984, serving as defense minister in Labor–Likud coalitions. During his tenure in office, he takes a strong stand against Palestinians rebelling against Israeli occupation of the West Bank and Gaza (the *Intifada* discussed earlier in this chapter). Finally, in 1991, Israel and the Palestinians begin to negotiate.

Rabin ousts Shimon Peres as Labor party leader in 1992 and leads Labor to victory in the national elections, becoming prime minister and defense minister. Israel and the Palestine Liberation Organization sign an agreement in an extraordinary ceremony on the White House lawn in 1993, allowing the Palestinians to slowly take over the Gaza Strip and the West Bank, with the exception of the Jewish settlements established in the regions. For their long work, Rabin, Peres, and PLO leader Yasir Arafat receive the 1994 Nobel Peace Prize.

Rabin also joins Jordan's King Hussein in Washington in July 1994, to sign a declaration ending a forty-six-year-long state of war. A formal peace agreement is signed in late October. Rabin also takes first steps toward defining the terms for an eventual peace with Syria.

Peace negotiations with the PLO meet with repeated setbacks and crises for more than two years following the 1993 ceremony. However, after a second White House formality in October 1995, Israel's army begins pulling back from major Palestinian towns in the West Bank. The agenda for the following months is to include Palestinian elections and the initiation of discussions about the fate of Jerusalem and the settlements. These matters are at the core of the most-heated controversy, not only between Israel and the Palestinians, but also within Israel itself.

On September 28, 1995, Rabin addresses a peace rally in Tel Aviv. After his speech, as he is walking to his car, he is shot by an Israeli law student with links to right-wing causes. He dies shortly thereafter in a nearby hospital.

Our Media Report Rabin's Assassination

The assassination of Yitzhak Rabin is a major news story in 1995, receiving less media attention than only two other events, both of which are given extraordinary coverage: the bombing of the Alfred P. Murrah Federal Building in Oklahoma City, and the O.J. Simpson trial. The substantial attention reflects the strength of the historical ties between the United States and Israel, expressed in U.S. foreign policy; the familiarity of the U.S. public with Rabin, because of his central role in one of the most regularly covered topics in international news for decades, the Arab–Israeli conflict and the struggle for peace in the Middle East; and the personal, dramatic, and somewhat surprising (he was killed by an Israeli) nature of the event.

The bond between the United States and Israel is expressed by the size and composition of the official U.S. delegation attending Rabin's funeral, by linking the assassination of the Israeli leader to culturally important assassinations in American political history, and by the statements of U.S. representatives.

Language employed by U.S. commercial news media to describe Rabin reflects his personal status in the United States as well as the geopolitical and cultural importance of Israel to this country. He is referred to as a "peacemaker," a brave and brilliant soldier, and a diplomat of towering achievement who will be mourned around the world (Moeller 1999, 168). Media call attention to his close personal ties to the United States and to U.S. political leaders. However, while American media construct Rabin as a heroic figure, they also note he was surrounded by controversy, not only in Israel, but in the United States as well.

U.S. news media coverage of the Rabin assassination follows conventions established after the assassination of President John F. Kennedy. Accounts focus on five moments of coverage: the shooting; the vigil at the hospital; the swearing-in of the successor; the identity and motive of the assassin, including discussion of the response of authorities and assessments of remaining threats; and the funeral, after which the media reassert the supremacy of the established political and social order (Moeller 1999, 164–167).

As noted, Rabin was a staunch ally, effectively working for a goal much desired by the U.S. government: political, economic, and military stability in the Middle East. While our commercial news media coverage of the *Intifada* had been generally sympathetic to the Palestinians, at the time of Rabin's death, the media appeared to be giving priority to establishing an orderly peace in the region over promoting a Palestinian view of justice. Now, opponents of such an order are labeled "extremists."

Language of the news of Rabin's assassination constructs support for Israel as being in the national interest of the United States (the expression of an ethnocentric concern). Rabin is described as a democratic leader who unselfishly pursued the interests of his nation. (His leadership was consistent with the news value of altruistic democracy.) His effort at establishing peace and order in the Middle East is presented as an unquestionable good—also in the interest of the United States (the expression of ethnocentrism and the importance of social order and national leadership).

An assassination, even that of a foreign leader who is assigned exceptional importance by U.S. news media, does not remain major news indefinitely. As Moeller observes about U.S. commercial news practice:

The coverage arbitrarily works to tidy up a complex event into a neat package of death, mourning and funeral. . . . In the world of international news, if the loose ends aren't tied up by the time the last story in the cycle is published or broadcast, the practice is that they are forgotten. (1999, 167)

The 1981 Assassination of President Anwar el-Sadat of Egypt

Like Yitzhak Rabin, Anwar el-Sadat is a soldier–statesman and a major participant in the most crucial events in his nation's modern history. As a military officer during World War II, he collaborates with the Germans to oust the British from Egypt. The British arrest and imprison him in 1942 for spying, but he escapes. He is arrested again in 1945 and released in 1949. When his army command is restored in 1950, Sadat joins Gamal Abdel Nasser's Free Officers Movement, and is involved in their bloodless coup that overthrows the Egyptian monarchy in 1952. He supports Nasser's election to the presidency in 1956.

Sadat holds various high positions, including chairman of the National Assembly from 1960 to 1968 and vice president (1964–1966, 1969–1970). He becomes acting president upon Nasser's death in 1970, and is elected president shortly thereafter, receiving more than ninety percent of the vote in a national referendum.

Egypt breaks formal diplomatic relations with the United States during the 1967 war with Israel, charging that the United States is providing direct assistance to Israel. However, in 1972, Sadat expels fifteen thousand Soviet technicians and advisors on grounds that he is receiving inadequate support from the Soviet Union in Egypt's struggles against America's ally. The following year he joins with Syria in launching an attack on Israeli forces, with Egypt striking those occupying the Sinai Peninsula and Syria assaulting Israeli forces occupying the Golan Heights. Egypt's surprise military action in the first few days of fighting retakes some land from Israel. Israel counterattacks and establishes forces on the West Bank. Nevertheless, Sadat's initial successes enhance his prestige throughout the Arab world.

In November 1973, Egypt and the United States restore diplomatic relations, and in December, the two nations participate in the Geneva peace conference. U.S. Secretary of State Henry Kissinger's shuttle diplomacy leads to Egyptian–Israeli and Syrian–Israeli disengagement agreements in 1974 and a second set of Egyptian–Israeli disengagements in 1975. The agreements return the Sinai Peninsula and secure a U.S. commitment to resume economic aid to Egypt, which had been suspended since 1967.

In search of a lasting peace with Israel, Sadat travels to Jerusalem in November 1977, and addresses the Israeli Knesset (parliament). The following September he meets with Israeli Prime Minister Menachem Begin and U.S. President Jimmy Carter at Camp David, Maryland, and establishes the foundation for the Egyptian–Israeli peace treaty finalized in March 1979. The treaty provides for the normalization of Egyptian–Israeli relations and establishes a framework for the Palestinian problem. However, issues concerning the status of the Israeli-occupied West Bank and Gaza territories and the question of Palestinian autonomy are to be negotiated.

Although he is viewed as an international peacemaker in the West (he is awarded the Nobel Peace Prize for his participation in the 1979 treaty agreement), Sadat fails to convince the Arab states that the Camp David agreements deal justly with legitimate Palestinian concerns. Egypt loses the financial support of the Arab states and, shortly after signing the peace treaty, is expelled from the Arab League. Egypt remains isolated from other Arab states, with the exception of Sudan and Oman, because of the Israeli treaty. Isolation ends only after Sadat's death, when Egypt opposes the June 1982 Israeli invasion of Lebanon.

Sadat is praised in the West, not only for his international peace efforts, but also for his attempts at domestic political and economic reforms. He works to remove the most oppressive features of Nasser's rule, with its heavy reliance on the military and security apparatus, and to establish a form of a multiparty system. He also pursues a course of economic revitalization.

Neither program achieves significant success. Economic conditions worsen and demonstrations erupt in Egypt's major cities. Widening class inequality threatens regime stability. In addition, opposition to the peace treaty remains. In September 1982, Sadat cracks down on public dissent by arresting more than fifteen thousand political opponents on grounds that they are fomenting sectarian strife and endangering his efforts to bring economic reform and democracy to his country. Prominent among those arrested are members of the Takfir, a Muslim group that, for generations, has been combating secularism and Western influence in Egypt and throughout the Middle East. In the context of this unrest, on October 6, 1981, Sadat is shot and killed by a group of men in military uniforms who fire rifles at him as he is watching an elaborate military parade commemorating the 1973 war against Israel.

Our Media Report Sadat's Assassination

Like the assassination of Yitzhak Rabin, that of Anwar el-Sadat is a major news story. It is third of the top ten news items of 1981, following reports on an assassination attempt on President Ronald Reagan and the return of U.S. hostages from Iran. One explanation for such media attention is that "due to his powerful personal leadership and his mastery of modern mass communications, Sadat's impact on world events was far beyond the norm for an Egyptian leader and beyond that of leaders of far more powerful nations" (*The Washington Post*, October 7, 1981).

From the perspective of U.S. geopolitical interests of the period, one of Sadat's accomplishments deserving considerable media attention is his leadership in transforming the nonaligned movement from its support of the Soviet-dominated eastern bloc to a more-balanced position, associated neither with the Soviet nor with the western blocs. The ideological shift is described by our media as one that will promote Egypt's modernization, increase its prosperity, and actually transform the nation into an ally of the United States. *The New York Times* notes that Mr. Sadat "was bent on moving the impoverished country into the late twentieth century, a drive that led him to abandon an alliance with the Soviet Union and embrace the West" (October 7, 1981). *The Washington Post* reports: "Since the fall of the shah and the Soviet invasion of Afghanistan, Egypt has become 'the pivot, the linchpin of our whole policy' in the Middle East and the Persian Gulf, according to a former American official" (October 8, 1981).

U.S. interest in good relations with Egypt also is tied to Egypt's providing a moderate voice in Arab councils. While such a role is routinely praised by U.S. commercial news media and is appreciated by the American public, the perspective is not shared by all in the Arab world. Sadat's assassination, publicly celebrated by many Arabs, provides U.S. media with an opportunity to construct several nations as enemies of reason in the politics of the Middle East—opponents of U.S. policies that would promote peace, economic development, and democracy in the region.

Behind the television images of Arab crowds celebrating the assassination of President Anwar Sadat that are horrifying Westerners who revered him as a statesman lie deeply held personal grievances and political antagonisms that made Sadat seem very different when perceived through the Arab prism. (*The Washington Post*, October 8, 1981)

Sadat receives favorable press in the United States not only for his moderating role in the politics of the Middle East, but also for the restraint he imposes on "Islamic extremists" struggling against secularization and Western economic and cultural influence throughout the region. His image provides a useful contrast to the images of the media demonized "Arab dictators" such as Ayatollah Khomeini, Mu'ammar al-Qaddafi, and Saddam Hussein. Ordinary Arabs who vehemently oppose Sadat are more easily typified as irrational supporters of "fanatical groups" who might be dismissed, at least on this occasion, in this way: "the anti-Sadat demonstrators were limited to Palestinian and left-wing Lebanese militants and gunmen whose principal accomplishment appeared to have been to wound civilians with stray bullets fired aimlessly in the air" (*The Washington Post*, October 8, 1981).

When we talk about internal wars in the Middle East, we inevitably discuss their implications for a crucial concern of the United States: use of military bases in the region to protect U.S. access to Persian Gulf oil. Coverage of the assassination of Anwar el-Sadat is no exception. In this context, news media report that the United States has sought a military base in Egypt since the late 1970s' discussions of developing a "rapid deployment force" and the need for staging, support, and military storage areas. According to press reports, the United States has shown an interest in an air facility, such as Cairo West or the air base near Nag Hamadi, or an air and sea base, such as the small Egyptian base at Ras Banas on the Red Sea. Shortly before Sadat's assassination, Egypt had agreed to allow the United States use of Ras Banas if an Arab state were threatened.

U.S. commercial news media coverage of the Sadat assassination begins with the use of dramatic imagery.

Early in the parade, a rocketlike object had been launched. It rained down Egyptian flags and portraits of Mr. Sadat hanging from tiny parachutes that were whipped by the wind. Most of them floated over a nearby housing development called Nasser City.

As the grounds were being cleared, one of the portraits was seen hanging from a flag pole on which it had become impaled in landing. The portrait of Mr. Sadat had been torn by the sharp tip of the Egyptian flag that was fluttering from it. (*The New York Times*, October 6, 1981)

Like their coverage of the assassination of Yitzhak Rabin fourteen years later, commercial news media Americanize the assassination by following conventions established after the assassination of President John F. Kennedy noted earlier (see Moeller 1999, 216). Media quote U.S. officials who refer to Sadat with phrases such as "a man of hope," "a close friend of America," "a man of great courage," and "a pillar of peace in the world," and to his death as "a tragedy for the civilized world."

Americanizing this event also involves locating it in the context of the Cold War. Representation of U.S. reaction to the assassination of "a pillar of peace in the world" is highlighted by placing it in sharp contrast to accounts of Soviet responses. These are reported by *The Washington Post* to emphasize that Sadat's assassination opens new opportunities for Russia to reassert its presence in Egypt (October 8, 1981).

Many of Sadat's policies were supported by the U.S. government and praised by U.S. commercial news media. The media created a symbolic universe in which Sadat represented reason and the quest for peace opposed by irrational and belligerent forces represented by militant Palestinians, several Arab states, such as Iran and Libya, and by the Soviet Union.

The 1984 Assassination of Indian Prime Minister Indira Gandhi

Indira Gandhi serves as prime minister of India for three consecutive terms (1966–1977) and a fourth term (1980–1984). She is the only child of Jawaharlal Nehru, the nationalist leader who, in 1947, becomes the first prime minister of independent India. The United States looks to India as a potential model of political democracy and economic development in the Third World. The United States also sees India as preventing the spread of communist China's influence, and consequently contributes substantial amounts of aid; but the Soviet Union also begins an effective aid program in 1955, and Nehru finds support from the USSR once the Sino–Soviet split becomes evident.

Independence from Britain for the ethnically and religiously mixed land was achieved only after a large portion of its territory was partitioned to form Pakistan. Independent India develops a predominantly Hindu leadership, although there is a significant Muslim minority; Pakistan has a Muslim government. Many members of India's Muslim population are vehemently opposed to the loss of land involved in the creation of Pakistan, and relations between India's Muslim and Hindu populations often are hostile and sometimes turn violent.

In addition to this chronic threat to political stability, Gandhi confronts the full range of problems associated with an impoverished economy straining to support approximately 750 million people.

Gandhi is a highly controversial figure in Indian politics. Her first five years of leadership of the Congress party, a position that makes her prime minister, are constantly challenged by the party's right wing. However, in 1971 she wins a landslide victory over a coalition of conservative parties.

She also concludes a twenty-year Treaty of Peace and Friendship and Co-operation with the Soviet Union. Later that year she supports East Bengal (now Bangladesh) in its secessionist conflict with Pakistan. The United States has been a major arms supplier to Pakistan since 1955, because of its membership in the Central Treaty Organization (CENTO). CENTO was founded at the urging of Britain and the United States to counter the threat of Soviet expansion into Middle East oil-producing regions.

In 1975 Gandhi is convicted of a minor infraction of election laws during her campaign. She maintains her innocence and charges that the conviction is part of an attempt to remove her from office. She refuses to resign and declares a national state of emergency. Although her conviction is soon overturned by the Indian Supreme Court, the state of emergency is continued. Gandhi imprisons thousands of her opponents, passes many laws limiting personal freedoms, and implements other unpopular policies, including a large-scale sterilization program as a form of birth control. Popular opinion turns against Gandhi; she is accused of being a dictator, concerned with enlarging her own sphere of power, undermining India's democratic system, and failing to attend to India's serious problems of economic development.

Despite signs of widespread dissatisfaction, Gandhi calls for a general election in 1977, hoping to demonstrate her popular support. However, she loses her seat in Parliament, the Congress party is defeated, and the Janata party seizes power. Nevertheless, Gandhi proves to be remarkably resilient. In 1978, she and her followers split from the Congress party and form the Congress I party; Gandhi subsequently wins a new seat in parliament. Dissention within the ruling Janata party leads to a fall of its government in 1979. When elections for the lower house of Parliament are held in 1980, Gandhi wins a decisive victory and is able to form a new majority government. Many see her as the "Mataji," or the Great Mother of India, and the single most stabilizing force in Indian politics.

During the early 1980s, Gandhi faces threats from several Indian states seeking greater independence from the central government. In the Punjab, many of India's thirteen million Sikhs, followers of an amalgam of the Muslim faith and Hinduism, express increasing dissatisfaction with their experiences of cultural and political discrimination.

Conflicts between Sikhs and Hindus become increasingly frequent; there are riots and other violent protests. Gandhi decides to suppress Sikh militancy and send troops into the most holy of all Sikh shrines, the Golden Temple of Amritsar. The shrine is suspected of harboring leaders of the Sikh terrorist movement and storing weapons. A battle erupts between the Sikh militants, and the military and at least five hundred people are killed in the fighting. The incident outrages many of India's Sikhs, who feel that the Indian government had used unnecessary force, had debased their most sacred shrine, and had shown a complete disregard for Sikh culture and religion.

Throughout the summer of 1984, Gandhi continues to clamp down on Sikh militants. Five months after the attack on the Golden Temple, she is assassinated in revenge by two of her own Sikh bodyguards. Her death is followed by widespread rioting.

India continues to be plagued by internal problems of political integration and extreme difficulties with Pakistan. Riots follow the destruction of a sixteenth-century mosque by Hindu militants in 1992. Thousands are killed in ethnic violence in Assam in 1993. Corruption and scandals dominate Indian politics in the mid-1990s. India conducts a series of nuclear tests in 1998, drawing worldwide condemnation and raising tensions with Pakistan.

Our Media Report Gandhi's Assassination

India is the world's most populous democracy. Its location under the shadow of the People's Republic of China, sharing the Asian subcontinent with the rival state of Pakistan, gives it enormous strategic importance, which is enhanced by its nuclear capability. Nevertheless, India tends to receive little attention from U.S. commercial news media. To be newsworthy during the Cold War, a nation had to be understood publicly as being allied unambiguously with either the United States or with the Soviet Union. This criterion produced an easily intelligible and dramatic world of politics in which audiences were prepared to react with varying degrees of approval or disfavor to allied nations and to ignore most other nations of the world. Events in other countries generally went unreported, even when they involved the lives or vast numbers of people or had implications for world politics.

On November 3, 1984, *The New York Times* publishes a variety of articles on the Gandhi assassination. There are reports on the reactions of world leaders familiar to U.S. audiences (Queen Elizabeth, Margaret Thatcher, François Mitterand, Pope John Paul II, Yasir Arafat) and less well-known heads of nations, who are of considerable concern to Washington at the time (the Soviet Union's Konstantin Cherenko, East Germany's Erich Honecker, Pakistan's Zia ul-Haq). Other articles note the "suggestion of U.S. government officials" that the assassination could eventually provoke a clash between India and Pakistan, "a matter of serious concern because the United States is a long-standing arms supplier to Pakistan and also because of the current tensions on Pakistan's border with Afghanistan." United States worry over future instability in India is expressed as the threat of "turning the Punjab into a Northern Ireland of the Subcontinent"—language making the problem more meaningful to the psychologically remote U.S. audience.

The New York Times also attends to what Soviet and Soviet Bloc media are saying about the assassination. For example, on November 1, 1984, the newspaper reports that the official Soviet news agency *Tass* is accusing the Central Intelligence Agency (CIA) and other Western intelligence services of carrying out a campaign of subversion in India through their links with Sikh extremist groups.

Moeller (1999) cites an additional factor elevating commercial news media interest in the assassination: It enables them to feature a sensational account of an event of apparent world importance though not of great interest to their mass audience.

It wasn't the fact of Gandhi's death that provoked the attention, it was the manner of her death. She died at the hands of her Sikh bodyguards—news that, when released, prompted Hindus to batter and kill more than a thousand Sikhs by the day of Gandhi's funeral. The assassination story, already of some interest, turned into a dramatic tale of religious violence. (1999, 175)

Dramatic presentations appear likely to attract interest in a war within a nation where politics are not easily explained in terms of the Cold War frame. However, audiences are informed that Soviet bloc media are suggesting that such framing might, in fact, be appropriate, though certainly not by imposing it in the manner uniformly employed by U.S. commercial news media.

Indira Gandhi's funeral was a *media event*, attracting the attention of audiences worldwide and affecting the international image of her nation. "For a given society, an event of this type is a 'cultural performance' . . . offering the opportunity of a solemn presentation of self to other societies. Major media events . . . picture societies at those moments when their actual practice and explicit ideals coincide" (Dayan and Katz 1992, 201). U.S. commercial news media do devote considerable attention to the ceremony and assign Gandhi's death some historical significance. Nevertheless, discussion focuses on the extent to which she promoted a social order congruent with American values and interests.

Part II

What Their News Media Say: Four Case Studies

Chapter 4

The United States as a Former Enemy: Russian National Television Construction of the United States after the Collapse of the Soviet Union

For four decades following World War II, when our commercial news media talked about the external wars of other nations, about their internal conflicts, and about the assassinations of their leaders, we invariably also talked about the Soviet Union. We noted that the lesson of the Falklands War was that the U.S. government was mistaken in its belief that the Russians wanted to create Marxist–Leninist states in the Western Hemisphere. On the other hand, we reported that there was good reason to conclude that the war offered the USSR a chance to enlarge its growing commercial and military ties with Latin America at the expense of the United States. When we did discuss the Iran–Iraq War, we expressed our concern over increased opportunities for Soviet encroachment in the Persian Gulf.

Our discussion of the *Intifida* noted that the Soviets were arguing that oppression of the Palestinians was the primary cause for all problems of the area, as part of their effort to undermine allied coalitions with other Arab states. Our commercial news media's Tiananmen Square narrative emphasized that young people the world over were rejecting Soviet-style communism and demanding that they live under American-style democratic rule. Reports of each of the three assassinations expressed concern for its impact on regional political, economic, and military order and stability—an order supported by the United States and found objectionable, if not directly opposed, by the Soviet Union. This was made particularly clear in news reports of Soviet response to the assassination of Anwar el-Sadat.

Mirroring the practice of our commercial news media, between 1945 and 1990, Soviet news media talked about us when discussing wars, internal conflicts, and assassinations—even those that directly involved neither the Soviet Union nor the United States. Like their American counterparts, Soviet media employed a conflict perspective in which the United States and Russia were seen as polarized forces, and one in which the political world was seen as an ongoing series of contests, each with a set of winners and losers (Davis 1990; Downing 1988; Hallin 1992; McNair 1988; Neuman, Just, and Crigler 1992, 64–65).

The importance of the conflict perspective adopted by U.S. and Russian media alike is suggested by research indicating that, while most media listeners/viewers retain little information from the news they encounter, what they do tend to retain are the generalized conceptions of the order of things that are embedded in the categories through which news events are presented (Morley 1990, 128). As discussed in Chapter 1, people's view of the order of things provides a frame of reference or orientation with which they can interpret objects and events as they conduct their everyday lives. The objects and events of the world have no inherent or universal meaning apart from this imposed framework. The meaning that is imposed is limited by, and relative to, the social context in which it is created. However, once meanings are learned through the socialization process, people tend to act on them without reassessment and without awareness of the social forces that created them. They come to identify truth with a particular learned set of socially shared meanings (Schutz 1932/1967).

As illustrated in Chapters 2 and 3, media organizations construct social reality as they select and prioritize some items of information, omit or ignore others, edit accounts together, and build a story, using particular types of exposition and articulating verbal discourse together to make a certain kind of sense (Entman 1993). The interpretive structure that governs the selection, omission, prioritization, and editing processes has been termed a "news frame" (Gamson 1991). A given frame can be used to structure numerous stories about a variety of actors, conditions, and events (e.g., diverse political and economic conflict occurring throughout the world). A particular story tends to evoke in an audience a distinct pattern of judgments and opinions about the actor, condition, or event that is its subject matter (Beckett 1995; Gamson and Lasch 1983; Gamson and Modigliani 1989; Iyengar 1988). Hall (1982) notes that

the more one accepts the principle that how people act will depend in part on how the situations in which they act are defined, and the less one can assume either a natural meaning to everything or a universal consensus on what things mean— then the more important, socially and politically, becomes the process by means of which certain events get recurrently signified in particular ways. This is particularly the case where events in the world are problematic (that is, when they are unexpected); when they break the frame of our previous expectations about the world; where powerful social interests are involved; or where there are starkly opposing interests at play. The power involved here is an ideological power; the power to signify events in a particular way. (1982, 69)

In 1989, a series of extraordinary events initiated changes in the world political–economic order that "broke the frame of our previous expectations about the world." The Soviet Union withdrew its troops from Afghanistan, the Solidarity movement ascended to power in Poland, and the mass political demonstrations that were staged in the heart of Beijing were followed by similar actions in East Germany, Czechoslovakia, Bulgaria, and Romania. Finally, on December 26, 1991, the Soviet Union itself was formally dissolved.

Although media analysts tended to agree that subsequent world events could no longer be signified by the Cold War news frame, there was no consensus among them concerning the future of news making. A few anticipated some continuity of the established practices which had proved serviceable for four decades, arguing that journalism would be the last fortification of the Cold War perspective (Eberwine, Manoff, and Schiffer 1991; Zassoursky 1991, 168). Others concluded that the Cold War news frame had been steadily losing its influence on journalistic practice in both Western and Soviet bloc countries since 1987 (Wallis and Baran 1990, 139–140).

Empirical studies of American media clearly suggested that the Cold War news frame was moribund. For example, Norris's (1995) content analysis of network news in the pre- and post–Cold War periods (1973–1995) found a reduction of interest in the old Soviet bloc, a reduction in the coverage of military–defense issues, and an increasing coverage of international economy.

A review of several works published in Russian during the Gorbachev era suggests that Russian media also had abandoned the well-defined Cold War framework.

Ghosts of the old order are present alongside signs of gradual, though chaotic opening of the news to less orchestrated patterns of elite conflict and debate. The proliferation of more voices in the news occurs in the absence of a clear framework providing citizens some understanding of what the voices are saying. (Alexseev and Bennett 1995, 410)

Such findings, though valuable, provide little detail about framing of news by Russian media in the post–Cold War—post-Gorbachev era (1990–2001). More adequate understanding of Russian media framing practices of this period requires answers to questions analogous to those raised by Norris (1995) in her study of American network news-framing practices after the Cold War.

1. What was the rate of international news coverage? What did this rate represent in historical–comparative perspective?

2. How much interest was displayed in Western nations? How wide was coverage of international concerns? What did these patterns represent in an historical–comparative perspective?

3. Was there a new focus on the world economy rather than on military–defense issues?

These additional inquiries still fail to confront the most fundamental aspect of the Cold War frame. Full understanding of Russian media framing practices necessitates asking one further question:

4. How did Russian media depict their own country and the United States—as intimately connected social constructions that constitute the core of the Cold War frame?

The study, described below, is designed to answer these four sets of questions, focusing attention on the social construction of Russia and the United States by the Russian national television news program *Vremya* (time). It investigates the selection, omission, prioritization, encoding, and editing processes that a major Russian news medium employed to tell stories about the two formerly antagonistic superpowers. It examines what Edelman (1988) termed the "political spectacle" that many Russian citizens routinely confronted.

VREMYA

For decades, the Department of Propaganda of the Central Committee of the Communist party operated as the highest authority within Russia's state-controlled media system. In the 1960s, the Central Committee created *Vremya* (time), the official, national evening television news program. Over the following twenty years, television emerged as the most widely used source of news in Russia, and, in 1987, the government estimated that ninety percent of the population considered *Vremya* their main source of information (Mickiewicz 1988, 32). Watching *Vremya* became a prime-time ritual; in 1988 an average of 150 million people watched the evening news daily—over eighty percent of the adult population (1988, 8).

Vremya captured an enormous audience, as early as 1973, but there were survey data indicating the Russian public's dissatisfaction with *Vremya's* lack of timely domestic news and, more fundamentally, with its single official point of view (1988, 30–34). With the rise to power of Mikhail Gorbachev, there was increasing pressure to change the character of broadcast news offered to the Russian people. The long-term public dissatisfaction was exacerbated by media treatment of Russian involvements in the long futile war in Afghanistan, and by its handling of the Chernobyl nuclear accident in April 1986.

In 1987, Gorbachev initiated a series of reforms aimed at expanding freedom and democratization of the political process through glasnost (openness) and perestroika (restructuring). Under the direction of Aleksandr Yakolev, Gorbachev's chief ideologist and propagandist, *Vreyma's* contents and framing processes change dramatically along with Gorbachev's reforms (Remnick 1993, 143). Yakolev introduced radical changes in media rhetoric about conflict between East and West. The image of the United States on *Vremya* no longer emphasized global military threat, monopoly capital, and the impoverishment of the proletariat. It no longer described the United States as a nation whose corporations were indifferent to the well-being of Third World workers and whose government might disregard the human rights of its military personnel. Rather, it depicted the United States as the one global actor—the puppet master pulling strings around the world. The United States was the state actor most responsible for problems of the world political economy (Mickiewicz 1988, 126–130).

Although such an image of the United States as an international actor served Gorbachev in the consolidation of power, another, more positive portrayal of America was used to motivate Russian workers. Stories about individual initiative and the rewards it brought the American worker were used to show that individual effort can be understood quite apart from the economic system in which it is imbedded and that success can be transplanted (1988, 74). Some aspects of America seemed worthy of emulation, even if *responsible capitalism* still was seen as an oxymoron.

Although *Vremya* delivered such carefully constructed images, under Gorbachev the program did offer a venue for some social criticism and for the promotion of democratization. Russian society was more realistically presented, no longer constructed by sharp contrast to the United States. It was not depicted as a society facing serious social, economic, and political challenges such as ethnic conflict, crime, unemployment, homelessness, and some social injustice. Glasnost progressed sufficiently that media in Russia, although not free of censorship or party interference, had some autonomy and popular support (Turpin 1995, 123).

By the beginning of 1992, the Soviet Union officially had been dissolved and Gorbachev's successor, Boris Yeltsin, launched a drive to privatize thousands of state-owned enterprises. A new law came into effect that extended press freedom and now included provisions against monopoly ownership. Russian news agencies underwent radical reorganization with the end in view of becoming politically independent news-gathering organizations like other world press agencies, such as Reuters and Agence

France Presse. Through several mergers, the ITAR–TASS agency was formed. Emphasis was placed on providing accurate "de-ideologized" news. The agency now was to compete with independent agencies, such as Interfax and Postfactum, which served the same market. From Brezhnev through Yeltsin "the media [had] moved from pedaling lies to pursuing profits, with an intervening stage of the enthusiastic half-truths of *glasnost*" (Sakwa 1993, 237). However, Yeltsin's continuing difficulties with conservatives, former communists, and ultranationalists led to a scaling back of programs for privatizing state-owned properties in 1994. In 1995, the historically unique level of media freedom was precarious.

In this uncertain political context, how far did *Vremya* move away from use of the Cold War news frame that structured Russian news media discourse (as well as media discourse throughout much of the world) for almost four decades? What did the political spectacle offered by *Vremya* to the Russian public look like in 1995? To answer this broad question, we now turn to find empirical answers to the four more specific questions noted earlier.

Procedures

Analysis is based on a twenty percent sample of all *Vremya* programs broadcast during 1995. Six days were randomly selected from each month. One additional day of the year was randomly chosen and added to bring the sample size to seventy-three (one-fifth of 365).[1] Video tapes of the *Vremya* newscasts were obtained from the C-SPAN Public Affairs Video Archives at Purdue University. The original broadcasts were received via satellite and provided with an English translation voice-over by C-SPAN in its Washington, D.C. studios.

Language plays a crucial role in mediating reality and therefore in structuring the presentation of news (GUMG 1980; Fowler 1991). This must be taken into account in any content analysis, particularly in studies involving translated news materials. However, the present research does not focus on nuances of language. Rather, the news item serves as its basic unit of analysis. Items were assigned to topical categories and then examined to determine themes that were expressed within these categories.[2] The coding procedures for news item contents and the themes they expressed were established on the basis of four considerations: theoretical interest in dissolution of the Cold War news frame; studies of media and social change in the former Soviet Union during the period (Sakwa 1993; Shane 1994; Turpin 1995); studies of *Vremya* newscasts (Mickiewicz 1988; Remnick 1993); and a preview of several newscasts randomly selected from the sample.

After deciding on the coding categories, as a test of the reliability of the coding mechanisms, seven newscasts (ten percent of the sample) were

viewed and coded in the manner suggested by Andern (1981). An intercoder coefficient of reliability (Holsti 1969) was found to be 0.92 with a
calculated Scott's pi of 0.91 (Scott 1955). To further check the coding
mechanism later during the study, three additional newscasts were dupli-
cate-coded. The intercoder coefficient of reliability for these newscasts was
0.93 and Scott's pi was 0.92. The majority of the programs were viewed by
a single coder, and findings were aggregated to construct the tables contained in the study.

Findings

Before Gorbachev's reforms, *Vremya* opened with a view of the Kremlin
as a symbol of empire and the flow of information from the government
downward. The approach to the news provided by *Vremya* was embodied
in the person of Igor Kirillov, who anchored the program for twenty years.
Kirillov "made the declarations of the Central Committee seem the revealed wisdom of heaven; he could also report the most ordinary events
in the Capitalist West as if there were scandals against humanity, a mock-
ing of all that was good and decent" (Remnick 1993, 145). News presentation was not oriented toward offering timely information but toward providing an official point of view about the Soviet Union and its enemies
(Mickiewicz 1988, 30–31).

In 1995, *Vremya* opened with a stylized representation of a clock and its
mechanical workings. At least, this symbolized the title of the program.
Perhaps it also was intended to suggest to viewers that the material it contained would be timely. The news was presented by a reader whose appearance and role closely resembled those of readers on CNN Headline
News.[3] In the sample, the average *Vremya* newscast was 39 minutes in
length (range: 29–46 min.) and contained 25.7 items (range: 14–33 items).[4]
Data in Table 4.1 provide answers to two of the four sets of questions
about *Vremya's* news-framing practices in 1995.

Question Set 1

What is *Vremya's* rate of international coverage? What does this represent in historical–comparative perspective? Data in Table 4.1 reveal that, in
1995, items about countries other than Russia constituted thirty-four percent of *Vremya's* news items and that twenty-five percent of the items were
about countries other than Russia and the former Soviet states (collec-
tively the former Soviet Union). Mickiewicz (1988, 89) reports that, a decade earlier, sixty-six percent of *Vremya* news items focused on countries
other than the Soviet Union. The dramatic shift away from international
news coverage can be seen as one indicator of the demise of the Cold War
news frame. In 1995, *Vremya* newscasts did relatively little to embed Russia in the world at large.

Table 4.1

Percentage of News Item Topics by Nation on Russian National Television[a]

Topics[b]	Russia	Former Soviet States[c]	United States	Other G-7 Nations[d]	Other Nations
Domestic politics/ economy	31.3	3.0	0.6	1.5	1.6
Domestic disorder	11.7	2.5	0.4	2.4	5.9
Foreign relations	10.8	2.5	2.1	1.4	2.8
Culture	10.4	0.9	0.6	0.7	1.0
Natural disasters	1.8	0.3	0.2	0.4	1.1
Other	0.2	0.1	0.1	0.1	1.8
Total percentage	66.2	9.3	4.0	6.5	14.2

[a]$N = 1,876$ items

[b]*Domestic politics/economy* includes items dealing with statements and acts of government officials, meetings of government organizations, elections, social programs, business, finance, and industry.
Domestic disorder includes items dealing with crime, civil unrest, corruption, rampant inflation, and challenges to established political authority.
Foreign relations includes items dealing with transactions, ongoing or anticipated, between or among nations.
Culture includes items dealing with the arts, science, education, history, entertainment, lifestyle, and celebration of holidays.
Natural disasters includes items dealing with earthquakes, fires, floods, damaging weather, and accidents such as mine explosions and plane crashes.

[c]Armenia, Azerbaijan, Belarus, Estonia, Georgia, Kazakhstan, Kyrgezia, Latvia, Lithuania, Moldavia, Turkmenistan, Ukraine, Uzbekistan

[d]Canada, France, Germany, Italy, Japan, United Kingdom

Question Set 2

How much interest is displayed in Western nations? How wide is coverage of international concerns? What does this pattern represent in historical–comparative perspective? Data in Table 4.1 show that, in 1995, items about the United States comprised about four percent, and about the United States together with other G-7 nations, about ten percent of *Vremya's* news reports. Approximately the same percentage of item coverage given to Western nations and Japan was also given to former Soviet states, as well as to the residual category of all other nations—excluding items about the war in Bosnia, which accounted for almost five percent of all items. (In 1995, Bosnia appeared to be more newsworthy than America.)

Table 4.2

Percentage of Foreign Relations Item Topics by Nation on Russian National Television

Topics	Russia	Former Soviet States	United States	Other G-7 Nations	Other Nations
Economy[a]	21.7	6.4	7.7	3.8	3.8
Military/defense[b]	18.2	36.2	35.9	30.8	24.5
Other	60.1	57.4	56.4	65.4	71.7
N	203	47	39	26	53

[a]*Economy* includes items dealing with business, finance, or industry.

[b]*Military/defense* includes items dealing with wars, border conflicts, armed forces training exercises, armed forces organizations, allocation of resources for armed forces, weapons systems, defense system.

The percentage of item coverage given the United States in 1995 was considerably lower (a forty-three percent reduction) than the seven percent figure for 1985 reported by Mickiewicz (1988, 89). *Vremya's* overall pattern of news coverage did not display the structuring of the dichotomized world of the Cold War news frame.

Question 3

In 1995, is there a focus on the world economy rather than on military–defense issues? In order to answer this question, items located in the foreign relations row of Table 4.1 were further classified. Table 4.2 presents the results of this analysis. Overall, data suggest that the answer to the question is a qualified "no."

For each nation or class of nations, *Vremya* dedicated more than half of its items to topics other than either economic matters or military–defense subjects (range: 56.4 percent to 71.7 percent). There were relatively few items about the international economic activities of nations or classes of nations other than Russia itself (range: 3.8 percent to 7.7 percent). For nations or classes of nations other than Russia, the ratio of military–defense items to international economic items ranged from approximately 5:1 to 10:1. For countries other than Russia, concerns with military–defense issues predominated. During 1995, *Vremya* paid considerable attention to the war in Bosnia, conflicts between Israel and its neighbors, Georgia and Abkazia, Armenia and Azerbaijan, Tajikistan and Afghanistan, as well as French nuclear testing and NATO troop exercises.

Vremya did devote a slightly higher percent of its items to the international economic affairs of Russia than to the country's military–defense issues. However, this amounts to very little support for the view that, in the post–Cold War era (or, at least, in 1995 in particular) there was a focus on international economic issues rather than military–defense concerns.

Question 4

How does V*remya* depict Russia and the United States in 1995? To answer the question, further analysis followed the suggestion that what reveals the meaning of a text "are the patterns, the wholes which can be made manifest by qualitative exegesis" (Kracauer 1953, 640) and that "an understanding of foreign countries as reflected in news coverage requires a much more delicate methodology than the simple question of counting how much attention is devoted to such categories as politics, natural catastrophes, etc." (Nordenstreng 1984, 141).

News items dealing with domestic politics/economy, domestic disorder and foreign relations of both Russia and the United States were examined to determine the frequency with which four general themes available for constructing stories about the two countries appeared:

1. Old Cold War Domestic Themes: Expressed in items offering the view of the order of things that dominated Russian media discourse during the Cold War. The United States is presented as troubled by a vast array of social and economic problems linked to the dynamics of its political economy. For example, a report of President Clinton's announcement of plans to close nine military bases points out that, in the United States, any reduction in military spending creates extensive job losses and presents political problems for the president (July 14). Russia is presented as relatively free from the domestic problems inherent in the social order of capitalist societies. For example, an item on organized crime in Russia links its increase to Russia's development of a market economy (March 7). A related item claims that "the furor over Russian Mafia in the West is a Western attempt at the political and economic isolation of Russia" (April 27).

2. Old Cold War International Themes: Expressed in items offering the view of the order of things that dominated Russian media discourse during the Cold War. The United States is presented as an imperialist power driven by military–industrial interests and threatening the security of nations worldwide. For example, an item identifying U.S. plans to build a military airbase in Pakistan notes that "it's unlikely this Pentagon decision is connected with striving to create order in this remote mountain valley which both India and Pakistan claim. Probably the purpose here is quite different—using the strategic location to take control of the situations in India, China, Afghanistan and the countries of Central Asia" (Dec. 13). Viewers are also reminded that American U-2 pilot Francis Gary Powers took off on his ill-fated 1960 spy mission from an airbase in this region

(Dec. 21). Russia is depicted as effectively checking the advance of Western imperialism through maintaining its military strength as the world's counterveiling superpower. An item on Russia's dismantling of its long-range strategic bombers in accord with the Start I Treaty suggests that Russia should remain prepared to meet Western military threats, now posed by the eastward expansion of NATO. "By the end of the year 2000, hundreds of heavy bombers of long-range aviation must be demolished. How reasonable today is compliance with this obligation in light of the problem of NATO?" (April 14).

3. Post–Cold War Domestic Themes: Expressed in items offering a view of the order of things incompatible with the perspective that dominated Russian media discourse during the Cold War. The United States is depicted as a nation with a high standard of living attributed to its market economy; criticisms of America's domestic order are conspicuously absent.[5] For example, an item on the heat wave that killed two hundred notes that "most victims were in Chicago where, due to the problems of local power stations, a lot of air conditioners and fans were out of order. One hundred thirty people died and hospitals are filled with victims" (July 17). The item did not mention that most victims were poor, members of racial and ethnic minority groups, and elderly. Consequently, it did not comment on America's history of discrimination and its relative lack of social programs for the poor and elderly found in other industrialized nations. Visuals showed working-class housing but not inner-city slums or "projects." Some citizens were victims of the processes of nature, not the processes of American capitalism.[6] Russia is depicted as a nation critical of its former (pre-1990) political order, and now plagued by serious domestic social, political, and economic problems, although some of these may be on the way toward eventual solution. For example, an item reports the results of a poll indicating that "forty-eight percent believe life in Russia today is difficult but tolerable" (Dec. 23). Other items report shortages of funds in Russia for basic scientific research (Feb. 20), for new medical technologies for hospitals (April 4), and even for school books (July 24).

4. Post–Cold War International Themes: Expressed in items offering a view of the order of things incompatible with the perspective that dominated Russian media discourse during the Cold War. The United States is presented as a nation which has numerous cooperative economic and military ties with Russia. The United States is also depicted as a major competitor with Russia for markets throughout the world (including Russia itself). For example, items report that General Motors plans to build an assembly plant in Russia, which will produce Chevy Blazers (Dec. 7); that the United States and Russia have decided to cooperate in building an in-

ternational space station (Aug. 15); that the United States and Russia are engaged in joint military peacekeeping exercises at Ft. Riley, Kansas (Oct. 27); and that United States and other Western aviation companies are reported increasingly to fly Russian air routes (Dec. 5). Russia is depicted as a nation with cooperative ties to the United States and the West, and with international concerns that are primarily economic rather than military. For example, an item discussing "the problem of broadening NATO to the east" concludes: "We have already lost much of the market of the former Eastern Bloc, as it was called, why should we, through broadening of NATO, lose this even further?" (Oct. 10).

Data in Tables 4.1 and 4.2 indicated the absence of systematic application of the Cold War frame in the sense that (1) There is relatively little international coverage to define Russia's and America's locations in the structure of the world political–economic–military relations; (2) There is little coverage of the United States to provide material for constructing, not only a clear view of America, but also for developing a contrasting view of Russia; (3) Data, however, did not indicate an overall refocusing of concern from military–defense issues to matters of the world economy. Data in Table 4.3 also indicate little use of the Cold War frame. The data suggest the way in which *Vremya* depicted Russia and the United States in 1995 by indicating the frequency with which each of the four themes was employed in presenting items about each of the nations.

Consistent with the suggestions of Tables 4.1 and 4.2, data in Table 4.3 indicate that *Vremya* used the Cold War frame very infrequently to tell stories about Russia. Only 1.3 percent of its items about Russian domestic life and foreign affairs offered a view of the order of things like that con-

Table 4.3
Percentage of Frame Use for Russian and U.S. Items on Russian National Television[a]

Frames	Russian	United States
Cold War domestic	0.3	5.9
Cold War foreign relations	1.0	19.1
Post–Cold War domestic	12.5	2.9
Post–Cold War foreign relations	7.6	30.9
Other	78.6	41.2
N	1,009	68

[a]Excludes items classified as *Culture, Natural disasters*, and *Other* in Table 4.1.

structed by Russian media prior to 1990. Also, while Cold War themes appeared with much greater frequency in its items about the United States, this was the case in only one out of four items. Very few items (5.9 percent of U.S. items) referred to what might be considered problems inherent in America's domestic order.

Post–Cold War themes appeared most regularly in items about U.S. foreign relations. To a large extent, this reflected reports of cooperative exchanges between the United States and Russia, and between the United States and former Soviet states. The second most common appearance of post–Cold War themes occurred in Russian domestic items, appearing in those dealing with economic shortages and failing industries.

Overall, data in the three tables indicate not only an absence of the Cold War frame but also the absence of a framework used to tell numerous stories incompatible with those told during the Cold War. With the Cold War over, *Vremya* displayed an awareness of the extent to which other pressing domestic problems and international issues had gone unattended.

Images of nations can be constructed incrementally over extended periods of time. Data presented thus far have concerned *Vremya's* patterns of topic selection and news item framing in order to detect images of Russia and the United States developed in this way over an entire year. National images also can be constructed through systematic framing of relatively few items that are attributed particular significance by the media of the subject nation and/or media worldwide. The full texts and analyses of four such items appear below. The qualitative material is intended to supplement the preceding analysis. The items report on the Republican party's assumption of control of the U.S. Congress (Jan. 4), an assessment of conditions in Russia and of Russia's place in the world scene on the occasion of the fifth anniversary of the independence of the RSFSR (June 13), the Million Man March (Oct. 16), and Presidents Boris Yeltsin and Bill Clinton's addresses to the UN (Oct. 23).[7]

Item 1: Republicans Assume Control of Congress

VERBAL	VISUAL
Today in Washington, the Congress of the United States began work. For the first time in 10 years in both chambers of the highest legislative body of the country, representatives of the Republican Party dominate. Our correspondent reports from Washington.	Capitol building Meeting of Congress
With this stamp at a price of 29 cents, one can't send a letter any longer. For the new year it's a different price—32 cents, although the new sum is not yet indicated.	29¢ stamp

The problem is not the mail but the fact that the very distant and very rich America, according to our standards, has its problems.	Mail moving along conveyor belt
Here there is no comment on the city streets, many can afford to have their own house and almost all good foods are available. What else does one need? But the Americans are not happy.	Street scene Men in business suits predominate
Almost each of these ordinary Washington residents, from approximately January to April works for the government. One quarter of their wages goes for taxes.	Traffic scene
The number of thefts and murders is growing, and it seems to have no limit. Central authorities are undertaking measures which, in the final analysis, procreate bureaucrats.	Car with shattered windshield Police cars with flashing lights
What is compared to a revolution did occur in November—the failure of Clinton's policies at local elections. The new bosses of the Congress are Republicans. During the first hundred days they promised to lower taxes, stop feeding the poor at the government's expense, and strengthen defense.	Newt Gingrich at rostrum erected in front of Capitol building Interior scene of Congress in session
Among new figures is Newt Gingrich from the state of Georgia, the tough Speaker of the House of Representatives. The Committee on International Affairs will be headed by Jesse Helms, a man without affection for Russia. Incidentally, regular Americans, because of reports of war in Russia, don't have much trust in us— although the White House representatives again implied Tuesday that Chechnya is Russian territory. Clinton himself said that anyone who loses in America has already been called a "lame duck" and therefore there is more tension for the position of leader of the Republicans in Congress, Robert Dole, and he has hinted relations can change.	Gingrich addressing Congress; Editorial cartoon depicting Gingrich with chain saw Newspaper featuring picture of Helms Building under attack in Grozny State Department briefing Clinton speaking Capitol building Dole speaking
American aid to Moscow can be stopped. The position of presidential influence in the United States has significantly weakened. It seems in the next two years before presidential elections, and even before that, Russian politicians will have to more often deal with those people who began work on Capitol Hill today.	*Vremya* reporter in front of Capitol building

According to this item, American citizens are rich by Russian standards but are dissatisfied with their heavy tax burden. The expanding U.S. government bureaucracy and weakened presidency are ineffective in dealing with a major problem facing American society—the increasing rate of serious crime. Americans remain distrustful of Russia, and their newly empowered political leaders threaten to bring to life the "ghosts of the old order." The item embodies Old Cold War themes, which, as data in Table 4.3 indicate, are more likely to appear in items about the United States (25 percent) than they are in items about Russia (1.3 percent).

Item 2: Independence Day Self-assessment

The five years which passed since the day of the first Congress of National Deputies of the RSFSR adopted the declaration on the sovereignty of Russia is a significant period of time to attempt to evaluate what independence has given Russia and the Russians. Probably the main positive result of the last five years is that we have finally rejected the utopia that was stubbornly propagated in the country over seventy years. It would, however, be naive to presume that from a totalitarian system something new would emerge over-night to suit everyone. And truly, for this something new during five years only the preconditions have been created. Its construction itself will probably take decades. Such is historical reality. But, unfortunately for many Russians, life is tight and for some of us it's extremely difficult. Within society the social differentiation is increasing. Forty percent of the employed Russians barely make ends meet. On the other hand, the class of those who have is growing and increasingly defining the paths of the country's economic development. Here one may probably add that this year for the economy of Russia is a breakthrough year—so Prime Minister Chernomyrdin assures.

Another significant aspect of time—contradiction between the center and the regions. Incidentally, the greater danger, and that was the collapse of Russia into many tens of principalities, which was still quite realistic one or two years ago, seems to have been avoided, although at times at very high prices.

With regard to the international arena, where during the last five years there were losses and subsequent gains, Russian politicians currently with intermittent success are struggling for the country regaining its almost lost status of a superpower.

Item 2 clearly expresses several post–Cold War themes: Russia has rejected its Marxist–Leninist ideology; the present period is one of economic hardship and increasing social stratification, but there are signs of a brighter future; Russia is struggling to remain a major player in world politics. The overall image is hardly one of a nation whose domestic order and international actions can and should serve as a model for evaluating all other nations. Rather, the image is one of a struggling nation facing serious domestic and international challenges with guarded optimism.

Item 3: The Million Man March

VERBAL

A major action by representatives of black America which has received the name "The Million Man March" in Washington is under way in the capital of the United States today.

This action was undertaken on the initiating of the leader of the religious organization the Nation of Islam, Louis Farrakhan, and officially states its purpose to be to unite all African Americans under the slogan of the self-affirmation of the American black population. In essence, it served as a type of reaction of the black minority of America to the change in the socio-political climate of the country as a result of the Republicans coming to power in Congress in November last year. This led to the closing of social programs and infringements on the achievements of national minorities in the last decade.

The current march does not receive unanimous support in the country as well as among black Americans foremost because of the odious identity of its organizer. The press broadly cites remarks made by Farrakhan in which he had declared the white residents of the country to be sub-human. Refusing to participate in the demonstration were many black organizations and also several prominent representatives of the African Americans, including the possible presidential candidate, the former Chairman of the Joint Chiefs of Staff General Powell.

In the beginning of the march today, prayers were held and later a mass rally was held which will end when it will be late at night in Moscow.

VISUAL

TV trucks with dishes
Single file line of black males marching, all wearing suits and bow ties

Black security guards; participants wearing "Wake Up" buttons
Individuals walking toward Washington monument

Close up of several marchers
Participant holding Million Man March flag, capitol building in background

Marcher being interviewed by off-camera reporter
Scene inside black church (sparse attendance); Rev. Al Sharpton (not identified) preaching in a church
Participants apparently being interviewed by off-camera reporter
Participants boarding bus

Two participants hold up Million Man March T-shirts
Group of marchers

Vremya's coverage of the Million Man March made no attempt to contrast favorable social conditions existing in Russia with conditions in the United States that violate values such as social equality. There was no use of stock film footage depicting the conditions under which, today, many African Americans live in the decaying centers of countless cities. No reference was made to America's long history of racial prejudice and discrimination. On the contrary, the item mentioned that the United States has social programs that have benefited African Americans, and that the last decade was one of achievement for minorities in America—although new programs were being curtailed.

As in the case of Item 1, limited social and political criticism was aimed at the Republican party rather than at the United States and its political economy. The event was described as "a type of reaction to the changed political climate of the country," rather than as a protest against an enduring structure of social inequality. There was no aerial view of the event (which might have been obtained from an American television producer) to give the Russian audience some sense of the vast number of participants in the event. Finally, the item explicitly noted that the Million Man March was not spontaneous. The item is noteworthy for its failure to employ Cold War narrative and supporting visual material, which could easily have been used in this case. As data in Table 4.3 indicate, this was the modal treatment of items about the United States by *Vremya*.

Item 4: Yeltsin and Clinton Address the UN

Relations between the United States and Russia today are at the crossroads. After the limited euphoria of partnership in relations between the two countries, a sobering period has come. In Moscow there is concern over the United States' claims of individual leadership in the world, the plans for broadening NATO to the east and NATO actions in Bosnia. In Washington concern is expressed over the continuing crisis in Chechnya, the sale of nuclear reactors to Iran, and an attempt to revive the old friendships with Cuba, Iraq and North Korea. Addressing the General Assembly, Presidents Clinton and Yeltsin confirmed the differences in their positions. Clinton is pleased with how the UN and NATO acted in Bosnia and is not pleased that the threat of international terrorism and the power of drug Mafia is increasing. Yeltsin is not pleased that the regional organization, circumventing the UN Security Council, made the decision to deploy force in the former Yugoslavia, and is pleased that prevailing in the world is the mood to prevent a resurgence of the spirit of enmity.

Item 4 rejects post–Cold War discourse. Reference is made to Russia's anxiety about U.S. world leadership, NATO expansion, and maintaining its Cold War alliance with Cuba, Iraq, and North Korea. Russia and the United States are said to have serious disagreements over the peacekeeping efforts in Bosnia. However, although the item begins by noting that "a sobering period has come," it concludes with the claim that "prevailing in the world is the mood to prevent a resurgence of the spirit of enmity." Like item 3, it expresses a sense of guarded optimism. Concern is noted over American claims to world leadership but not to the threat of U.S. world domination. The story that is told is more complex than those resulting from the imposition of a consistent set of Cold War or post–Cold War meanings. It does not provide an unambiguous perspective for routine understanding and evaluation of Russia and the United States as actors on the world political scene.

Discussion

Whatever else might be said about *Vremya's* social construction of Russia and the United States in 1995, it seems clear that the images of the nations and their relationship were more complex than the images it once broadcast. *Vremya* no longer offered the view of a dichotomized world that depicted Russia as progressive and equalitarian and the United States as reactionary and unjust, and that described virtually all major world events in terms of conflict between communist and capitalist–imperialist forces, led by Russia and the United States, respectively. The earlier constructions were central features of a framework with which *Vremya's* viewers easily could make sense of domestic and international politics. It provided them with a sense of political reality. It also offered them an unambiguous framework for evaluating this reality.

In 1995, *Vremya's* account of the order of things was neither entirely compatible nor entirely incompatible with its earlier version. Perhaps this was because Russia, the United States, and the structure of international relations all had changed so dramatically. Obviously, remarkable changes had occurred in Russia between the dissolution of the Soviet Union and 1995, but the presence in Russia of political infighting, resource shortages, ethnic conflicts, and the struggle to compete in world markets predate 1990. However, these matters previously were ignored in favor of reporting others, which together built the story of the Cold War. The reality of Russia had not become more complex. Rather, long ending features of the nation now came into view with the abandonment of the Cold War frame.

The United States certainly changed between 1990 and 1995. But many of its features, such as racial conflict, homelessness, crime, social and economic inequality, and social injustice unfortunately did not come to an end during the period. Nor had the influence of military–industrial interest on national and international policy terminated. Rather, they were of less interest to *Vremya*, which had reduced its coverage of events in the West and, more generally, its reporting of international news, as it refocused on Russia's domestic issues.

In 1995, most of the items reported by *Vremya* fell outside the Cold War frame. They also fell outside a news frame that told a clear story about a post–Cold War world. The apparent absence of such simplifying frameworks left viewers without a clear sense of the order of things and without a basis for making systematic judgments about the domestic and international scene.

To *Vremya* viewers, the political world must have seemed much more complicated than it did before the end of the Cold War. It was now harder for them than it once was to make sense of daily happenings in domestic and international politics. What had changed was the political spectacle offered to them by *Vremya*. As philosopher of science Abraham Kaplan once pointed out, simplicity and complexity are not qualities inherent in a subject matter. Rather, the terms refer to the manner in which a subject matter is treated (Kaplan 1964). The principle is consistent with the contention of Edelman (1988), Hall (1982) and others that media news accounts evoke a spectacle that is an ideological product, not a set of facts.

NOTES

Barbara Ruth Burke, University of Minnesota, contributed to this chapter.

1. The study analyzed *Vremya* programs broadcast on these dates in 1995:

Jan.	4, 9, 11, 17, 20, 31
Feb.	3, 6, 7, 9, 10, 20
Mar.	2, 7, 8, 14, 16, 22
Apr.	4, 12, 13, 14, 18, 20, 27
May	2, 3, 4, 12, 17, 19
June	1, 6, 9, 13, 15, 16
July	12, 13, 14, 17, 24, 27
Aug.	1, 3, 7, 14, 15, 23
Sept.	1, 8, 15, 22, 27, 28
Oct.	3, 10, 16, 19, 23, 27
Nov.	2, 7, 8, 9, 15, 28
Dec.	1, 5, 7, 13, 21, 23

2. For another thematic study of Russian media using translated material, see Downing (1988).

3. The individual news readers: Tatyana Kamarova, Aleksander Panov, Nelle Petkova, and Igor Bihuholev appeared to be counterparts of *CNN Headline News* readers such as David Goodnow, Bob Losure, and Lynn Russell. Their role was considerably more limited than that of American news anchors such as Tom Brokaw, Peter Jennings, Ted Koppel, and Dan Rather. The era of Igor Kirillov clearly had ended.

4. The fifteen-minute newscast of September 15, shortened to permit coverage of a Russian hockey match, was the only program to fall outside these ranges.

5. Some criticisms do appear, though infrequently. Three items do mention high taxes and an apparent shortage of government funds to support popular social programs.

6. Due to space limitations, items dealing with culture and sports are not discussed in this chapter. However, it is worth noting that no *Vremya* item appeared to disparage American popular culture by contrasting it with Russia's interest in opera, ballet, films, museums, etc. On the contrary, considerable attention was paid

to events such as the Detroit Auto Show (Jan. 4), Diana Ross's tour of Eastern Europe (June 16), and Frank Sinatra's birthday celebration (Dec. 23). Russian street scenes commonly showed children wearing clothing decorated with Walt Disney characters. Highlights of National Hockey League and National Basketball Association games were common features of the sportscast.

7. Visual as well as verbal contents are reported for both U.S. items. The items dealing with the fifth anniversary of the RSFSR and the Yeltsin–Clinton speeches presented little more than "talking heads," pictures of arrivals and departures of diplomats, views of formal meetings, and pictures of interiors and exteriors of government buildings and the United Nations building.

Chapter 5

The United States as a World Military Power: An Indonesian Newspaper's View of the United States in the Persian Gulf Crisis

Given the vast amount of media coverage throughout the world, reports on the Gulf crisis provide considerable material for studying alternative ways in which political events can be socially constructed by the media of different nations. This chapter presents a comparative study of how a leading American newspaper, *The New York Times*, and a leading Indonesian newspaper, *Kompas,* accounted for the situation in the Persian Gulf between August 2, 1990, when Iraqi tanks and infantry entered Kuwait, and January 16, 1991, when a military assault was initiated by forces of the United States and a coalition of other nations with the explicitly stated objective of driving Iraqi forces out of Kuwait.

Like the studies reported in Chapters 2, 3, and 4, this research explores the ways in which news reflects and serves national political, economic, and ideological interests. In addition, the research deals with a topic that received little attention in the preceding chapters: the impact on media content of the different normative systems under which the media of various nations operate. *The New York Times* works within the context of a free-press system, whereas *Kompas* functions as a developmental press.

THE POSITIONS OF THE GOVERNMENTS OF THE UNITED STATES AND INDONESIA

The position of the United States toward Iraq's military thrust into Kuwait was unambiguous. On August 2, 1990, President George Bush denounced Iraq's action as "naked aggression" against a sovereign state, signed executive orders banning most trade with Iraq, and froze Iraq and Kuwait's assets in the United States. An aircraft carrier battle group was dispatched to the Persian Gulf. Addressing the American people on August 8, President Bush said he sought the withdrawal of Iraq from Kuwait, restoration of the Kuwait government, stability in the Persian Gulf region, and protection of Americans living in the region. In an August 15 speech, Bush stressed "access to vital resources" and "our jobs, our way of life" as factors related to U.S. military deployment in the Gulf.

As an active member of the Association of Non-Allied Countries, and as a member of the United Nations, Indonesia did not support Iraq's invasion of Kuwait and called for the withdrawal of Iraqi forces. However, before the outbreak of war on January 16, Indonesia did not favor the use of military force to bring about Iraqi withdrawal. Indonesia maintained an extensive and complex set of political, cultural, economical, and organizational ties to both Iraq and the United States. These ties made problematic the meanings that the Indonesian media were to impose on events occurring in the Gulf.

Politically, it would have been difficult for Indonesia to criticize the military action by Iraq. Indonesia itself had engaged in somewhat similar action. In 1975, East Timor declared itself the Democratic Republic of East Timor, no longer an overseas territory of Portugal. Subsequently, Indonesia invaded and occupied East Timor and, in 1976, declared it a province of Indonesia.

Culturally, both Iraq and Indonesia are Muslim nations. Eighty-eight percent of Indonesia's 191.3 million inhabitants share the religion, giving Indonesia the largest Muslim population outside the Arab world. This linked Indonesia to the Middle East generally, but particularly to Iraq. Both nations had been highly critical of sheiks in Kuwait and Saudi Arabia who, they claimed, had exploited poor Muslim workers from other countries. Although Indonesia did not support Iraq's attempted annexation of Kuwait, neither did it support the U.S. presence in Saudi Arabia. Furthermore, since the 1979 Iranian Revolution, the United States has been pictured in many Muslim nations as the enemy of Islam. The weekly Indonesian newsmagazine *Tempo* commented in September 1990: "The great Satan of the Ayatollahs is growing into a medium-sized Satan in Indonesia" (quoted in Vatikioitis 1990, 20). Economically, Indonesia and Iraq were trading partners. Indonesian trade with Iraq was increasing at a more rapid rate than it was with other Middle East countries as a result of a bilateral trade agreement between Indonesia and Iraq signed in 1989 (Djiwandono 1990, 79).

Indonesia's ties to the United States also were extensive. Politically, Indonesia enjoyed good diplomatic relations with the United States as a result of its noncommunist stance. Through the Association of South East Asia Nations (ASEAN), it took a firm stand against Vietnam's invasion and occupation of Kampuchea, and in 1989–1990, Indonesia played a major part in exploring the possibilities of a negotiated resolution of the Indochina problem. Many members of the Indonesian government and military were educated in American colleges and universities. Indonesia and the United States have an active cultural-exchange program. Next to Japan, the United States was Indonesia's leading trading partner. In 1989 trade with the United States accounted for twelve percent of Indonesia's imports and for sixteen percent of its exports. Indonesia also receives economic aid from the United States. In 1989 it totaled approximately $35 million.

COMPARING *THE NEW YORK TIMES* AND *KOMPAS*

The New York Times and *Kompas* are their nation's leading newspapers in terms of their circulation, prestige, and apparent influence. In 1989, *The New York Times* had a circulation of approximately 1,068,000, fifth largest in the United States. No other American newspaper possesses comparable resources (e.g., a news staff of 650); esteem (e.g., it has won more Pulitzer Prizes than any other newspaper); or influence (e.g., most presidents of the United States look at page one of *The New York Times* even before their morning coffee; Salisbury 1980, 5). *Kompas*, published in Jakarta in the national language, Bahasa Indonesian, is the largest newspaper in Indonesia, with a circulation in 1989 of about 600,000. It is generally considered the most reliable newspaper in the country and is routinely referred to by Indonesian intellectuals, religious leaders, and political elites, including the president of Indonesia (Sutopo 1983).

The New York Times operates within a free press system that, as an ideal type, can be defined in terms of these norms: (1) Publication should be free from any prior censorship; (2) Attack on any government, official, or political party (as distinct from attacks on private individuals or treason and breaches of security) should not be punishable; (3) There should be no compulsion to publish anything; (4) No restriction should be placed on the collection, by legal means, of information for publication; and (5) Journalists should be able to claim a considerable degree of professional autonomy within their organization (McQuail 1988, 115).

As numerous analysts have pointed out, a variety of interacting and mutually reinforcing social conditions work to make the actual operation of Western media diverge in important ways from the ideal type of a free-press system. First, in the West, the mass media are almost entirely commercial, profit-making organizations. As capitalist endeavors, they prosper by legitimizing the political–economic system of which they are a part (Croteau and Hoynes 2001; Entman 1989; Gans 1979, 46–48; Qualter 1985; Tuchman 1978, 210).

Second, Western media are not independent of government. "The political system endorses the media system by granting it constitutional and other legal rights to operate as an information system on the grounds that the media are essential to the conduct of a democratic society. If the media system were denied access to these resources, its stability and economic welfare would be seriously jeopardized" (DeFleur and Ball-Rokeach 1989, 305).

Third, Western media rely on information provided by government, business and "experts." At least in the United States, the vast majority of news stories are drawn from situations over which such news sources have either complete or substantial control (Sigal 1973, 124). In the West, "the typical news fare covers only a narrow range of issues from the viewpoint of an even narrower range of sources . . . " (Bennett 1996; ix). As discussed in Chapter 1, the enduring values of journalists are political values that imply the advocacy of one kind of social order. Because news has political implications, and because journalists choose the news in response to source power, they are unwittingly part of the political process (Pedeltry 1995).

Kompas operates within a developmental press system that, as an ideal type, can be defined in terms of these norms: (1) Media should accept and carry out positive development tasks; (2) Media should give priority in news and information to links with other developing countries which are close geographically, culturally or politically; (3) Journalists and other media workers have responsibilities as well as freedoms in their information-gathering and dissemination tasks; (4) In the interest of development ends, the state has a right to intervene in, or restrict, media operations, and devices of censorship, subsidy, and direct control can be justified (McQuail 1988, 121).

MEASURES AND FINDINGS

To what extent did *The New York Times* and *Kompas* present differing accounts of the Gulf crisis? Were the differences systematic? If they were systematic, how are they to be explained? To answer these questions, every issue of *The New York Times* and *Kompas*, from August 2, 1990 (the date of the Iraqi invasion), until January 16, 1991 (the date of the initiation of direct military action by the United States and a coalition of nations aimed at driving Iraqi forces from Kuwait), was subjected to content analysis.

In his early survey of the state of the art, Berelson (1952, 18) defined content analysis as a research technique for or involving "the objective, systematic and quantitative description of the manifest content of communication." Almost immediately, critics of the approach noted its limitations. For example, Kracauer (1953, 640) argued that the frequency counts of items out of context often produce little by way of revealing the meaning of a text. "What is relevant are the patterns, the wholes which can be made manifest by qualitative exegesis and which can throw light upon a textual characteristic which is allergic to quantitative breakdowns." More recent critics (e.g., Hall 1982) have added that the subtle biases embodied in the language of media presentations often are not measured by current quantitative research.

Such possible limitations of content analysis are acknowledged. This study focuses on the overt meaning of the newspapers' contents. It does not deal directly with the latent connotative meanings which may or may not have been intended by those responsible for the newspapers' contents or that derived by newspapers' audiences. Nevertheless, the study indicates that content analysis can reveal linguistic constructions of political reality, indicate the systematic biases they express, and suggest the political and economic interests they serve.

Three dimensions of news coverage were examined: the amount of attention or relative importance assigned to the Gulf crisis, the relative amount of coverage given to the official positions on the Gulf crisis of the governments of the United States and Iraq, and the particular themes that each newspaper developed.

Importance

The importance or "newsworthiness" of an event is not a quality intrinsic to the event itself, but rather is defined by interested parties. "Newsworthiness is a negotiated phenomenon rather than the application of independently derived objective criteria to new events" (Tuchman 1978, 46). Because the United States had heavily invested in the Gulf crisis (troops, money, war materials) whereas Indonesia had no comparable investment, *The New York Times* might be expected to define the event as more important than did *Kompas*. However, explanation of the attribution of importance to the event by the American newspaper is not entirely self-evident. Was the crisis defined as important by *The New York Times* because the government of the United States heavily invested its resources (including the serious risk of loss of countless lives)? Or, beyond this, had the government of the United States heavily invested its resources because the "crisis" was important (i.e., the United States had much at stake, such as access to essential resources, regional influence, and international image, and/or because higher issues were involved, such as the principle of sovereignty of nations and the protection of human rights)? To the extent that *The New York Times* was emphasizing the second set of reasons in its account of the Gulf crisis, it was legitimating government policy. It was constructing a symbolic universe in which U.S. policy was linked to maintaining a humane and stable international order.

Four comparative measures were used to investigate the relative importance attributed to the event by *The New York Times* and *Kompas*: (1) number of items concerned with the Gulf crisis; (2) number of days on which

Gulf crisis items appeared; (3) number of leading headlines; and (4) percent of foreign news items dealing with the Gulf crisis.

The New York Times is a larger newspaper than Kompas, having an average of forty-eight pages per weekday edition, compared to Kompas's sixteen pages. During the period studied, The New York Times published 1,176 items relating to the Gulf crisis whereas Kompas published 195 items. Hence, although The New York Times is 3.1 times the size of Kompas, it published 6.0 times the Gulf news items. Also, during the period of August 2, 1990 to January 16, 1991, the period covered in the study, The New York Times carried items relating to the Gulf crisis on 168 days as compared with Kompas's 155 days.

The Gulf crisis was the subject of leading headlines 104 times in The New York Times, but it was given that status 29 times in Kompas. During the period of the study, Kompas published 1,162 news items that focused on nations other than Indonesia. Of these, 195, or 16.8 percent, concerned the Gulf crisis. In the same time period, The New York Times published 3,505 items that focused on nations other than the United States. Of these, 1,176, or 33.6 percent, concerned the Gulf crisis.

By all four measures, then, The New York Times clearly defined the Gulf crisis as more important or newsworthy than did Kompas. If newsworthiness were an intrinsic quality of an event, this would have been reflected in the more or less equal attention given the situation by the two newspapers. What the data reflect, however, are differences in the material resources invested in the Gulf crisis by the government of the United States and Indonesia, and possibly differences in the political perspectives of the governments as well.

Balance

In American journalism, the appearance of political balance is assigned considerable importance. Displaying some effort to present both sides of a political conflict equally is made on grounds that failure to do so will lead to accusations of bias and undermine credibility (Gans 1979, 75). However, as many analysts have pointed out, American media are participants in a symbiotic relationship with government and with corporations that results in its continuously confirming the legitimacy of the state and corporate capitalism (Bagdikian 1997; Bennet 1996; Fishman 1980; Herman and Chomsky 1988; Schudson 1983; Sigal 1973; Tuchman 1978).

Several studies have shown that American media coverage of the Gulf conflict (including The New York Times coverage specifically) was subject to various forms of censorship. Among the most important of these was the practice of pooling. Media were prohibited from having direct access to the troops and to certain geographic areas. Journalists were organized into pools and were taken to sites selected by the military itself, and then were permitted to interview troops and others, such as shopkeepers, or to make observations of military activity only with the military escort present. Reporters then were allowed to forward their material only after it had been subjected to security review (Cockburn 1992; Cohen 1992; Cumings 1992; Fialka 1992; Kellner 1992, 80–85; MacArthur 1992; Nohrstedt 1992). On January 10, 1991, a group of publishers sued the Pentagon in New York federal court, claiming that the Pentagon rules regulating the media were unconstitutional. *The New York Times* declined either to join the suit or to contribute to friend-of-the-court briefs once the suit was filed (MacArthur 1992, 34). This does raise some question about the strength of commitment of *The New York Times* to a balanced presentation of the Gulf crisis.

Working within a developing nation, Indonesian journalists are participants in a guided media system normatively committed to assigning priority in their news to the established policies of their government (Hachten 1987; Righter 1979). Operating within the framework of *Pancasila*, the Indonesian national ideology, newsmakers are required to reflect the interests of their government in their information coverage and reportage (Department of Information, Republic of Indonesia 1988).

Two comparative measures were used to explore the balance of the newspaper accounts: (1) percentage of Gulf crisis items in which there appear direct quotations of George Bush and Saddam Hussein, and (2) percentage of Gulf crisis items using U.S./Coalition, Iraqi, or other information sources.

Despite the normative context of a media system emphasizing balance, *The New York Times* quoted George Bush almost twice as frequently in its "Gulf crisis" items as it quoted Saddam (Bush 13.9 percent; Saddam 7.5 percent—a ratio of 1.9 to 1). *Kompas* quoted Saddam more frequently than Bush (Saddam 17.4 percent; Bush 12.8 percent—but with a lower ratio of 1.4 to 1). Data in Table 5.1 also show that *The New York Times* relied exclusively on U.S./Coalition sources of information for more than half of its Gulf crisis items (52.9 percent), whereas *Kompas* relied exclusively on this source in fewer than fifteen of its items (14.4 percent). (*Kompas's* level of exclusive dependence on U.S./Coalition sources appears to be remarkably low in light of the prominence of U.S. government sources in the world information system.) Data in Table 5.1 further indicate that *The New York Times* published a smaller percentage of items citing "other sides" than did *Kompas*. Although 18.5 percent of *Kompas's* Gulf crisis items cited both U.S./Coalition and Iraqi sources, the corresponding figure for *The New York Times* was a mere 3.1 percent.

As a leading Western newspaper, *The New York Times* is normatively committed to balanced presentations of international affairs. Yet, data indicate that its pattern of reporting the Gulf crisis supported the position of the U.S. government. As a leading Third World paper, *Kompas* is norma-

Table 5.1
Source of Information Cited within Item in Indonesian and U.S. Newspapers

Source	The New York Times		Kompas	
	Number of Items	Percent	Number of Items	Percent
U.S./Coalition[a] only	622	52.9	28	14.4
Iraqi[b] only	91	7.7	19	9.7
Other[c] only	334	28.4	78	40.4
U.S. + Iraqi	36	3.1	36	18.5
U.S. + other	68	5.8	18	9.2
Iraqi + other	20	1.7	9	4.6
U.S. + Iraqi + other	5	0.4	7	3.6
Total	1,176	100.0	195	100.0

[a]Includes White House, state department, Pentagon, U.S. military command, coalition military command, governments of coalition nations

[b]Includes ministry of information, foreign ministry, Parliament, Iraqi radio, interviews with Baghdad residents

[c]Includes Organization of Petroleum Exporting Countries, United Nations, International Monetary Fund, Amnesty International, the Pope, oil industry analysts not having direct government connection, Palestine Liberation Organization, Israeli government, interviews with Iraqi military deserters and prisoners of war

tively committed to supporting the policies of its government. Data indicate that its pattern of reporting of the Gulf crisis was comparatively balanced. That balance appears to have been a reflection of the officially neutral position of the Indonesian government.

Western and Third World Media

Research on the structure and operation of international communication (McPhail 1987; Rosenblume 1978; Schiller 1976; Smith 1980) indicates that one important dimension for comparing Western and Third World media messages involves the extent to which each emphasizes its national interests and the interests of other nations at similar locations in the world political economy. Western media, including the major wire services, tend to socially construct political conditions and events in ways promoting self-serving values, ascribing legitimacy to the present structure of the world political economy and supporting existing forms of world domination and control (Giffard 1984; Masmoudi 1978; McPhail 1987; O'Brien 1984; Rosenblume 1978). The media of Third World nations tend to construct news in accordance with the foreign policy interests of their individual governments and, to a lesser extent, in accordance with the political and economic interests they share as occupants of the periphery of the world political economic system (Fox 1988; Hedeboro 1982). The Gulf crisis presented a situation in which the West and several rich oil emirates and kingdoms were aligned against a comparatively poor Third World country. To some, it signaled a threat to build a new post–Cold War order on repeated recourse to military force against Third World nations (Frank 1992, 3).

Drawing on suggestions in this literature on international communications, three comparative measures were used to examine the framing of the Gulf crisis by *The New York Times* and *Kompas*: (1) percentage of Gulf crisis items referring to the implications of the Iraqi invasion for the political economy of Western industrial nations; (2) percentage of Gulf crisis items referring to the implications of the Iraqi invasion for the political economy of Third World nations; and (3) percentage of Gulf crisis items referring to the Iraqi invasion as a threat to the existing world order.

Data in Table 5.2 show that, proportionately, *The New York Times* referred to the implications of the Gulf crisis for the political economy of Western nations 2.7 times as often as it referred to its implications for the political economies of Third World nations. *Kompas* did almost precisely the opposite, referring to the implications of the Gulf crisis for the political economies of Third World nations 2.6 times as often as its implications for the Western nations. Given the practically limitless number of frames that might have been employed to discuss the Gulf crisis, the fact that each newspaper presented one-fourth of its total Gulf crisis articles in terms of the event's impact on Western and Third World political economies suggests that this was an important frame used by media throughout the world in their construction of the Gulf crisis spectacle.

The international communication literature suggests that *The New York Times* would tend to focus more on the implications of the Gulf crisis for the existing world order than would *Kompas*. Because of their economic and political interests in maintaining a system that supports the existing structure of inequality in the distribution of the world's wealth, Western nations seem more likely than other nations to view an event such as Iraq's invasion of Kuwait—which would have increased Iraq's ability to block Western access to important oil resources—possibly a threat to the world order.

Data in Table 5.2 do not conform to this expectation. At least two possible explanations of the data merit attention. First, *Kompas* might have presented numerous discussions of the world order from a Third World per-

Table 5.2
Topic References in Articles in Indonesian and U.S. Newspapers

Reference	The New York Times		Kompas	
	Number of Articles	Percent	Number of Articles	Percent
Western political economy	196	16.7	12	6.2
Third World political economy	86	7.3	38	19.5
Threat to world order	281	23.9	57	29.2
Other[a]	559	47.5	84	43.1
Western and world order	11	0.9	1	0.5
Western and other	2	0.2	1	0.5
Third World and world order	2	0.2	—	—
Third World and other	3	0.3	—	—
Western and Third World	2	0.2	—	—
World order and other	34	2.9	2	1.0
Total	176	100.0	195	100.0

[a]Includes historical information; military strategy; biographies of Saddam Hussein, Tariq Aziz, Colin Powell, Norman Schwartzkopf, Brent Snowcroft; customs in the Arab world; hostages; human interest; international efforts to solve crisis

spective. For example, it might have called attention to the possibility of Iraq's developing the capability of placing some limitation on Western exploitation of Third World resources. Data, however, do not support this interpretation. *Kompas* did not offer a single article that linked Third World interests in any way to the existing world order. A second explanation is that *Kompas's* frequent description of the Gulf crisis as a threat to the world order is a reflection of the newspaper's extensive reliance on Western news agencies. The framing may represent an unintended consequence of a Third World nation's dependence on an information system dominated by the West.

Several additional indicators were used to identify historically specific aspects of the approaches employed by *The New York Times* and *Kompas*. Two items examined the frequency with which each newspaper presented information that could be construed as critical of United States policy that led to the military buildup in the Gulf. First, how many items did each newspaper publish noting that, during the Iran–Iraq War, the United States had provided military intelligence and technology to Iraq? (Such aid not only strengthened Saddam Hussein in his struggle against Khomeini's Shiite legions, but against other regional adversaries as well; it also provided him with additional means to pursue further oppression of Iraq's own Shiite and Kurdish minorities, ultimately enhancing the capabilities of his military, which directly confronted the forces of the United States in the Gulf.) Second, how many items did each newspaper publish that referred to dissent against direct U.S. military involvement in the Gulf? (In retrospect, there appears to have been few large public anti-war demonstrations in the United States. However, a number of leading intellectuals such as Noam Chomsky, Barbara Ehrenreich, Edwin Knoll, and Edward Said wrote and spoke extensively in opposition to America's military involvement.)

Data indicate that *The New York Times* published nine articles in which there was reference to support for Iraq in the Iran–Iraq War. This constituted less than one percent of the total number of its Gulf crisis items. *Kompas* published five such articles, which comprised 2.6 percent of its Gulf crisis items (almost three times the *New York Times*'s percentage). In sixteen of its articles (1.4 percent of its total), *The New York Times* made some reference to dissent (domestic, foreign, individual, or collective), whereas the corresponding figure for *Kompas* was nine articles (4.6 percent of its total; again, more than three times the *New York Times*'s percentage). Hence, neither paper described the buildup to the Gulf War as involving U.S. government policy about which serious questions could be or, in fact, were being raised. However, insofar as some reference was made to problematic aspects of prior American foreign policy or to ongoing policy debate, *Kompas* was more likely than *The New York Times* to do so.

Two final issues relevant to the symbolic construction of the Gulf crisis merit consideration. Iraq's military incursion into Kuwait represented a violation of the principle of the sovereignty of nations. In recent decades, this principle has become increasingly important within world organizations, such as the United Nations, as a criterion for evaluating the actions initiated by nation states toward one another (McNeely 1993). *The New York Times* repeatedly referred to Iraq's violating Kuwaiti sovereignty in items discussing the rationale for the military buildup in the Gulf. Of its items, 195, or 16.6 percent, contained such references. In sharp contrast, only one item in *Kompas* (or one half of one percent of its Gulf items) referred to the principle of national sovereignty.

During wars or during periods immediately preceding them, accounts of atrocities are common (Jowett and O'Donnell 1986, 130–132). The Gulf crisis was no exception. For example, on January 12, 1991, *The New York Times* carried excerpts of a speech delivered to the House of Representatives by John Edward Porter (R, Ill.) in which Porter claimed that Iraq had undertaken "the most sadistic, cruel, barbaric, brutal, and vicious program of torture and repression against the people of Kuwait that can be imagined." Although *The New York Times* referred to human rights violations committed by Iraqi troops in forty-six of its items (3.9 percent of its coverage), *Kompas* carried only three such items (1.5 percent of its coverage). Allegations of atrocities, made by the Bush administration and reported by media throughout the world, were part of the government's campaign to demonize Saddam Hussein, making him the "target of terse rhetoric and by implication, his destruction the raison d'etre of the War" (Kellner 1992, 336). *The New York Times* coverage reflected a tendency of American media to report human rights violations when they occur in nations outside the U.S. sphere of influence, but to overlook atrocities occurring in client states (Herman and Chomsky 1988, 37–86).

Whether intentional or not, the *New York Times's* relatively frequent reference to violation of Kuwaiti sovereignty and to Iraq's human rights violations supported the U.S. government policy of troop buildup in the Gulf. A free press is not always a critical press. However, questions can be raised about *The New York Times's* apparent willingness to discuss such matters in the case of the Gulf crisis and its apparent unwillingness to do so in the context of the few items it published in 1975 on Indonesia's invasion of East Timor; or, perhaps more pointedly, the infrequency with which the paper referred to Iraqi human rights violations after 1984 when the Reagan administration "tilted" toward Iraq and against Iran (MacArthur 1992, 37–77).

DISCUSSION

The Gulf crisis was typical of political conflicts; its importance, the justness of the causes of the contending nations, and the meaning of the conflict itself were not qualities inherent in the conflict as an objective social reality. Rather, they were attributes of the various symbolic realities constructed by media to represent it. At some time in the future, historians and social scientists might reach some sort of consensus on how important the Gulf crisis was, and what the crisis was really about. Those judgments, which themselves will be social constructions, might vary considerably from those offered by *The New York Times* and *Kompas* that were identified in this chapter.

In both Indonesia and the United States, there was some division of opinion over the proper response to Iraq's incursion into Kuwait. As noted above, Indonesia's ties to both the United States and Iraq led its government to adopt a neutral position in the unfolding conflict. *Kompas*, as a developmental press normatively committed to supporting the policies of its government, reported the crisis in ways that helped legitimate this stand.

Although *Kompas's* coverage certainly indicated that the situation in the Gulf was important, it did not invest the event with as great an importance as did the American newspaper. *Kompas* discussed the position of the Iraqi government more frequently than did *The New York Times*. *Kompas* described the news of the Gulf crisis in terms of its implications for the political economies of Third World nations more than twice as often as it identified its implications for the West. In addition, *Kompas* failed to cover alleged human rights violations and made no reference to the principle of sovereignty of nations in explaining the crisis. Such omissions strongly suggest the point made by Gamson (1989, 158) that the *absence* of certain facts can reveal a story line that favors the interests of a partisan agent whom a medium is representing.

Undoubtedly, such coverage by *Kompas* angered some Indonesians who, above all else, saw the United States and its Western allies as seeking to establish a new world order based on the use of military force to intervene in Third World political affairs in ways serving Western political–economic interests. They well might have preferred a spectacle that created Saddam Hussein as some sort of Third World hero, George Bush as personifying an imperialist enemy, and an emerging neocolonial ambition on the part of Western industrial nations as the problem.

Undoubtedly, such coverage also troubled other Indonesians, such as members of the military, business, and intellectual elite, who would have preferred a more pro-Western orientation and disliked the publication of material potentially useful to the country's Muslim opposition parties. However, because of its status as a noncommercial, developmental press, it was not incumbent upon *Kompas* to take into account such conflicting attitudes of its readers. Rather, the media system within which the paper operated prescribed the role of *Kompas* as an instrument of the state, imposing constructions of political reality consistent with and supporting state policy.

The New York Times reflected the position of the American government. The newspaper's accounts of the conflict emphasized its importance, thereby justifying investment of vast economic, military, and symbolic (U.S. international prestige) resources. *The New York Times* discussed the position of the American government more frequently than the position of the government of Iraq. Over forty percent of *The New York Times's* accounts of the Gulf crisis framed Iraq's action as a threat to the political economy of the West and more generally as a threat to world order, thereby legitimizing American policy—at least in some Western eyes. Emphasis on violation of the principle of sovereignty of nations reinforced the theme of Iraq's threat to world order. References to human rights violations added an emotional thrust possibly lacking in other components of the legitimizing frame. Exhibiting its own pattern of selective omission,

The New York Times paid little attention to expressions of dissent over U.S. policy in the Gulf region prior to the outbreak of war. There were few discussions of the Bush administration's support of Iraq's government immediately prior to the war (Graber 1993, 160).

Such coverage by *The New York Times* certainly appealed to sectors of American society whose interests were served by a military solution to the situation, and more generally by establishing a strong U.S. presence in the Middle East. Such interests included defense contractors, big oil, banking, and finance. Policy seen as forcefully stabilizing the area also was favored by stock and commodity markets, which operate erratically during periods of global uncertainty. On the other hand, the newspaper's coverage certainly distressed those opposed to the developing government policy. These included members of a growing peace movement, veterans of the 1960s' antiwar movement, environmentalists, feminists, and other social movements opposed to war, as well as those wanting to see a "peace dividend," supposedly acquired by the ending of the Cold War, invested in various social programs rather than in new military undertakings.

A model that focuses on the operation of media as instruments of the state may be useful for analyzing the contents of a newspaper, such as *Kompas*, which is part of a developmental press system. However, such a model may not be as helpful in analyzing the contents of a newspaper, such as *The New York Times*, which is part of a commercial, free-press system. Differences in the operation of a developmental press system and a commercial free-press system may be particularly pronounced during the coverage of a crisis event about which there is some substantial dissent over government policy.

Kellner (1992, 59) has suggested that a hegemonic model of the media is useful for understanding American media discourse about the Gulf crisis. The model "represents society and culture as contested terrain and depicts various social groups and movements struggling for power, rather than seeing society as merely a site of manipulation and domination (though ... such manipulation of the public does obviously occur). . . . Because an aggressive interventionist policy and war in the Gulf was opposed by powerful forces, it was crucial that the Bush administration enlist mainstream media support in establishing their intervention as a hegemonic project."

Although ideologically committed to the norms of a free press, commercial news media in corporate–capitalist nations nevertheless tend to provide support for the policies of their governments. The "balance" they supposedly exhibit to express their independence, but also to attract and maintain the largest possible audiences as a commercial necessity, gives way to skewed presentations when this becomes a political necessity—particularly when access to information is tightly controlled by the government and the military. In the particular case of the crisis in the Gulf, commercial and political interests coincided. As Kellner (1992, 61) notes, "during times of crisis, especially with late-breaking stories, the media are especially dependent on official sources which are thus able to manipulate and control the agenda. If the public . . . tends to support official policy, this is another incentive for mainstream media to privilege the views of the administration in power, for going against popular policies could lead to loss of audience and revenue."

Media in Third World nations are ideologically committed to the norms of a developmental press that support the social and economic needs of their nation and give priority to news and information that links their nation with other developing countries. These media, too, tend to provide support for the policies of their governments. This is not to claim that important differences between Western and Third World media systems do not exist. Nor is it to claim that different models of media discourse are not required for the analysis of developmental and commercial media systems. It is to claim, however, that some of the differences might not be as great as commonly assumed and that the supposed critical function of Western media is more realistically understood as what Bennett (1996, 83) termed a "ritualistic posture of antagonism."

Future comparative research is required to determine more precisely the nature of difference between developmental and commercial free-press systems. Studies might investigate these questions. Within a specific time frame or for a specific event, will developmental media tend to report a greater proportion of their news that is consistent with the expressed official position of their governments than will commercial media? Are there systematic differences between the reactions of Western and non-Western governments to the media of their countries on any occasions on which their news presentations contain material that runs counter to their expressed positions? Answers to these questions will suggest the amount of sovereignty actually enjoyed by media in the various media systems. In particular, data would show how a commercial free press behaves at the uncomfortable intersection of journalism, commerce, and politics.

NOTE

Arie S. Soesilo, University of Indonesia, contributed to this chapter.

Chapter 6

The United States as a World Economic Power: Radio Japan's View of the United States in International Trade Disputes

"In an increasingly interdependent world in which mass opinion power-fully shapes public policy, a government's ability to sell its position to for-eign elites and mass publics is an increasingly vital source of power. No country has been more successful in propagating its position abroad than Japan" (Nester 1993, 174–175). This chapter reports on the way in which Radio Japan, one of Japan's official media of international political com-munication, constructs ideologically useful images of Japan and its chief trade rival, the United States, in the context of its newscasts. It is an exami-nation of broadcast news in the post–Cold War period in which power ap-peared to depend as much on the ability of nations' banks and corpora-tions to capture market share and defeat foreign trade rivals as it did on the capabilities of its military.

International radio broadcasting during times of war provides some of the most clear examples of the uses of news in the service of state objec-tives. The history of international radio broadcasting is particularly in-structive for what it reveals about media construction of the image of an enemy. A brief history serves as a point of departure for analyzing the so-cial construction of international trade rivals during times of peace.

NEWS IN THE SERVICE OF WAR EFFORTS

As early as World War I, radio was employed by both Russia and Ger-many to encourage mutiny of enemy soldiers (Radio Nederland Werel-domroep 1982). During this period, the uses of radio were limited because transmissions largely had been confined to Morse code. Nevertheless, even with this limitation, the potential of international radio broadcasting had been sufficiently well appreciated that the representatives of the Allies at Versailles prohibited German broadcasting and the construction of any new station for a period of three months after the peace treaty had been signed (Short 1983).

During World War II, radio served as Germany's instrument of choice for presenting the views of the Third Reich to the world (Zeman 1964). In its discussion of the war, German international radio placed greater emphasis on adversary qualities than on the qualities of its own nation. Efforts were made to weaken Allied conviction of the right to victory by reporting Allied acts of brutality, while describing German military action in terms of attributes such as bravery. The pattern of messages on German international radio was, "We are strong and you are immoral." Broadcasts aimed at convincing citizens of Allied nations, particularly the French, that they were divided socially from other allied nations, such as Britain. They also attempted to depoliticize Allied audiences by emphasizing nonpolitical values and loyalties as more important that political ones. For example, there were numerous discussions of the senselessness of war (Speier and Otis 1979, 223).

In a similar manner, Fascist Italy's Radio Bari broadcast verbal assaults against its wartime enemies, particularly the British, portraying them as imperialistic oppressors and Italy as the protector of Islam (MacDonald 1977). Italian international radio also emphasized that the prevailing world political–military order served the narrow self-interests of Russia and the West and was created and promoted through the provisions of the Treaty of Versailles and the establishment of the League of Nations (Grandin 1939/1971, 61).

During World War II, Japanese radio depicted Western nations as aggressors in the Far East with ambitions of conquering the world. It emphasized the need to liberate Asians who lived under European colonial rule and domination. Western influence was equated with decadence, laziness, and lack of national pride (Daniels 1983).

International radio broadcasting also was used extensively by the Allies during World War II. The British Broadcasting Corporation (BBC) responded to the fascists by attempting to discredit them as intentionally deceitful and malicious and to present their news program as depictions of the truth about the war (Abshire 1976, 201; Balfour 1979). Although the British officially took a no-propaganda policy toward its coverage of the war, one of its major tasks was to overcome American isolationism in order to involve the United States directly in the conflict. In part, this was achieved by disseminating the view that Germany clearly had shown itself to be the enemy of democracy and capitalism and would, in the event of victory, jeopardize the American economic system (Cull 1995, 67). (As discussed in Chapter 2, when the BBC actually did adopt what amounted to a no-propaganda policy decades later, toward reporting the Falklands War, it was severely criticized by the British government.)

In 1942, under the auspices of the Office of War Information, the Voice of America (VOA) went on the air. In its newscasts, the United States was idealized as a land of freedom and mobility where unity of will existed alongside diversity of background. America's goals were depicted as the liberation of Europe from Axis tyranny and the achievement of the four freedoms enunciated by President Roosevelt in 1941: freedom of speech and worship, and freedom from want and fear (Schulman 1990, 71).

World War II culminated in the emergence of the United States and the Soviet Union as the two most powerful nations in the world, with each nation working to consolidate leadership within its political–economic bailiwick. In 1950, the VOA became part of President Truman's Campaign for Truth program, which was intended to serve as an integral part of the administration's "struggle against Communism" (Browne 1982, 101; Alexander 1988, 10–11).

From World War II to 1989, media throughout the world tended to frame international news items "in terms of a dichotomized view of Communist and anti-Communist power, with gains and losses allocated to contesting sides and rooting for 'our side' [was] considered entirely legitimate news practice" (Herman and Chomsky 1988, 30–31). A conflict frame resulted, in which the United States and its allies and the Soviet Union and its allies were polarized forces. In this conflict frame, private enterprise Capitalism was pitted against Communism in a media discourse that focused on the Cold War, which transformed events into stories (Davis 1990; Neuman, Just, and Crigler 1992, 64–65; Real 1989, 195–186). The media of both the United States (commercial news media as well as the VOA) and the Soviet Union told stories in which images of the self and of the enemy played major roles. The symbolic universe of the Cold War, with its typifications of allies and enemies, is even more apparent in both Western and Soviet news coverage of conflicts (e.g., the Korean War, the uprisings in Poland and Hungary in the mid-1950s, the 1956 Suez crisis, the Bay of Pigs and the Cuban missile crises, the Soviet invasion of Czechoslovakia in 1968, and the Vietnam War) than it is in their reporting of the wars, internal struggles, and assassinations, which are here considered in Chapters 2 and 3.

Just as the media process of socially constructing allies and enemies did not end after World Wars I or II, the practice did not end with the termination of the Cold War. As discussed in the last chapter, during the 1991 Persian Gulf War, Western media portrayed Iraq as an aggressor that had violated the sovereignty of another nation and threatened Western access to vital resources.

War Stories

The transformation of events into stories is a necessary part of the act of communication (Hall 1982). In reporting political and military conflicts, media constructed enemies and allies as central components of the stories they told. War lends itself particularly well to appropriation by such narrative.

The use of a given narrative structure determines the shape of the actors, conditions, and events to be judged, and thereby often the judgment that is to be rendered. In the context of reporting political and military conflicts, the acts of one's state and its allies generally are reported as necessary and ethically justified. For example, throughout most of its course, American commercial media coverage of the war in Vietnam took for granted that the United States had intervened in the service of generous ideals, with the goal of defending South Vietnam from aggression and terrorism and in the interest of democracy and self-determination (Herman and Chomsky 1988, 169). The vocabulary used by our commercial news media to describe the war is revealing. "Throughout the Vietnam War, the insurgent forces were described as the 'enemy' although it was never explained why they deserved to be so considered; it being assumed that the 'Communist' label was a sufficient explanation. Reporters who prided themselves on their 'objectivity' saw cities 'fall' to the 'enemy' when they could have as easily viewed them as 'liberated' or merely changing political hands" (Parenti 1986/1993, 175).

The legitimacy of the war as a response to a clearly defined enemy was rarely subject to question by American media. When early dissent found public expression in the form of organized protest of student, church, union, and peace groups, it was occasionally treated with some sympathy. However, the cumulative impact of media coverage was to discredit protest (Gitlin 1980; Hallin 1986). Discussion of opposition tended to focus, not on the legitimacy of the war, but rather on the possibility of military success. A 1968 survey by *The Boston Globe* of thirty-nine leading newspapers with a combined circulation of twenty-two million showed that not one advocated withdrawal from Vietnam (Aronson 1973). Other data indicate that commercial media coverage did encourage a decisive majority of readers, viewers, and listeners to support the war (Epstein 1975).

Socially constructed allies and enemies not only help media tell their war stories, they also serve to legitimate the actions of one state toward another, and do so for both domestic and international audiences. This is the process of incipient legitimation discussed by Berger and Luckmann (1966, 94). Experiences of war make it clear that no country can afford to ignore the effects that its foreign policy will have on world opinion, as well as on the states directly affected by it (Hale 1975).

Trade Stories

In 1990, more than one political pundit wryly commented: "The Cold War is over—Japan won." As illustrated by the study of Russian national television newscasts in 1995, with the dissolution of the Soviet Union and the Soviet bloc, journalists worldwide lost the explanatory framework for constructing stories about international conflicts that had served them well for four decades. International events could no longer be constructed as parts of the global geopolitical struggle between capitalist and communist allies and enemies. Lack of a clear interpretative structure for presenting events reduced the likelihood they would be reported (Tuchman 1978). By 1995, with the exception of coverage of strife in Somalia, Haiti, and Bosnia, American network news reported fewer international events. Coverage of those conflicts that were reported tended to be shorter and were given lower priority (Norris 1995).

Although highly serviceable frameworks for telling war stories were developed for both world wars and for the Cold War, media worldwide entered the 1990s with no comparable framework for describing and explaining the economic conflicts that had become dominant in shaping the world order. It was not clear how *trade* stories were to be told. In 1995, the government of Japan had considerable interest in telling such stories effectively, in order to legitimate its trading practices to both domestic and foreign audiences. Japanese citizens were deeply concerned with the perceived loss of personal and economic security, which they saw as partly the result of global economic competition. Dissatisfaction found political expression in the frequent replacement of prime ministers and in the creation of a highly unusual coalition of liberal Democrats and Socialists (Carnegie Endowment 1995, 18–19). In the international arena, Japan sought acceptance of its trading practices by the newly established World Trade Organization. It also sought to maintain its shares in international markets—particularly in the huge American automobile market. (In 1994, Japan had exported 1.49 million new passenger cars to the United States.)

NEWS IN THE SERVICE OF TRADE EFFORTS

Opponents are not necessarily enemies, for some opponents are respected and accepted as legitimate. According to Edelman (1988, 66–89), enemies are characterized by a set of traits that mark them as evil or immoral and, therefore, a continuing threat, regardless of what action they pursue, regardless of whether they win or lose in any particular encounter, and even if they take no action at all. "The distinction between unacceptable and acceptable opponents, or between *enemies* and *adversaries*, lies in whether the focus of attention is upon the inherent nature of the antagonist, or instead, upon the tactics an opponent employs" (1988, 67).

Media seem most likely to construct serviceable images of international trade competitors during trade disputes. In this specific context, a number of interrelated questions, which have received little attention in the research literature, can be explored.

1. In their newscasts, do media, during international trade disputes, tend to focus on characterizing the trading practices of their nation's rival, or do they also construct a multidimensional integrated image of the competitor? If a set of general traits is ascribed, the difference between constructing an enemy and constructing an adversary would not be so great as Edelman suggests; trade stories would not be very different from war stories.

2. In their newscasts, do media, during international trade disputes, tend to assign to the practices of their nation's rival, or to the rival itself, qualities that are opposite those they assign to the acts of their own nation or to their own nation itself? (As noted above, this pattern of enemy construction clearly influenced the Cold War news reporting of media in both Western and Soviet bloc countries. However, during World War II, the pattern was not present in newscasts of Nazi Germany, which emphasized its military *strength* but Allied *immorality*.)

3. During international trade disputes, do news media attempt to symbolically isolate their nation's rival by claiming that the rival lacks international support? Efforts to perform this function were seen during World War II in German radio's attempts to divide France from the other Allies, and in Italian radio's effort to separate Islamic nations from Russia and the West. In their coverage of the Gulf War, American commercial media frequently mention the incompatibility of the goals of the government of Iraq and the governments of the other Arab states (Frank 1992; MacArthur 1992). American commercial news media routinely continue to mention the political and economic isolation, not only of Iraq, but also of Cuba, Libya, and North Korea, when these nations are mentioned in their newscasts (Lee and Solomon 1991). In reporting America's new war, news media emphasize that the views of those accused of plotting the September 11, 2001, attacks on the United States are shared by very few Muslims throughout the world.

4. In the context of international trade disputes, how is constraint on the construction of a rival expressed? Unlike war, the object of trade disputes is not to destroy an enemy. The other nation is likely to represent an exploitable market for a variety of goods and services, can engage in joint international economic ventures of mutual benefit, and can form military al-

liances, also of mutual benefit. Furthermore, "increases in the cost of developing new technologies (safety, environment, and energy consumption) have increased the desirability of sharing risks" (Utagawa 1992, 28). Hence, there must be some limits on what can be said about the rival.[1] In addition, statements may be made to encourage future cooperation on the part of the rival.

This chapter addresses these four questions. It does so through an analysis of Radio Japan's coverage of a major economic conflict between Japan and the United States from mid-April to the end of July 1995. A dispute between Japan and the United States was selected for study because of the dominant role the nations play in today's world economy. Together, the countries account for nearly two-fifths of the world's gross national product (Benjamin 1991, vii).

During the approximately one-hundred-day period selected for study, a major trade dispute broke out, ran its course, and was resolved. Also during the period, two additional trade disputes arose. Each of these involved many of the same issues as the major conflict. A Japanese, rather than an American, media source was selected for study because of the relative paucity of research on media in countries other than the United States and the United Kingdom. It also was chosen because Japanese media construction of the United States are less familiar to Western audiences than is American media construction of Japan. Newscasts of Radio Japan were selected for study because the international broadcasting organization reflects the views of the Japanese government and business, and because it broadcasts worldwide in English.

RADIO JAPAN NEWSCASTS

Radio Japan is the international shortwave service of Nippon Hoso Kyokai (NHK), Japan's public broadcasting organization. The source of NHK's revenues (domestic receiver's fees) and a legal stipulation that the organization is to operate in accord with the wishes of the public through a review of business operations by the people's elected representatives are aimed at minimizing direct government supervision of NHK's affairs (Japan Broadcasting Corporation 1981, 78). On occasion, NHK has expressed opposition to major policies of the Japanese government. For example, in 1988 it objected to aspects of a new consumption tax enacted to provide resources to cover expenditures for pensions and welfare in an aging society. The organization was criticized by the Ministry of Posts and Telecommunications. However, the attack was effectively rebuffed precisely on grounds of government interference, and the ministry withdrew its statement (Ito 1993, 270).

Although NHK's domestic service has exercised such independence from the government, its international broadcasting operation, Radio

Japan, has a different structure, a different audience, and a different responsibility. Structurally, Radio Japan has an advisory council (the Overseas Broadcasting Program Council) made up of prominent officials, representatives of industries, and others involved with foreign trade and foreign relations. Radio Japan administrators also meet routinely with officials from the Ministry of Foreign Affairs and the Ministry of International Trade and Industry (MITI) (Browne 1982, 210). As an official external service, Radio Japan's newscasts are aimed at foreign countries and function as an arm of Japanese diplomacy (Head 1985, 342). These conditions suggest that the materials broadcast by Radio Japan, including official statements, proposals, and decisions, will be constructed in a manner sensitive to the concerns of MITI and to those of the ruling and opposition party leaders.

Radio Japan broadcasts a total of sixty-five hours daily in twenty-two languages. The international broadcasting organization "presents news about Japan and other countries, as well as Japanese life and culture, politics and economics, and the present circumstances in society, industry and science. It tries to correctly explain Japan's positions and opinions regarding important international issues, thereby contributing to international understanding, friendship and cultural exchange" (Radio Japan Program Schedule, April–September 1995). Radio Japan's English language newscast to North America is transmitted at noon (JST), 10:00 P.M. (EST).[2] The newscasts alternate between nine and thirteen minutes in length and, during the period that was studied, average 12.4 items per newscast.

PROCEDURES AND FINDINGS

To investigate the process of socially constructing rival notions during trade disputes, the English-language evening newscasts of Radio Japan were recorded and transcribed from April 13, 1995, through July 31, 1995.[3] During this time, a major dispute arose between Japan and the United States over trade in automobiles and auto parts. The period of the study extends from the initial low-level technical talks to one month after the dispute had been formally resolved through high-level diplomatic negotiations between the trade representatives of the two nations. During this time, two additional trade disputes arose. The first involved granting U.S. air cargo companies the right to fly new routes to Asia via Japan. The second involved the complaint filed by an American corporation, Eastman Kodak, alleging that Japan's film market was closed to foreign firms.

In order to understand the relative importance Radio Japan attributed to the auto trade dispute during the period of study, it is necessary to place the dispute in the context of other events that were of major concern to the international broadcasting organization at that time. Description of this context is also important to understand historically specific constraints on Radio Japan's construction of the United States as a rival nation. The 108 monitored newscasts contained 1,344 items. The two most frequently mentioned subjects, appearing almost every day, involved items reporting on the performance of the U.S. dollar against the Japanese yen on the Tokyo Foreign Exchange Market (N = 97) and share prices on the Tokyo Stock Exchange (N = 93). Beyond these routine items, the topic receiving the greatest amount of coverage concerned events surrounding Aum Shinrikyo (Supreme Truth), a sect implicated in numerous acts of terrorism in Japan, including the March 20, 1995, nerve gas attack in the Tokyo subway system that killed eleven and injured an estimated five thousand (N = 88). This was the only nonroutine topic receiving greater attention that did Japan's auto and auto-parts trade dispute with the United States (N = 72).

If Japanese–U.S. conflicts over air routes (N =16) and Japan's film market (N = 6) are added to this, items dealing with trade disputes between Japan and the United States (N = 94) appear as frequently as the most routine items. By way of contrast, the next two topics, in terms of frequency, were the war in Bosnia (N = 63) and events affecting North Korea (the replacement of North Korea's graphite-mediated nuclear reactors with light-water reactors, which produce less plutonium, and negotiations involving Japan, South Korea, and UNESCO in shipping thousands of tons of rice to alleviate North Korea's food shortage) (N = 27). The high frequency of items concerning Japanese–U.S. trade disputes indicates the great importance Radio Japan attached to broadcasting its construction of the dispute to its worldwide audience.

The monitoring period coincided with the fiftieth anniversary of the end of World War II. At the time, Japan's governing coalition was having difficulty drafting a resolution renouncing war to mark the anniversary. The two main governing parties, the Liberal Democratic Party and the Social Democratic Party, were sharply divided over the issue. The Social Democrats argued that the resolution should recognize Japan's past colonial rule and acts of invasion as historical facts. They also contended that it should include phrases expressing repentance and renunciation of war. A group of Liberal Democrat members of parliament opposed such wording, calling instead for expressions of condolence and gratitude for the war dead. In this context, constructing an image of the United States was a difficult task for Radio Japan. A highly negative image might appear inconsistent with the spirit of the Social Democrats' intent, as well as with their efforts to maintain generally good and highly beneficial relations with the United States. Failure to construct any sort of critical image of the United States would be likely to displease many of the more conservative Liberal Democrats.

As a first step toward specifying the image of the United States constructed by Radio Japan newscasts during the Japanese–U.S. trade dispute, verbs that consistently appeared in the narrations were identified.

Frequent repetition of certain words imposes a value-laden organization on the news in the process of articulating it. Repeated use of a set of verbs can enhance the likelihood that an audience will adopt a given framework for understanding particular actors, conditions, and events, rather than assign alternative meanings to them. Although texts inevitably contain some incongruent material, the basic interpretation imposed by a pattern of verb use constitutes a symbolic universe that provides a consistent meaning to a variety of news items (Entman 1991, 7; Fowler 1991, 82).

Employing a particular pattern of verb use is one method of encoding news that effectively conceals the assumptions underlying what appear to be empirically based, ideologically neutral reports. The dynamics of such encoding have been explored extensively by the GUMG. In their analyses of British media coverage of collective bargaining between labor and management in Great Britain, the researchers conclude that

the language . . . conforms to a logic that is not simply a reflection of the reported events or relationships per se but one that pertains to a more general cultural 'code'. The absurdity of applying concepts like 'offer' and 'demand' to the 'wrong' side shows how this code works to legitimate the side that responds and makes concessions rather than the side that make requests as though of right. (GUMG 1980, 185)

Concerning this method, the Glasgow investigators note that in reaching their conclusions they did not rely "on an examination of what some might consider exotic or provocative terms, but rather the constant reposition of the small stack of descriptive terms which form the meat of the bulletins' language" (1980, 401).

Radio Japan reported acts of the United States ($N = 194$) more often than it reported acts of Japan ($N = 168$). Table 6.1 identifies those verbs that were used with quite different frequencies when describing either acts of Japan or those of the United States. The United States is depicted clearly as a demanding and threatening trading partner. In addition to the twenty-seven uses of *demand*, six of the U.S. *announcements* involved detailing sanctions that the United States would apply should Japan fail to meet the demands. Each of the nine *threats* made by the United States referred to these sanctions, and five of the eight times *use* appeared, it did so in the context of using sanctions. United States plans to *impose* sanctions were mentioned nineteen times.

The following two news items illustrate the manner in which the United States was depicted as *demanding* and *threatening*. In the first, the verbs *fight*, *hit*, and *force* dramatically convey this perspective. The second item suggests that within the U.S. government itself, major political figures viewed America's negotiating stance as excessively demanding and threatening.

Table 6.1
Verbs Used with Much Different Frequencies to Describe the Acts of Japan and the Acts of the United States on Radio Japan

Verb	Japan	United States
announce	—	14
appeal	5	—
ask	12	2
buy	6	1
demand	1	27
grant	7	—
impose	1	19
refuse	9	2
threaten	—	9
use	1	8
violate	—	7
want	1	6

Note: In all, 167 different verbs were identified. "Much different frequency" was defined as a difference of at least five occurrences. Verbs were not counted when they were used to refer to a joint activity (e.g., both sides agreed). Those verbs were: agree, avoid, continue, decide, discuss, end, exchange, hold, meet, reiterate, resume, settle, take part, toil. The count also excluded verbs denoting the travel of officials: arrive, attend, leave. The use of a verb modified by "not" was counted as an occurrence of its opposite.

U.S. President Bill Clinton said that the United States won't hesitate to fight to open Japan's market to U.S. autos and auto parts. In his weekly radio speech, President Clinton said that he had asked for a list of possible punitive sanctions against Japanese imports because U.S. negotiators were hitting a brick wall in the dispute with Japan over auto trade issues. U.S. Trade Representative Mickey Kantor said earlier that Washington was ready to hit Japanese imports with punitive duties and would challenge Tokyo's trade practices in a new world forum in order to force Japan to open its market to U.S. cars and parts. (May 13)

The Speaker of the United States House of Representatives says the United States should apply trade pressure more subtly to maximize pain in Japan with minimum public relations. Speaking at the National Press Club in Washington on Wednesday, Mr. Newt Gingrich said President Bill Clinton's tactic of threatening sanctions was wrong in that it would lead to recession and the start of a global trade war. The House leader said that it was absolutely insane in the long run to get into public fight after public fight with the Japanese. In applying pressure to open Japan's closed markets, Mr. Gingrich said the United States should take a low key approach rather than use highly charged public rhetoric which often results in the Japanese negotiators losing face. But he said the approach should be of maximum pain to the Japanese. Mr. Gingrich is seen potentially as one of the Republican Party's leading candidates for the U.S. presidency next year. (July 5)

Constructing an opponent as *demanding* and *threatening* in itself suggests only that the adversary is tough. The construction conveys nothing about how *fair* the other party is being in making the demands, nor how *reasonable* it might be for the adversary to impose particular sanctions should the demand be rejected. In the context of war stories, it is useful to depict the enemy as *immoral*. In the context of trade stories, it is useful to depict the adversary as *unfair* and *unreasonable*.

Radio Japan's use of the verbs *violate, refuse,* and *appeal* served to assign these attributes to U.S. trading practices. In seven of its news items, Radio Japan claimed that U.S. threats to impose sanctions were unfair in the sense that imposing the sanctions would violate international trade rules. In addition, five of the nine times Japan was reported to have refused U.S. demands, the refusal also was based on the claim that the threatened sanctions violated international trade law. Each of the remaining four times Japan was reported as having refused a demand of the United States, the refusal was presented as justified in terms of the demand being unfair.

The following news item constructed U.S. trading practices as unfair, both in the sense of violating international trade law and in the sense of potentially forcing Japan into unfair discriminatory practices of its own:

During a meeting with new French Trade Minister Christine Chauvet, Japan's Trade and Industry Minister Ryutara Hashimoto sought French support for Japan's position in the trade dispute. He explained that the demand for increased purchase of foreign auto parts by Japanese companies would lead to preferential treatment of U.S. products. Mr. Hashimoto also said that the unilateral announcement of a list of U.S. trade sanctions against Japan violates international rules. Japan took the case to the World Trade Organization last week. The French Trade Minister supported the Japanese stance, saying international sanctions run counter to international rules. Mr. Hashimoto also met with Mexican Commerce and Industry Minister Herminio Blanco, and reportedly won his understanding of Japan's position in the trade dispute with the U.S. (May 22)

The point that U.S. threats might force Japan into unfair discriminatory trade practices with other nations appears again in this brief item:

Australian Industry Minister Peter Cook has asked Japan not to discriminate against Australian auto parts in favor of American products. (July 11)

Radio Japan's use of *appeal* also called attention to the characterization of U.S. practices as unfair. In each of the five uses of the verb, Japan was appealing the U.S. threat to impose unilateral sanctions on grounds that this would go against international trade rules. The appeals were made to the World Trade Organization and at a ministerial meeting of the Organization for Economic Cooperation and Development.

Although a practice or set of practices might be judged unfair by some criterion or set of criteria, it is not thereby unreasonable as well. A practice or set of practices is likely to be judged as unreasonable by an observer if it is shown to produce costs, or to have potential costs, that appear to outweigh its rewards for the actor who intends to initiate or to continue the practice. Radio Japan was considered to be characterizing U.S. trade practice as unreasonable when it presented news items specifying negative consequences or potentially negative consequences for the United States itself if the practices were continued or were initiated. Radio Japan presented eight such items. The following two items serve as examples:

U.S. auto dealers say they are against imposing sanctions on Japan. The opposition was expressed in a statement issued on Tuesday by the American International Auto Dealers Association. This statement says potential U.S. sanctions against imported Japanese autos will devastate thousands of small U.S. auto dealers, and their workers will lose their jobs. It says that if sanctions are imposed, U.S. consumers will find themselves paying thousands more dollars for their new cars. (May 9)

Our reporter says Japan's Trade and Industry Minister, Ryutara Hashimoto, rejected a U.S. demand to set a numerical target for expanding purchases of foreign auto parts by Japanese auto makers. The trade chief explained to the U.S. negotiator that Japan thinks the talks will fail if the U.S. continues to stick to this demand. Mr. Hashimoto called on the U.S. to take a realistic approach to the dispute. He stressed that if the U.S. side withdraws the numerical target demand, Japanese car makers in North America will expand their local production, resulting in a boost in purchases of U.S. made auto parts. (June 26)

Findings reported thus far have indicated that Radio Japan depicted the United States as *insisting, demanding, threatening, unfair,* and *unreasonable.* Each of these individual attributes does refer to specific trading practices with Japan. However, together they constitute a rather clear multidimensional image of the United States as an actor in the world political economy. This particular image does appear in six additional news items that report on U.S. economic transactions with nations other than Japan. For example,

the European Union has criticized the United States for its growing tendency to resort to unilateral sanctions in bilateral trade disputes. The European Commission

on Thursday released its eleventh annual report on barriers to trade and investment. The report says the Commission is concerned about Washington's application of unilateral sanctions in disputes over access to E.U. markets for Latin American bananas and U.S. beef. The report also faults the United States for its stance in
multinational talks on trade and financial services. Washington has balked at offering nondiscriminatory access to its markets in return for what it sees as inadequate
offers from other countries. The report also highlights problems that the U.S. trade
embargo of Cuba has created for European companies. The E.U. regards the U.S.
tactics as a threat to the credibility of the World Trade Organization, a new international trade watchdog that replaced the General Agreement of Tariffs and Trade.
(July 6)

As noted earlier, one process by which a social actor is socially constructed as an *enemy* is to attribute to that actor qualities that are the opposite of those one attributes to oneself or to one's allies. In times of war, we
are *moral* and they are *immoral*.

Radio Japan newscasts suggest that a similar, though not identical, process goes on in the context of reporting international trade disputes. In stories about trade wars, concepts of *fairness* and *reasonableness* take the place
of *morality* and *immorality*. Table 6.1 shows that, in sharp contrast to the
United States, Japan is never depicted as *violating* or as *threatening*, only
once as *demanding* and only once as *imposing*. Japan was constructed as
trading in a fair and reasonable manner by way of contrast. Such a method
of communicating ideas is common in Japan, though not in the United
States (Gudykunst and Nishida 1994, 40–53).

The difference between Radio Japan's characterization of American and
Japanese practices in trade negotiation is illustrated below. The routine
presentation of such contrasts conveys a sense of which partner in the negotiation is fair and reasonable and which is not.

Japan and the United States will start consultations in Geneva on Monday on the
legality of the U.S. plan to impose sanctions on Japan following the breakdown in
auto trade talks. Australia is expected to send an observer to the first consultation
under the new World Trade Organization. Following the breakdown of auto trade
talks, the United States announced the plan to impose a one hundred percent tariff
on Japanese luxury cars. Japan appealed to the World Trade Organization, saying
that the unilateral sanctions would violate W.T.O. rules. At the consultations, Japan will ask the United States to withdraw its planned sanctions on the grounds
that Japanese auto companies have begun voluntarily restricting exports on luxury cars to the United States. The United States is expected to insist that Japan's
closed automobile market is the biggest problem. Our reporter says that the views
of both sides will differ greatly at the consultations in Geneva. Attention is now focused on whether Prime Minister Tomiichi Murayama and President Bill Clinton
can break the deadlock at their talks at the Group of Seven summit in Halifax Canada this week. (June 11)

In addition to characterizing U.S. trade practices as demanding and threatening, and the United States as unfair and unreasonable, Radio Japan newscasts also presented nine items that symbolically isolated the United States from other nations. The following is an example:

The European Union has indicated that it might file a complaint with the World Trade Organization if Japan bows to the U.S. demand to give American auto makers access to the Japanese market. Japan's Trade and Industry Minister, Ryutara Hashimoto, visited E.U. headquarters in Brussels on Friday. He discussed the Japan–U.S. auto trade dispute with trade commissioners. The E.U. officials severely criticized the U.S. for its move to impose unilateral sanctions, and they indicated that the E.U. will support Japan in bringing the case to the W.T.O. They also criticized Washington, which demanded that Tokyo should see to it that Japanese auto makers buy U.S. made auto parts. But the E.U. officials expressed the concern that if Japan bows to the U.S. demand that would discriminate against European firms. (May 19)

The distinction between *enemies* and *adversaries* has been overdrawn. Nevertheless, for reasons cited earlier, in trade stories, media seem more likely to construct a rival of their nation as an *adversary* than as an *enemy*. In its newscasts, Radio Japan presented three types of items, in addition to its trade stories, that imposed some limitations on viewing the United States as an *enemy* of Japan.[4] First, four items reported that Japanese Prime Minister Tomiichi Murayama urged the adoption of a parliamentary resolution on the fiftieth anniversary of the end of World War II, spelling out Japan's antiwar policy and apologizing for Japan's act of aggression.[5]

Second, Radio Japan exercised constraint in the construction of its rival by including five items that identified apparently legitimate worries of both Japan and the United States in the trade dispute. The following is an example:

During a meeting of the World Trade Organization, delegates from the European Union, Australia, India and South East Asian countries expressed grave concern over planned U.S. sanctions against Japan. Japan says the one hundred percent punitive tariffs on Japanese luxury cars violates W.T.O. rules. Conference sources say, however, that the E.U. delegates at the same time criticized the closed nature of Japan's auto market and supported the market-opening intentions of the United States. (May 29)

A third method employed by Radio Japan to keep the construction of their trade *adversary* from becoming the construction of a national *enemy* was to emphasize repeatedly the ongoing, mutually beneficial cases of cooperation between the two states. Trade wars may have something of a zero-sum-game quality. Nevertheless, each side is seeking only limited economic objectives. The goal of the conflict is not to destroy a nation, replace its regime, or discredit its ideology. Radio Japan newscasts contained seven items reminding listeners of the mutual interest of Japan and America. The following is an example:

Japanese Prime Minister Tomiichi Murayama hopes to confirm with U.S. President Bill Clinton that the auto trade dispute will not worsen all bilateral relations. The two are expected to hold talks in Halifax Canada on Thursday of next week, just before the annual summit of the G-7 industrial nations. Mr. Murayama will call on Mr. Clinton not to take unilateral action against Japan. In mid-May, the U.S. government announced a list of sanctions against Japanese cars following the breakdown of discussions of trade talks on autos and auto parts. Mr. Murayama will seek Mr. Clinton's understanding, noting that Japan's trade surplus with the United States is on the decrease. The Japanese Prime Minister will also call for strengthening the Japan-U.S. security framework and increasing cooperation for success for the summit of the Asia-Pacific Economic Cooperation Forum in November in Osaka. (June 8)

CONCLUSION

War stories locate nations in a symbolic universe that legitimates or condemns their actions. Such stories, told by the media of a nation in its newscasts, bolster its government's efforts to win both domestic and international support for its actions. In war stories, there is a threatening enemy who must be opposed—not merely out of self-interest, but as a moral imperative. The image of the enemy has a moral dimension, because it incorporates the opposites of those qualities that are used to define one's own nation and that serve to locate it in the realm of the "Good." As in many matters associated with war, there is little restraint on action—in this case, the act of socially constructing an enemy. In the universe of Good versus Evil, little subtlety is to be found.

The research reported earlier suggests that trade stories also symbolically locate nations—not in the clearly defined domains of good and evil, but rather in the somewhat less sharply defined realms of the fair and unfair. Like war stories, trade stories that appear in the news produced by a nation's media organizations work to win support for the actions of their government. However, opposition to the nation's competitor is not presented as a moral imperative so much as a matter of self-interest. Although the rival nation is not only unfair but unreasonable and tough as well, it can be kept in line by a community of fair nations working together through the aegis of international organizations.

In the case of trade wars, there is clear constraint on the social construction of the rival. Although conflict in a particular sector of trade might make overall relations between nations difficult, other areas of joint activity can make continuation of cooperation imperative. Therefore, trade stories are likely to be accompanied by other news items that remind audiences of the history and probable future of mutually beneficial collaborations with the presently troublesome nation. War stories are told with the flourish of explicit moral discourse. Trade stories are told with the patient repetition of words suggesting, but not directly stating, that the rival nation is unreasonable and unfair. Numerous news items are presented that illustrate these qualities.

These findings do not mean that those who are responsible for telling war stories or trade stories are necessarily conscious of what they are doing. The news they report may well represent the world as they see it. This is likely to be the case for Japanese journalists, when not only their government, but also the Japanese public, share perceptions of and attitudes toward an issue. Then, *kuuki*, or a dominant air or atmosphere, is present in their society, which functions as a social pressure on the Japanese media for compliance (Ito 1993). Whatever the prevailing political culture in Japan in the summer of 1995, the language consistently used by Radio Japan in reporting the news, and the explanatory framework it assumed in telling Japanese–U.S. trade stories, produced discourse of ideological service to the government of its sponsoring state.

Future research might inquire into the manner in which Japan's commercial media report the trade disputes between Japan and the United States. Other investigations might explore how other official external service (particularly the Voice of America, but also international broadcasting organizations, such as the BBC and Deutsche Welle) talk about the disputes. Comparative studies might reveal general processes by which official media socially construct their sponsoring state, their state's competitors, and other nations with which their state has various kinds of political, economic, and military interactions. Findings are likely to suggest similarities of the products of state-sponsored and commercial news organizations and to indicate again just how tenuous is the distinction between *news* and *propaganda* during times of peace as well as times of war.

NOTES

1. Several analysts (Conteh-Morgan 1992; Hersh 1993; Nester 1993) claim that the political rhetoric of both Japanese and American officials has already contributed to serious difficulties in maintaining mutually beneficial relationships between the two countries.

2. Japan and the United States are on different sides of the international dateline. Dates used in this study refer to those on which newscasts were recorded in the United States.

3. In total, 109 newscasts were recorded. However, one newscast was not relevant to the study. On May 15, 1995, a report on the arrest of Aum Shinrikyo cult leader Shoko Asahara preempted the regular news program.

4. Although Japan was demonized by American media during World War II, its social construction changed drastically immediately after the war. In the processes of demilitarization, democratization, and economic reconstructing of Japan during the 1945–1952 occupation, the overriding objective of U.S. policy was to transform the country into an economically strong and stable ally against America's new, aggressive and expansionist political and ideological archenemy—the Soviet Union. Even American business presses of the period, such as *Barrons, Business Week, Forbes, Fortune, The Harvard Business Review* and *The Wall Street Journal,* looked beyond the economic and competitive dimensions of relations between Washington and Tokyo. The former enemy was depicted as the key to America's Cold War policy in Asia. Japan now was to be understood as one of the major nations supporting the American value of democracy, free trade, and capitalism (Higenberg 1993).

5. The United States was not absolved of all responsibility for the evil that befell Japan during the war. The historical wartime enemy image of the United States was not thoroughly dispelled. Radio Japan reported that the prime minister's resolution was not supported by the opposition party in the ruling coalition. Radio Japan also presented two items detailing controversy within the United States over a proposed Smithsonian display of the airplane that dropped the nuclear bomb on Hiroshima. An additional item reported a recent revelation from a declassified historical document indicating, that in 1943, most U.S. military planners thought it best to drop the atomic bomb on a Japanese naval fleet in a western Pacific harbor, rather than on a Japanese city.

Chapter 7

The United States as a Friend-at-a-Distance: Views of the 1996 Presidential Nominating Conventions and the Presidential Inauguration on British, Canadian, and French Television

In a manner much more apparent than in their routine newscasts, our commercial media promote national self-images on their live, remote broadcasts of certain public occasions such as U.S. presidential nominating conventions and presidential inaugurations. Such broadcasts constitute a genre of electronic communication that Dayan and Katz (1992) have termed *media events*. As conceptualized in their study, the organizers of media events typically are public bodies, such as governments and political parties, with whom the media cooperate. Such bodies are at the core of the institutionalized order, stand for received ideas and consensual values, and have the authority to command our attention. The events are preplanned and facilitated by the broadcasters. Their broadcasts interrupt routine programming. The broadcast events are presented with unusual seriousness and ceremony; the journalists who preside over them suspend their normally critical stance and treat the subject with respect. Even when media events address conflict, they attend not to the conflict but to reconciliation. "This is where they differ from daily news events, where conflict is the inevitable subject. Often they are ceremonial efforts to redress conflict or to restore order or, more rarely, to institute change" (1992, 8).

The events are proclaimed historic and are characterized by the presence of norms according to which people tell each other that routine concerns should be put aside in order to view the event. Finally, according to

Dayan and Katz's characterization, media events integrate society and evoke a renewal of loyalty to the society and its legitimate authority.

FOREIGN MEDIA COVERAGE OF U.S. MEDIA EVENTS

The current status of the United States as the world's one remaining superpower represents some threat to the political, economic, military, and cultural autonomy of the other Western democracies, and serves as an enduring source of distance between them and the United States. The distance may not be great, and undoubtedly varies from time to time in response to international events.

Throughout the 1990s, worldwide appreciation of the United States seems to have diminished. There are several possible origins of the apparent disenchantment.

Maybe it was the dawning realization that people around the globe are all flicking on the same Windows operating system in the morning, on their way to navigating an Internet dominated by American innovations and business and driven by Intel inside everything. Maybe it was when the United States, in the wake of the Asian economic crisis, began offering tutorials on American-style capitalism, and insisting that the world's financial architecture be rebuilt to American building codes. [Maybe it was when] allies and potential adversaries alike [understood] how much more formidable American military technology has become since the Persian Gulf War. Europeans got a rude awakening when they learned that the gap between the United States' capability and their own had so widened. (Sanger 1991, 1)

The impact of U.S. media monopolies has also generated considerable resentment.

The United States' global industrial pre-eminence may be slipping, but the domestic output and international sale of one of its manufacturers is booming—packaged consciousness. Packaged consciousness—a one-dimensional, smooth-edged cultural product—is made by the ever-expanding goliaths of the message and image business. . . . Gigantic entertainment-information complexes exercise a near-seamless and unified corporate control over what we think, and think about. (Schiller 1996, 16)

Such concerns make nations, even those having long histories as political allies and generally cooperative trade partners, such as Canada, France, and Great Britain, America's friends-at-a-distance. It seems likely that the terrorist attacks in 2001 reduced the salience of the issues. However, throughout the 1990s, the distance between those countries and the United States may have been great enough to discourage the presentation of any U.S. political events by their commercial news media as media events, which draws attention to them as the only legitimate events on the world's political agenda and enhances the international image of the United States.[1]

This chapter examines British, Canadian, and French television coverage of U.S. political events routinely presented by U.S. television networks as media events, such as presidential nominating conventions and presidential inaugurations.

The following analysis is guided by the perspective, developed in the preceding chapters, that media impose meanings on events that serve identifiable material and ideological interests. Based on this theoretical work as well as that of Dayan and Katz (1992) and Bourdieu (1996), it offers an explanation of why foreign media coverage of U.S. media events can represent more than alternative accounts of these political happenings. They present images that can actually *subvert* the meaning of the occasions intended by their official organizers and routinely imposed by U.S. media.

NOMINATING CONVENTIONS AS MEDIA EVENTS

Aside from reporting occasional presidential debates, coverage of nominating conventions used to be the most important media activity of presidential campaigns (Graber 1993, 259). In the 1950s, 1960s, and 1970s, America's major television networks generally provided gavel-to-gavel coverage. Programs received high television ratings, attracting nearly eighty percent of American households for some part of the proceedings (Ansolabehere, Behr, and Iyengar 1993, 165). The convention coverage appears to have benefited each party. Data gathered from 1952 through 1988 indicate that, immediately following a convention, the average surge for its nominee in the polls was seven points (Gelman and King 1992).

By the 1980s, convention telecasts appeared to the commercial television networks to have lost much of their appeal, and they sharply reduced their prime-time coverage. However, as Smith and Nimmo (1991, 5) point out, commercial media coverage of the conventions continued to maintain a forty-seven to forty-eight percent audience share, which is not meager either in terms of proportion or as a total number of viewers. Furthermore, this figure ignores the large number of citizens following the party conventions via C-SPAN, CNN, PBS, regional television consortia, the plethora of television news organizations originating coverage from convention sites, and by assorted daytime and nighttime programs (also see Graber 1993, 259).

The usual explanation of apparent declining public interest in the nominating conventions is that those conventions no longer worked out internal party differences nor chose party leadership. Lacking political substance, they had become merely publicity events for the parties, explicitly packaged for television with a heavy emphasis on fast pacing, visually compelling imagery, and other "production values" (Hallin 1992a).

Those who dismiss the political importance of nominating conventions and their television representations fail to recognize that the conventions always have tended to be both less and more than they had appeared to be.

That the party conventions are not decision *makers* is, in itself, not new. Conventions have always tended to be decision *ratifiers*—that is, they put the party label on decisions made elsewhere: compromises and deals struck in state legislations in an earlier era, then in state conventions run by party machines, in smoke-filled rooms, but rarely on the floor of a national convention. Furthermore, they have been decision *publicizers* as well, "sculpturing" convention events for dissemination by newspapers, then radio, now television. (Smith and Nimmo 1991, 4)

In competitive party systems, each political party organization must construct a reasonably coherent image of itself that it can use in its appeal for popular support. In systems with two dominant parties, such as that of the United States, each party must seek support from highly diverse segments of society. Hence, the image each constructs must emphasize ratification of a set of principles (i.e., those describing the substantive ends toward which the party's platform and its candidates are directed and in terms of which the policies proposed by the part are justified) that express a symbolic consensus (see Elder and Cobb 1983, 119–121).

Each political party has considerable interest in potential voters learning of and accepting the constructed image of what it and its candidates stand for. Effective promotion can no longer be accomplished, as it once was, by the parties themselves through the mobilization of their grassroots organizations. Publicity now depends on achieving some cooperation with mass media organizations. In the United States, one component of this cooperation has involved media coverage of nominating conventions as media events.

Although political changes may have reduced the impact of nominating conventions as media events, they do not appear to have subverted the images of the events intended by their producers. That is, data do not indicate that media now promote public understanding of the events that is contrary to the interests of the two dominant political parties.[2]

PRESIDENTIAL INAUGURATIONS AS MEDIA EVENTS

Media coverage of the inauguration of a president of the United States would seem to epitomize a media event. Inaugurals unify the country by reconstituting supporters, opponents, and undecided citizens into the people who officiate over the investiture of power in their President. Inaugurals characteristically discuss shared values and standards, rather than divisive issues. They interpret and announce the new administration's general principles and themes, grounding them in shared values. Inaugurals praise the presidential office, the nation, and the American people and their values and fuse the nation's past and future in a ceremonial and contemplative present (Campbell and Jamieson 1986; Paletz 1999, 245). Political inauguration involves legitimation of power via political ritual. Presidential inauguration is, by far, the most important and most spectacular of the political rituals of the United States (Combs 1980, 31; Gronbeck 1990, 204).

FOREIGN MEDIA COVERAGE OF CONVENTIONS AND INAUGURATIONS

Every four years, domestic television presents nominating conventions and presidential inaugurations in a routinized way—from the opening speeches of the nominating conventions to the parade following the swearing-in ceremony. Although formulaic coverage of these events is particularly noticeable, it is also a feature of daily news presentation that employs numerous typifications. "Familiar narrative frameworks are central to making the world of news so recognizable. We can miss most of the factual information and not even realize it because the narrative elements in themselves are so recognizable" (Dahlgren 1995, 59).

Domestic TV coverage of political conventions and inaugurations, offering familiar political images and ideas, requires little effort at understanding on the part of its viewers; but other modes of coverage, which eschew emphasis on legitimating symbols and rhetoric and tell different stories, cultivate in their audiences a more analytic orientation toward the televised events and encourage them to question "what is going on" (see Goffman 1974: especially Chapter 10). As Bourdieu points out, such questioning is subversive.

When you transmit a "received idea," it's as if everything is set, and the problem [of meaning] solves itself. Communication is instantaneous because, in a sense, it has not occurred; or it only seems to have taken place. The exchange of commonplaces is communication with no content other than the fact of communication itself. The "commonplaces" that play such an enormous role in daily conversation work because everyone can ingest them immediately. Their very banality makes them something the speaker and the listener have in common. At the opposite end of the spectrum, thought, by definition, is subversive. It begins by taking apart "received ideas" and then presents the evidence in a demonstration, a logical proof. (1996, 29)

There are three defining qualities of media events that foreign media seem unlikely to impose on nominating conventions and presidential inaugurations: treatment of their ceremonial features with an unusual sense of seriousness, suspension of criticism customary in their reporting of political affairs, and emphasis on reconciliation rather than conflict. These are properties of domestic TV coverage that construct the legitimating symbolic universe supplying the taken-for-granted meaning of the events for the domestic audience. Failure to include these features would result in the presentation of images and ideas that subvert U.S. political party and national ideological interests.

Subverting images of an event results from adopting a mode of coverage that departs from the mode conventionally used to report that type of event. Treating a nominating convention or inauguration as *news* rather that as a media event is the present example. It is not the treatment of any event as news per se that produces subversive images. For example, in the United Kingdom in the 1960s and 1970s, reporting industrial conflict as news, but from the perspective of labor rather than management, produced ideas and images that challenged received ideas about the legitimacy of Britain's political economy—a consequence quite different from what resulted from conventional British media news coverage (see GUMG 1976).

There are other factors, in addition to concerns over the present dominant position of the United States in the world political economy and associated U.S. cultural imperialism, that could predispose foreign journalists to avoid treating U.S. political events, such as nominating conventions and inaugurations, as media events.

Robert Bellah (1975) observed that in the United States, despite separation of church and state, politics has a religious dimension. There are, he pointed out, certain common elements of religious orientation that are neither sectarian nor in any sense Christian, which the majority of Americans share, and which provide a basis for national religious self-understanding. America's "civil religion" provides much of the content of the symbolic environment that shapes conventions and inaugurations. Political leaders, addressing these events, come to the people and, literally surrounded by national symbols, rhetorically celebrate democracy, the people, peace, progress, prosperity, and other received ideas of the political culture of the United States (Combs 1980, 141). Such rhetorical presentations are responded to with some degree of seriousness by those socialized into this political culture (see Osborn 1986, 82). They tend to experience the ceremonial features of the events with a sense of respect that would seem less likely to be common among foreign journalists who did not undergo their early political socializations in the United States.

The generally cooperative relationship between U.S. news media and the political elite often is masked by media's taking what Bennett (1996, 82) termed a "ritualistic posture of antagonism," rather than a genuinely adversarial stance. Features of this posture include the tendency to report interelite confrontation, rather than directly expressing criticism. When any criticism is expressed, it is directed at individuals, rather than their offices, organizations, or the institutions they represent. Because they are not integral parts of the U.S. "public-relations state," foreign news media are more free than their U.S. counterparts to move beyond "ritualistic antagonism" to confront elites directly and challenge the claims they make on behalf of themselves, their organizations, and their institutions (see Deacon and Golding 1994, 7; Negrine 1996, 10–14).

Foreign journalists would seem to be less likely to experience a sense of great seriousness and be more willing and able to move beyond "ritualistic antagonism" in their reporting. Likewise, they would seem to be less interested than their U.S. counterparts in promoting images of the internal harmony of the dominant political parties and affirming the earnest commitment of its newly elected leaders to the pursuit of consensus values. They would appear to be more likely to attract audiences with reports of unresolved political conflicts than they would with descriptions of rituals of political legitimation and integration.

The following study examines the way in which British, Canadian, and French television covered some of the most important political events of the United States. At issue is whether they told stories that raised questions about what was going on, and that subverted some of the received ideas of the U.S. political culture. If the media of the friends-at-a-distance of the United States are found consistently to construct subverting images of these events, it takes little effort to imagine the character of media coverage throughout the rest of the world. It would suggest that there are clear limits on the ability of the United States to establish the legitimacy of its globally dominant political, economic, and cultural position.

COVERING POLITICAL CONVENTIONS IN THE UNITED STATES

Procedures

The public television corporations of Britain (BBC), Canada (CBC), and France (FRANCE 2) each presented a series of items on the Republican National Convention in its evening newscasts during the four days of the mid-August party meetings in San Diego. The broadcasting organizations provided similar coverage for the late-August Chicago meetings of the Democratic National Convention. Each broadcaster also televised and discussed America's presidential inauguration. Video recordings of these newscasts were obtained from the C-SPAN archives at Purdue University, and provided the material for the study. In all likelihood, the BBC, CBC, and FRANCE 2 presented materials related to the conventions and the inauguration in additional news programs. Data are not available to determine whether the news items that are analyzed are representative of the entire news offerings of each of the national television corporations. However, consistency in the pattern of coverage, reported later, suggests that there is little reason to believe that consideration of data from other news programs would result in significantly different conclusions from those that are stated.

As conceptualized by Dayan and Katz (1992), media events cannot be newscast items. Indeed, they argue that treating an event as a news item keeps it from being experienced as an occasion. In this study, media events will be understood in a more modest sense. A newscast item will be considered a media event if it has several of the qualities specified by Dayan and Katz as characterizing media events: commanding attention, emphasizing consensus, evoking support, legitimating authority, and enhancing the image of a social unit.

Four coders watched each of the newscasts together. For each newscast item reporting on a convention or convention-related event, they were to decide on (1) a brief specification of the topic or topics it addressed; (2) a brief specification of what was said about the topic or topics; and (3) a brief specification of any evaluative statements made by an on-the-scene reporter, and/or news anchor, and/or correspondent. (Evaluative statements were understood as those that expressed a favorable or critical attitude toward an actor or event or toward an anticipated consequence of an action or event.) When the four coders could not agree unanimously on all three specifications for a given item, the newscast item was dropped from further consideration.

A second phase of coding convention and convention-related items involved determining if each of the items eligible for analysis was presented as a media event. Coders were asked to determine whether the item

1. *commanded attention* ("Was the general content of the item presented as the most important matter on the world's political agenda of the day?");
2. *emphasized consensus* ("Did the item emphasize party unity as opposed to disagreement within the party?" [or, where applicable] "Did the item emphasize that a party leader or position was likely to find broad social support as opposed to finding significant social opposition?");
3. *evoked support* (determined by reference to the specific evaluative statements identified in the first phase of the coding);
4. *legitimated authority* ("Did the item present information generally supporting a party leader or position?");
5. *enhanced the image of the party and/or nation* ("Did the item convey an overall favorable impression of the party and/or the United States?").

An item was considered to be presented as a media event if the coders unanimously agreed that the item had at least three of these qualities.

For each newscast item reporting on the presidential inauguration or an inauguration-related event, other than the presidential inaugural address itself, the coders followed the procedures they used for the convention and convention-related events. For the inaugural address, they were to decide on a brief specification of any evaluative statements made by an on-the-scene reporter, and/or news anchor, and/or correspondent, both before and after the address. Then they were to determine whether the overall presentation had each of the five qualities of a media event used in coding convention and convention-related items. As in the earlier analysis, the presentation was considered to be scripted as a media event if the coders unanimously agreed that it had at least three of the qualities.

Findings

Republican National Convention

BBC

Item 1.

(1) Topic: Speech by General Colin Powell, former Chairman of the U.S. Joint Chiefs of Staff. (2) What we said: Powell represents sections of the Republican party whose voices are not often heard. Powell stresses inclusion: the Republican party should not forget the immigrants and the minorities. Powell supports affirmative action and a woman's right to abortion—positions not widely popular in the Republican party. It is in the interest of the Republican party to move toward the center of the political spectrum and away from the Far Right, which has been dominant for the last two or three years. (3) Evaluative statements: It was a good night for the Republicans, the night they needed. The party has moved too far to the Right and has little chance for electoral success. It does not have a credible leader in Dole.

Item 2.

(1) Topics: Gender gap; interviews with Gov. Christine Todd Whitman (R, N.J.), Sen. Nancy Kassenbaum (R, Kans.); keynote address by Rep. Susan Molinari (R, N.J.). (2) What was said: Opinion polls show that while Clinton's lead over Dole is around six points, with women it is almost four times as great. Whitman says gender gap stems largely from the perception that the Republicans are treating a hard stand on social issues such as abortion and the environment as a litmus test for membership in the party. Kassenbaum argues that gender gap is a result of the belief that the Republican party somehow is opposed to measures that help working women. Molinari claims Republican tax breaks would help career women. She also tries to placate those religious conservatives who believe woman's place is in the home. (3) Evaluative statements: It's not only the minorities—African Americans, Hispanics, and Gays—that mistrust the Republicans, it's also the daunting prospect of America's women.

Item 3.

(1) Topics: Role of Elizabeth Dole in campaigning; media treatment of Dole. (2) What was said: Elizabeth Dole attempts to court elusive female vote. The Republicans need a new appeal to women. Perhaps Elizabeth Dole could make that appeal, but she's not the candidate. Media decided long ago that Dole was a lost cause. (3) Evaluative statements: Uncertainty of how to portray Elizabeth Dole reflects the difficulties Bob Dole has with America's women voters. It will take a superhuman effort on Dole's part to reverse media's view of him. This has been a good convention in part because it has managed to suppress open dissent.

Item 4.

(1) Topics: Dole's acceptance speech; convention staging; poll results. (2) What was said: Dole calls for greater emphasis on moral values and criticizes Democrats' preoccupation with the economy. He promises an administration that would cut taxes and eliminate intrusive government. He promises a hard line on trade, a crackdown on illegal immigration and equal opportunity for all Americans regardless of race, but no special treatment for anyone. Dole also promises stronger national defense and greater American leadership in the world. The last time Dole addressed the nation was after Pres. Clinton's State of the Union Speech in January, and performance was universally described as awful. The main aim of the Republicans was to avoid the mistake of four years ago when the party came across as harsh and doctrinaire. A daily tracking poll yesterday showed President Clinton's lead widening by five points to nearly seventeen percent despite Dole's selection of Kemp. (3) Evaluative statements: The Republican Convention this year has been reduced to a television occasion. The delegates were props who were told not to argue in public. The object was to make the party look open. The American media are not quite sure how to handle this sophistry. This will have been good television for the Republicans that will have softened their image.

CBC

Item 1.

(1) Topics: Protests by Hispanic immigrants; party platform on immigration; Powell speech. (2) What was said: Everyday this week Hispanic immigrants have been protesting outside the Republican convention. They accuse the party of pushing anti-immigrant measures from the convention floor, while preaching tolerance from the podium. On the Mexican border, immigrants staged another in a series of demonstrations to denounce the Republicans as racists. The demonstration turned violent. Earlier, delegates had approved a policy platform calling for cuts in illegal immigration, the exclusion of illegal immigrants from schools and social services, and the denial of citizenship to children of illegal immigrants.

Latino leaders claim they will punish the Republicans at the ballot box. Powell urges the party to reach out to immigrants. (3) Evaluative statements: If the last election was any indication, the Hispanic vote will be overwhelmingly for Bill Clinton and the Democrats.

Item 2.

(1) Topic: Dole's tax proposal. (2) What was said: Some delegates believe his fifteen percent tax cut proposal might be the issue to get Dole elected. Few delegates are troubled by the fact that the proposal represents an extraordinary conversion for Dole and congressional Republicans, whose top priority long had been cutting the deficit and balancing the budget. (3) Evaluative statements: Many economists note that a similar tax break by Ronald Reagan in 1980 tripled the national debt. They say Dole's proposal could do the same and that it helps the rich more than less affluent Americans. Polls show that the public is skeptical.

Item 3.

(1) Topic: Speech by Elizabeth Dole. (2) What was said: Dole's speech was a flawless, riveting performance, but it again raised the question of how minutely the convention is scripted. The irony of this made-for-television convention is that it is all for the benefit of a candidate who loathes the slickness and packaging of modern political campaigns. (3) Evaluative statements: None.

Item 4.

(1) Topic: Dole's acceptance speech. (2) What was said: Dole presented himself as a plain-speaking man from the American heartland who would restore America to the country of his youth. He portrayed an America of crime, drugs, illegitimacy, abortion, and devastated families. He called for a greater emphasis on moral values and criticized the Clinton administration's preoccupation with the economy. (3) Evaluative statements: Dole's chances of defeating Clinton remain slim. He is a weak campaigner, and Republicans privately worry about what the President could do to him in this autumn's debates. Dole is also gambling on his tax cut promise when the economy is doing very well and voters may be reluctant to risk such a radical move.

FRANCE 2

Item 1.

(1) Topics: Colin Powell, Nancy Reagan, and George Bush appear at convention to push up Dole's ratings; delegates are optimistic with the arrival of Jack Kemp; NOW protests the Republicans' stand on abortion. (2) What was said: The party wants to outlaw abortion in all cases and also wants to abolish automatic citizenship for all babies born in the United States. Powell expresses faith in the "American dream," but offers views that are controversial within the party. Pro-life supporters and advocates

of prayer in the schools finished the day in silence. (3) Evaluative statements: The party is standing behind a hard-line platform. Polls show Dole twenty points behind Clinton, but Clinton once lagged twenty points behind George H. W. Bush.

Item 2.

(1) Topic: Keynote address by Rep. Susan Molinari (R, N.J.). (2) What was said: By emphasizing how tax reductions promised by the Republicans will help working mothers "make two ends meet," Molinari avoided those issues that women doubt the Republicans at the moment of voting: the right to abortion; equality of the sexes (that many women think has progressed, thanks to affirmative action); gun control; and the role of the state in education, immigration, healthcare, aid to the poor, and the environment. American women continue to believe in the positive role of the state and are more critical of private enterprise. (3) Evaluative statements: The majority of American women are hostile to the Republicans.

Item 3.

(1) Topic: Convention security. (2) What was said: As a reaction to the Atlanta bombing, delegates are happy with convention's tight security. (3) Evaluative statements: None.

Item 4.

(1) Topics: The Christian Coalition; interview with Jordan Bonfonte (*Time Magazine*). (2) What was said: The Christian Coalition claims to stand up for America's true values. Supporters are numerous at the convention and emphasize that the Republican party is a pro-life party. Bonfonte says the convention has given the Republican party a unified and centrist image. He claims the Christian Coalition was kept in the background. (3) Evaluative statements: The Christian Coalition is characterized as ultraconservative. The convention has heard more about "real values" than about the details of the party platform. A speech (outside the convention) by Christian Coalition leader Ralph Reed was a response to Colin Powell. Reed's view is that tolerance won't be tolerated.

Item 5.

(1) Topics: Convention staging; party platform; Dole's position on party platform. (2) What was said: The Republican party affirms its unity but forbids expression of its diversity. Pat Buchanan, who four years ago gave the convention an image of extremism and intolerance, was not permitted to address the convention. Gov. Pete Wilson (R, Calif.) was kept from speaking because of his position on abortion. Republican vice-presidential candidate Jack Kemp had to compromise the expression of his position on affirmative action. Newt Gingrich adopted a low profile. There are, in fact, two Republican parties. The first is that of the delegates who put together

Table 7.1
British, Canadian, and French Television Coverage of the 1996 Republican National Convention

	Item	Atten-tion	Con-sensus	Support	Author-ity	Image	Event	Evalua-tion
BBC	1	x			x			±
	2	x						—
	3	x						—
	4	x			x			±
CBC	1	x						—
	2							—
	3		x	x				
	4	x		x				—
FRANCE 2	1	x						±
	2					x		—
	3							
	4							—

a radical platform. The second is that of the general Republican electorate who often have difficulty finding themselves in the first. American political history shows that once in office, American presidents distance themselves from dogmatic principles. What is interesting here is that even before being nominated candidate, Dole is saying he will not feel bound by an extremist program. With such a message, can Dole hope to act as a unifier? (3) Evaluative statements: The party platform is a catalog of ultraconservative principles that poorly represent the more moderate views of the majority of the party.

As Table 7.1 suggests, the image of the Republican party, constructed by British, Canadian, and French television, consistently emphasized that the party was not responsive to the concerns of immigrants, minorities, women, or less affluent U.S. citizens. Legitimating symbols and rhetoric were seldom in evidence; viewers were told that the party was dominated by its most conservative segment. Such presentations did not reflect well on one of the two dominant parties in the U.S. political system; they were not likely to enhance the international image of our country.

Democratic National Convention

BBC

Item 1.

(1) Topic: Interviews with David Maraniss (Clinton biographer) and James Carville (Clinton's 1992 campaign strategist). (2) What was said: Maraniss believes Clinton may be the best campaigner in the history of American politics. He claims Clinton has co-opted the Republicans on all their issues. However, this year he has embraced a change in the welfare system that repudiates most of what the Democratic party has stood for for a long time. This has deeply divided the party. Carville admits Clinton's welfare bill is controversial, but he emphasizes that during Clinton's administration the economy improved, the crime rate dropped, and that the things we measure the nation by became stronger. He praises Mrs. Clinton as a symbol of hope and opportunity to American women and condemns attacks on her by Dole's campaign manager as malicious. (3) Evaluative statements: Clinton is agreeing to withdraw the welfare net from America's poor. Hillary Clinton may be an election liability for the president. Just like the Republicans at their San Diego convention, the Democrats are suppressing genuine debate. There, the forbidden topic was abortion. Here, it's welfare reform.

Item 2.

(1) Topic: Interview with Rep. Pat Schroeder (D, Colo.). (2) What was said: It's difficult to say what is reducing voter turnout. What now unites the Democratic party is largely opposition to the extremism of the Republicans. There have not been meaningful fights over the party platform, because the Democrats are more ideologically united than they were before some of the Southerners became Republicans. (3) Evaluative statements: We did not see the liberal wing of the Democratic party at this convention any more than we saw the Christian Right at the Republican convention. The Democrats are as bland as the Republicans.

Item 3.

(1) Topic: Speeches by Rev. Jesse Jackson and former Gov. Mario Cuomo, (D, N.Y.). (2) What was said: Jackson praises Clinton as a first line of defense against Republican extremism. He strongly supports Clinton's stand for the end of assault weapons and his efforts on behalf of voting rights, raising the minimum wage, affirmative action, social justice, and social equality. He notes he disagrees with Clinton on the critical issue of welfare, but maintains that the party must protect one big tent. Cuomo credits Clinton for the party's remarkable recovery since its 1994 defeat in the midterm election, but he admitted he had misgivings about the price the president has paid, particularly in terms of his signing the Welfare Reform Bill. (3) Evaluative statements: Does President Clinton really want the

Democrats to recapture Congress? In that event, it would put a lot of senior liberals back in charge of congressional committees.

Item 4.

(1) Topic: Interview with John Prescott (Deputy Leader, British Labour party). (2) What was said: Prescott credits Clinton administration with getting ten million people back to work in four years and improving the minimum wage. He expresses concern over the Democrats' discussion of public expenditures. Their arguments, he says, are geared to a middle-class vote. In Britain, such an appeal has dispossessed the poor of political influence. (3) Evaluative statements: Democrats have increased support from those whose natural leaning is to the Left, even while the party has moved toward the Right. Bill Clinton has pulled it off, in part because he's fortunate in his enemies—the conservative Republicans. Congress may have upset the Democrats, but it has worried much of Middle America and terrified the unions, who have all come to regard Clinton as their "defender in chief."

Item 5.

(1) Topic: Clinton's relation to his own party. (2) What was said: With victory likely and with few disputes over the party platform, the stage should be set for the Democrats to show unity and confidence. However, there are deep concerns because of the distant relationship between Clinton and his party. He has only once called upon the American people to elect a Democratic Congress. He appears to regard associations with them as disadvantageous to his electoral interests. The distance between the president and the party has created uncertainty about what the Democrats stand for. He has declared that the time for big government is over and that he wants to unite public-sector goals with private-sector techniques, but he has not enlightened Americans or anyone else as to exactly what this means. (3) Evaluative statements: From tax and spending to welfare reform, the divisions in Democratic party voting on the congressional floor reflect this basic confusion.

CBC

Item 1.

(1) Topic: Role of Hillary Clinton in campaign. (2) What was said: Although she is adored by the Democratic faithful, for many others, mainly Republicans and men, she is vilified as being everything from a crook to a pushy feminist. She received bad publicity over her central role in forging the administration's botched health-care reform and her involvement in the Whitewater real estate scandal. Her husband's advisors are watching the polls, trying to soften her image and steer her away from any kind of controversy. (3) Evaluative statements: She may have become a political liability for her husband.

Item 2.

(1) Topic: Clinton's political success. (2) What was said: The key to Clinton's political recovery was the chameleon-like political act embodied in his State of the Union address last January. Clinton shed his liberal image and stole one Republican theme after another by promising leaner government, stronger family values, and a crackdown on crime. The hard-edged conservatism of Republican leaders has enabled him to position himself as a bulwark against extremism. He also has the advantage of a strong economy and the ability to project an image of caring and compassion more effectively than Dole. (3) Evaluative statements: Clinton has been shrewd (co-opting Republican positions) and fortunate (the state of the economy and the extremism of his opponents).

Item 3.

(1) Topic: Speeches by Rev. Jesse Jackson and former Gov. Mario Cuomo (D, N.Y.). (2) What was said: Mario Cuomo, the liberal champion who delivered the 1992 keynote speech, is plainly unhappy with what he refers to as Clinton's "stepping-stone" approach to politics. He no longer holds any office, anymore than does the former firebrand, Jesse Jackson. Today Jackson is tamed to the point of talking about his party as "one big tent." (3) Evaluative statements: Clinton and the convention managers will not want to stifle liberal and progressive dissent entirely, even on welfare. It is bound to make him look good, as a centrist who solidly holds the line, even against his own party's extremists.

Item 4.

(1) Topics: Advisor resignation; Clinton speech. (2) What was said: The resignation of Dick Morris, President Clinton's top political advisor, marred what was to have been a night of triumph. The convention united powerfully behind Clinton's leadership and became confident of electoral victory. Clinton's message was that he is the man of tomorrow; Dole belongs to yesterday. Although it is a simple message, the president is counting on it more than any other to carry him to victory in November. (3) Evaluative statements: When Mr. Clinton got to about his thirtieth proposal, you could almost sense his audience getting away from him. We got the speech of a political engineer. The bridge he was building into the twenty-first century had so many struts and girders that one begins to wonder whether it would ever be open in time for the millennium.

France 2

Item 1.

(1) Topic: Speech by Hillary Clinton. (2) What was said: She emphasized family values and called for maternity leave. Her fans find that she now addresses more narrow issues. By doing so, she avoids charges she's run-

ning the show. (3) Evaluative statements: Her speech was a great success. Will husband Bill be able to measure up?

Item 2.

(1) Topic: Support of African American community. (2) What was said: Despite their disagreements on welfare, Democrats unite behind Clinton. Special efforts are being made to gain support of the Black community. However, African American residential areas surrounding the site of the Democratic convention have not benefited from Democratic Mayor Richard Daley's politics of rehabilitation. Poverty, unemployment, gang violence, and drugs are common here. Despite their sense of betrayal, African Americans probably will vote for Clinton in November. They are not his most stable base of support. (3) Evaluative statements: Although they vote for the Democratic party, African Americans have no respect for the Democrats, local or national. The welfare reform measures approved by Mr. Clinton will push an estimated additional 1.2 million children into poverty.

Item 3.

(1) Topic: Problems facing President Clinton. (2) What was said: The president's popularity is higher than ever. However, if re-elected, he will have to deal with a Congress still dominated by the Republicans. He also will have to deal with the scandals that shook his first term: Asian campaign contributions, Whitewater, and Paula Jones. (3) Evaluative statements: Scandals threaten to limit Clinton's ability to maneuver politically.

Item 4.

(1) Topic: Clinton speech. (2) What was said: The Democrats pretended to ignore the Dick Morris sex scandal. They celebrated the "bridge" they erected to the twenty-first century. The president promised to bury no issue. A balanced budget, safeguarding health insurance and retirement benefits, drugs, violence, and education top the list. His speech can be seen as a response to the criticism that he has no great scheme but simply an ability to preserve the status quo. America is seeing a resurgence of two opposing currents that have existed since its founding. One tells it to rediscover its sense of compassion toward its weaker members. The other convinces it that it is time for every citizen to accept individual responsibility in order to merit the concern of the nation. Mr. Clinton embodies this duality. (3) Evaluative statements: Mr. Clinton's speech was based on the first consideration, but his actions often speak to the contrary.

As Table 7.2 suggests, each of the public television corporations of Britain, Canada, and France gave the Clinton administration some recognition for increasing the minimum wage, lowering unemployment, and support-

Table 7.2
British, Canadian, and French Television Coverage of the 1996 Democratic National Convention

	Item	Atten-tion	Con-sensus	Support	Author-ity	Image	Event	Evalua-tion
BBC	1	x						—
	2		x					—
	3	x			x			—
	4	x						±
	5							—
CBC	1							—
	2		x					±
	3		x		x			—
	4	x			x			±
FRANCE 2	1				x			±
	2							—
	3							—
	4	x			x			

ing affirmative action. However, all also noted that Clinton's Welfare Reform Bill, his uncertain taxation policy, and his vaguely articulated program for public-sector spending made unclear what the Democratic party stood for. Media of the friends-at-a-distance of the United States portrayed our competitive two-party system as one that offers citizens a choice between one party unconcerned about immigrants, minorities, women, and the poor, and one party with a rhetoric of compassion but without matching policy proposals. The broadcast organizations told a story about a competitive two-party system that was not likely to be attractive to their audiences. It hardly seemed to be the image of a democratic political system worthy of the world's dominant nation.

The Inauguration

BBC

For all the bright hopes of today, President Clinton's page in history could be colored, not by achievement, but by the shame of the many scandals that surround him (interview with David Gergan, Clinton advisor 1993–1995). Gergan says he cannot remember the inauguration of a new president that has been surrounded by so many question marks. He argues that the president could best serve the country and best serve his place in history if he acted boldly now, before these issues must be confronted. The BBC commentator says that even without the scandals, Clinton's wish to attain the peaks is a long shot. Second terms are at best an anticlimax.

CBC

Clinton's speech was forceful but perhaps not the stuff of history. It drew a mixed reaction from spectators. Second terms are rarely ones of great achievement for American presidents. That might be especially true of a president facing a lawsuit, investigations, and a tough agenda at home and abroad. President Clinton has invited Canada's Prime Minister Chrétien to Washington for a big visit in March or April. Obviously, there are a few differences—Cuba, trade issues—but Chrétien is probably feeling pretty good about dealing again with a man who, more than any other previous American president, has supported Canadian unity.

FRANCE 2

Recent events in the news sum up what awaits Mr. Clinton in the coming years: Israel withdrew from Hebron under pressure from Washington. The Clinton sex scandal has resurfaced. Clinton wants to pursue the pacification of Bosnia and the Mideast peace process. The expansion of NATO and relations with China could cause friction between Paris and Washington.

The most spectacular of the political rituals of the United States was treated by the BBC, CBC, and FRANCE 2 as an occasion for discussing political scandals and limitations (see Table 7.3). They did not tell the story of a ceremony that renewed the hopes of U.S. citizens for achieving some of their shared traditional values so much as an event that presaged little national accomplishment.

Table 7.3
British, Canadian, and French Television Coverage of the 1996 U.S.
Presidential Inauguration

	Atten-tion	Con-sensus	Support	Author-ity	Image	Event	Evalua-tion
BBC	x			x			—
CBC	x			x			±
FRANCE 2	x			x			—

DISCUSSION

The BBC presented four items, each of which attributed considerable importance to the Republican National Convention. Its coverage of the convention's first night, featuring a speech by Gen. Colin Powell, came close to being a media event, at least in the modest sense in which the concept is defined in this study. Coders agreed that the item enhanced the image of the party and, possibly, even the image of the United States. However, the report made it clear that Powell's message of inclusion was not being heeded by his party. All four BBC items concluded with some critical statements. The general thrust of the comments was that the Republican Party had moved too far to the ideological Right and (for apparently good reasons) had lost the support of women, minorities, and the poor. Furthermore, the BBC concluded that Robert Dole was unlikely to win the presidential election.

Powell's speech was the only event of the Republican convention to which the CBC and FRANCE 2 paid much attention. The CBC juxtaposed the views expressed by Powell with a vivid depiction of Latino protest of the Republican positions on immigration and citizenship that Powell himself repudiated. Similarly, FRANCE 2 juxtaposed Powell's views on abortion with coverage of a NOW protest of a Republican position that, once again, Powell himself rejected. The FRANCE 2 items on Molinari's keynote address and the Christian Right, and the CBC items on Dole's proposed tax cut suggested, as did the BBC, that the principles ratified and publicized by the Republicans at their convention did not serve the interests of women, minorities, or America's less affluent.

These verbal and visual images produced by the public television corporations of friends-at-a-distance subverted the interests of the Republican party by identifying and vividly portraying widespread opposition to what the party itself said it stood for. The media did not support the principles the Republicans had ratified within and publicized through their convention. They called the principles into question. They also subverted party interests by casting serious doubt about the likelihood of the electoral success of its nominee.

The BBC devoted three long items to the Democratic Convention. None had more than two of the qualities used here to define a media event. BBC items credited President Clinton with improving the U.S. economy, particularly through the creation of new jobs. Reduction of crime during his first administration also was mentioned. Clinton was depicted as the likely winner of the November election, but not so much because of what he stood for, but because of the extreme positions endorsed by his Republican opposition. Clinton was credited with considerable political acumen, but his political success was depicted as being achieved at the cost of seriously compromising liberal principles he supposedly once had. Clinton's program for welfare reform received no support. References to the scandals he was expected to face were numerous.

Not one CBC item concerned with the Democratic National Convention approximated a media event. Unlike the BBC, the CBC had little to say about accomplishments of Clinton's first term in office. Rather, it reminded viewers of the Clinton administration's failed health-care proposals and the Whitewater and Dick Morris scandals. Clinton was termed an ideological "chameleon" whose probable electoral success could be attributed to the extremism of the Republicans and to his ability to present an image of himself as a compassionate individual. Clinton's proposals were not described as those of a national leader with an inspiring political vision for the twenty-first century, but as those of a "political engineer" with a number of individual policy proposals that somehow made him more forward looking than his opponent.

Like the BBC and the CBC, FRANCE 2 reiterated the problems and scandals facing Clinton in a second term. None of its items approximated a media event. What distinguished FRANCE 2's coverage was its treatment of the perceived change in Clinton's ideological stance. Rather than dismissing this as a political expedient, FRANCE 2 referred to the African Americans' sense of betrayal by the Democratic party and to the devastating consequences of the inconsistency between Clinton's rhetoric of compassion and policy initiatives on welfare.

The verbal and visual images produced by the public television corporations of America's friends-at-a-distance subverted the interests of the Democratic party with their greater emphasis on the past, present, and anticipated problems of the president, rather than on the accomplishments of his first administration. They said relatively little about party principles expressed in the formal speeches presented to the assembled delegates. After all, the broadcasters pointed out, during this presidency, political rhetoric largely has been divorced from administrative action. In light of this, principles ratified within and publicized through the convention appeared to mean little.

British, Canadian, and French coverage of the presidential inauguration did little more than repeat the observation that President Clinton would face an assortment of problems as he began his second term. These, it was noted, are likely to limit the opportunity for genuine accomplishment. To this the broadcasters added that, in general, the second term of U.S. presidents do not tend to be marked by major successes.

Very little was said by any broadcast organization about its own country's relationship with the Clinton administration. More generally, there was a remarkable absence of any discussion of U.S. foreign policy by any of the organizations during its coverage, either of the nominating conventions or of the presidential inauguration.

CONSTRUCTING IMAGES OF FRIENDS-AT-A-DISTANCE

The public television corporations of Britain, Canada, and France did not treat the ceremonial features of U.S. political conventions and the inauguration of the president of the United States with a sense of great seriousness. Rather, they tended to ignore them. The broadcast organizations did not suspend criticism of America's political officials during these occasions. Rather, they moved beyond a "ritualist posture of antagonism" and, on several occasions, took genuinely adversarial stances. For example, the BBC asserted that Dole simply was not a credible candidate. FRANCE 2 doubted that Dole could unite the party. Similarly, the CBC characterized Clinton as a shrewd and lucky politician, rather than as a visionary leader. FRANCE 2 pointed to the contradiction between Clinton's rhetoric of compassion and the actual policies he is advancing. Similarly, the BBC and the CBC pointed out that Clinton had abandoned the liberal wing of the Democratic party.

As data in Tables 7.1, 7.2, and 7.3 indicate, the public television corporations of Britain, Canada, and France did not treat our political conventions or the inauguration of our president as media events. Concern over the global domination of the United States in the 1990s, the political socialization of foreign journalists, and their less-than-complete integration into the U.S. public-relations state, as well as the widespread use of a conflict frame to tell stories about political events, were cited as reasons to anticipate this finding. Beyond this, data indicate that the media organizations constructed images that subverted the ideological interests of both political parties and did not enhance the image of the United States. Explanation of why the broadcast ideas and images should be understood as *subversive* rather than merely alternative to those appearing on U.S. domestic television can be located in the theoretically converging writings of Berger and Luckmann (1966) on symbolic universes and Bourdieu (1996) on questioning received ideas.

In Britain, Canada, and France, obviously, the United States was not portrayed as a morally reprehensible *enemy*. Nor, in 1996, was it depicted as an *ally* in an alliance against a common international threat. Nor was it characterized as an *adversary* in international trade who sometimes engaged in unreasonable or unfair practices. Rather, the United States was presented by all three broadcasting corporations as their respective nation's friend-at-a-distance. The major feature of such a nation–construct appears to be a focus on the social, cultural, and ideological cleavages that divide it, rather than on the symbols that unite it, or on political, economic, military, cultural, humanitarian, or other goals it is pursuing in the global arena. In the specific case of the United States, British, Canadian, and French constructions of their friend-at-a-distance makes their relationships with this country more symbolically equal than having to understand it as "the world's one indispensable nation."[3]

Further research might determine other features of friends-at-a-distance constructs by investigating the ways in which pairs of nations symbolically define one another in their news media. Such research could produce new insight into somewhat subtle forms of nationalism and propaganda. The next chapter will raise new questions about what happens to a friend-at-a-distance construct employed by the media of one nation to characterize another country when historical circumstances are changed by the emergence of a perceived common international threat.

NOTES

1. Individual nations also have specific grievances with the United States. For example, Canada views free trade in entertainment and telecommunications technology, strongly supported by the United States, as a threat to its cultural identity. France has denounced U.S. law providing for sanctions against foreign companies that invest in energy products in Iran and Libya. British leadership was highly critical of President Clinton's close, personal support of Sinn Fein President Gerry Adams.

2. Even calling attention to the contrived nature of the conventions does not necessarily undermine the intent of their producers. "In some moods we are connoisseurs of slickly produced images whether in political ads, pop art or popular movies. . . . Fascinated though we are with the process of image making, the other side of us believes the images we see. . . . Calling attention to the image as an image may not be enough to dissolve its hold. The reason is not that images are more powerful than words, but that certain images resonate with meanings and ideas that run deep in American culture" (Adatto 1993, 167–168).

Meaning and ideas expressed during nominating conventions, such as dramatically staged symbolic affirmations of commitment to consensus values by the dominant political parties, may "resonate" in this manner. To the extent that they do, their media coverage will perform the ideological functions of media events.

3. In his inaugural address, Bill Clinton used this phrase to describe the United States.

Part III

Implications

Chapter 8

Reassessing Our News Media and Our Understanding of Others and Ourselves

Over time, when we talk about ourselves, we tend to tell a rather consistent story about the world's most important nation whose democratic political system is the model for all other societies. In the narrative, our government is responsive to citizen interests; widespread expression of discontent with either domestic or foreign policy is rare. There is little argument in the country for long-range political and social goals that offer a vision of a social order substantially different from that of the present. Of those domestic problems that are generally recognized, most are understood as stemming from the acts of specific irresponsible agents—sometimes individuals and, less frequently, particular companies. Those that are acknowledged to have structural origins can be dealt with through slight adjustments in patterns of public spending.

Over time, our commercial news media also tend to tell a rather consistent story about the economic system of the United States in the global political economy. In the story, America's system of corporate capitalism has given U.S. citizens the world's highest material standard of living. It has created jobs throughout the world—more jobs at better pay than those available in many economies. It has made most commodities more affordable for everyone everywhere. All this has been accomplished without unreasonable corporate profit, worker exploitation, or unfair international trade practices. These achievements of American corporate capitalism stand in marked contrast to the worldwide failure of Communism and Socialism.

According to our commercial news media narrative, the United States is the world's most militarily powerful nation; we are the one remaining superpower. As such, the United States is prepared to respond to any serious threat to its national security and to the American way of life. From the end of World War II until 1990, most foreign conflicts were explained as episodes of the Cold War. Given sufficient consensus among political and economic elites, this would legitimate some form of intervention as a continuation of our fight against Communism in defense of freedom and American-style democracy. After the collapse of the Soviet Union, defining a situation as a threat to the nation became more difficult, though not exceedingly so, as coverage of the Gulf War illustrated.

The subsequent bombing of the World Trade Center in New York City in 1993, bombings of U.S. embassies in Tanzania and Kenya in 1998, an attack on the U.S. destroyer *Cole* in the port of Aden in Yemen in 2000, and then the devastating attacks on the World Trade Center and the Pentagon on September 11, 2001, followed by continuing threats of additional bombings and biological and chemical assaults on the United States, have now created an extraordinary and widely shared concern for the security of our nation. Whether a dominant news frame comparable to the Cold War frame will develop as a response remains to be seen. The preceding discussion suggests that such a frame would focus news attention on America's war against terrorism, prioritizing items that report domestic and international efforts to respond to our nation's new threat. The frame would employ a vocabulary constructing other nations as allies or enemies in this war. For some time, factors making the category friends-at-a-distance analytically useful probably would be assigned less importance. This would be ironic, for some of these factors, such as the global political, economic, and military power of the United States, and the worldwide influence of American popular culture, are among those commonly cited as sources of the deep resentment and hostility to which terrorist attacks are attributed. Adoption of the new frame also would be likely to promote selection of particular occurrences to characterize broad features of the war in ways generally supportive of official U.S. policy, and it would report domestic and international public opinion as generally favorable to that policy.

Given America's new war on terrorism, the probability of direct U.S. military involvement for peacekeeping or humanitarian purposes anywhere in the world is extremely low. Lack of elite consensus over the appropriateness of involvement in any nation not viewed as obviously relevant to U.S. political, economic, or strategic interests offers our commercial news media an opportunity to present a broad spectrum of views on the desirability of our engagement in the particular situation and, more generally, on the global responsibilities of our country. However, as long as the probability of direct U.S. military participation remains almost nonexistent, the American public is unlikely to see such genuine political debate in the media, because the conflict itself is unlikely to be considered worthy of media discussion.

Apart from the war on terrorism, there is one emerging international conflict to which our commercial news media might devote some attention. This is the struggle between supporters and opponents of economic globalization. Supporters include the U.S. government (or, at least, the most recent Clinton and Bush administrations) and major U.S. corporations. Opponents include a variety of socialist, labor, and environmental organizations in numerous countries. The preceding pages of this book suggest that our news media will talk in a reassuring manner about economic globalization, describing the process as a natural, inevitable, and universally beneficial extension of corporate capitalism, generally welcomed by citizens the world over. The preceding pages also suggest that such a media construction will become part of our stock of social knowledge, requiring no further analysis. Those raising critical questions about the desirability of globalization are likely to be marginalized by the mass media. Their claims, contradicting what have become typifications, generally will be dismissed as lacking credibility. Beyond this, the actions of globalization opponents might be described as weakening the economic prospects of the United States and, therefore, supporting a major goal of America's newly designated terrorist enemy. (These suggestions are, of course, hypotheses subject to verification or falsification by future empirical media research.)

REVISITING OUR TALK ABOUT THEM

British news media generally support their nation's involvement in the Falklands War. Such backing is illustrated by their reporting of the *General Belgrano* incident, Britain's approach to peace talks, and their characterization of public opinion on the war in Britain. Yet, despite the political socialization of British journalists, Britain's Lobby System, and enormous pressure exerted by the Thatcher government, British media, including the BBC, do express serious reservations about the legitimacy of the war. They do not systematically tell a war story of "us versus them" in which our use of military force is entirely appropriate, and in which our side obviously deserves the support of all our people. When they talked about their war, they occasionally overcame cultural and structural obstacles and accepted serious risks to their organizations, in order to facilitate and encourage active and critical public discussion of the policy of the British government.

U.S. commercial news media provide extensive coverage of the Falklands War, a brief conflict fought for vague purposes on a few small obscure islands. Our attention to the war, apart from its surprising occurrence, its drama, and the fact that it involves two U.S. allies, is associated with the practical and ideological interests of the U.S. government and business, which are best served by understanding particular aspects of the event. The U.S. military and the U.S. arms industry are concerned with the performance of various weapons systems under actual battle conditions. Also of interest to the Pentagon are the outcomes of various combat strategies employing new military technologies. U.S. businessmen and bankers are concerned with the effects of the war on the stability of international trade patterns.

Reporting the Falklands War gives U.S. news media the opportunity to remind audiences of Britain's colonial heritage and to renew the myth, maintained in their coverage of America's military involvements in Vietnam, Chile, Nicaragua, El Salvador, and the Persian Gulf, that our country's history bears few traces of such imperialism. Myths of this sort are a part of our national self-understanding. They are generally taken-for-granted features of the symbolic universe that legitimizes our highest political authority and the actions taken by our highest public officials. Falklands coverage also offers an opportunity to treat our closest ally as a friend-at-a-distance, at a time when there is some concern here over the degree of influence of Prime Minister Thatcher on the Reagan administration.

Discussions in previous chapters suggest two hypotheses concerning the consequences of media claims that Soviet interest in the Falklands War focused on matters of trade rather than on establishing Socialist states in the Western Hemisphere. First, in materials produced by U.S. government information agencies, there was a subsequent shift away from emphasis on the political aims of the Soviet Union and toward an emphasis on the benefits of a free-market economy, economic globalization, and free trade. Second, there was a subsequent shift in the relative importance of the various values that structure our news, with greater emphasis being placed on *responsible capitalism* and less on *altruistic democracy*. Findings supporting these hypotheses would also constitute further evidence that the line between *news* and *propaganda* is very fine.

Our commercial news media provide little coverage of the Iran–Iraq War, a prolonged and devastating conflict, but one that involves people and governments unlikely to be of great interest or concern to the American public at the time. However, over the eight-year course of the war, some events do attract media attention. None of these is directly related to the overall welfare of the citizens of Iran and Iraq.

Undoubtedly, many of our citizens are troubled by the possible consequences of the war for the fate of the U.S. hostages taken by Iran, and saddened by the deaths of U.S. sailors aboard the frigate *Stark*. Certainly, many are interested in learning why the *Stark*'s sophisticated warning system failed. More generally, they want to know who has authority to commit U.S. forces, and on what basis such decisions are made. More practically, many members of the American public are likely to be concerned about the possibility of a world oil crisis and the consequences of such a situation for prices they will pay for energy. Probably fewer had some concern about issues, such as the rise of Muslim militancy, political instability in the Persian Gulf region, and the increasing threat of international terrorism.

A review of public opinion polls taken over the eight-year period of the war would indicate the relative importance citizens actually attached to each of these topics. An analysis of leading news publications over the period would indicate the relative importance these media attached to each of these events and issues, and the terms in which each was discussed. The possible relationship between the two sets of findings might then be considered. Such analysis would reveal the nature and extent of any "disjunctions between the morselized and personalized language of private thought and discussion, and the official and public discourse that dominates the language of journalists and politicians" (Neuman, Just, and Crigler 1992, 112).

As discussed in Chapter 3, an unusual feature of U.S. commercial news media coverage of the 1987–1993 Palestinian uprising is the construction of the event that runs counter to U.S. government policy and is dissonant with public opinion in this country. The media's understanding is not produced primarily through the choice of vocabulary to describe events, nor through the repetition of political arguments, but is conveyed visually through the selection and repeated presentation of pictures showing Palestinian children fighting Israeli soldiers to characterize the conflict and support a dramatic David-versus-Goliath narrative.

Preceding chapters indicate that our news media can and do produce material opposing government policy during periods of elite dissensus. They do not suggest any hypotheses to account for the media's favorable coverage of the Palestinians' resistance to Israeli rule at a time when there is no apparent disagreement among political and economic leaders over America's support for Israel. Why our media offered such a pictorial representation of this internal war and not of others, such as the 1976 war between the government of Indonesia and the people of East Timor, in which an estimated 200,000 die as a result of famine, oppression, and fighting, remains unclear.

What we say about the Tiananmen Square uprising illustrates our commercial news media's inconsistent attachment to the value of objectivity, in any of its conventional interpretations. We praise members of the Chinese media who willingly risk serious personal and organizational consequences to report events at Tiananmen Square as they see and understand them. The potential consequences of their resistance to Chinese government pressure to promote an understanding of events sympathetic to government actions obviously are far greater than those faced by the BBC journalists who questioned their government's policy during the Falklands War—an effort to assert media independence we had congratulated five years earlier. Accordingly, our highest media accolades appear to have gone to those Chinese reporters who laid down their notebooks and joined students and workers in their protest of government policies.

Offering such praise of efforts to exercise autonomy, U.S. commercial news media proceed to tell a story of a struggle of Chinese youth for American-style democracy in their country. This construction misrepresents what the protesters themselves say are their goals. It expresses the ideological position of the U.S. government in the context of the Cold War. In the U.S. media's view, Communism is collapsing the world over, and people in all nations desire some form of political economy not substantially different from that of the United States. They want increased productivity from their economies and expanded popular participation in their governments. They are no longer motivated by the ideals of strong political integration, national power, and social equality.

Discussions in earlier chapters suggest that media narrative provides a frame of reference for understanding all of the countless individual events that comprise the Tiananmen Square uprising; none is in need of further explanation. Hence, the most celebrated news photograph taken during the conflict, that of a young man standing alone facing a stopped column of tanks, is understood in what seems to be a commonsense fashion. It is a picture of an extremely brave act of individual defiance of the power and authority of the Communist Chinese government. Any alternative interpretation is unthinkable. It is not, for example, a picture that calls attention to the restraint of the Chinese military and employs language to suggest that the Chinese Communist government has concern for the well-being of all of its citizens—including dissidents.

When we talk about the assassination of the democratically elected leader of a foreign nation, we tend to focus attention on four topics: (1) the historic ties between the United States and the leader's country; (2) the role of the fallen leader in pursuing objectives consistent with the interests of the United States, as defined by our administration at that time; (3) our interest in continuing support of the country; and (4) our renewed concern about threats to regional political and economic stability raised by the assassination. The leader is described as having charismatic qualities, and the assassination is presented as a *tragedy* for his/her nation. Those aspects of the assassination that are highlighted are dramatic and convey a sense of the fragility of democratic rule. U.S. and international public opinion about the leader is reported as mixed, but overall favorable, because he/she pursued policies supported by the United States. The state funeral for the leader is presented as a *media event* (Dayan and Katz 1992) rather than merely *news*.

This pattern of coverage of the assassinations of democratically elected foreign leaders further suggests the enduring nature of several of the news values identified by Gans (1979) more than two decades ago. Ethnocentrism is seen in the emphasis on the historic ties between the leaders' nations and the United States, in the identification of the importance of the leaders whose pursuit of policies is consistent with the international objectives of the United States, and in the need to continue supporting the nations, to ensure that their successors will continue these policies.

The presence of a democratic political system (if not entirely altruistic democracy) is understood as a major reason for our support of the nations. The fallen leaders of Israel, Egypt, and India are praised for their resistance to the pressure exerted by various antidemocratic movements (often termed *extremist*), who are opposed to the continuing recognition of the political rights of minorities in their countries.

Though none of their nations has a free-market economy equivalent to that of the United States, each of the leaders favored some form of privatization. Furthermore, each had been reported as positively favoring economic reform, particularly improving housing and health conditions and generating jobs for the poorest segments of their populations. That might be understood as moving their economies in the direction of *responsible capitalism* and segments of their populations away from hostility toward the United States.

News media biographies of each of the assassinated heads of state reflect the values of individualism, moderatism, social order, and national leadership. Each is characterized as an extraordinary person who, over decades, played a unique and decisive role in shaping the course of his/her nation's history. Each is credited with successfully opposing political and religious zealots in his/her nation. Each is recognized for having built and maintained a viable political coalition that made the orderly conduct of state affairs possible. To an extent beyond that realized by most American presidents, each leader came to represent his/her nation symbolically, as well as politically, in the international arena.

The analysis of our commercial news media's Americanization of the state funerals of Rabin, Sadat, and Gandhi (Moeller 1999) provides additional graphic evidence of ethnocentrism. It illustrates how our media can revitalize our civil religion (Bellah 1975) by recalling our martyrs, national ceremonies, and sacred places. It suggests that news media can remind us of our sense of a shared history and of the socially constructed vision of "who we are" and "what we stand for."

REVISITING THEIR TALK ABOUT US

Prior to 1990, the United States was understood as an enemy of Russia, and consequently received considerable attention on *Vremya*. The negative image of the United States was useful in Soviet construction of a positive national self-image. America was depicted as seeking global political, economic, and cultural domination. Our political system, described as run by and in the interest of corporate elites, was anything but an altruistic democracy. Our capitalist economy was reported to produce great wealth for a small ownership class at the expense of workers, not only in America, but particularly in Third World nations; American capitalism was not socially responsible. Those able to do so were said to be fleeing America's largest cities, leaving behind African Americans and other minorities whose chances in life continued to diminish. Individualism and competitiveness, characterological counterparts of capitalism, were identified as sources of popular support for leaders and policies exhibiting little compassion for the society's less fortunate members.

During the Cold War, the Russian government's definition of the United States as an *enemy* influences the language choices its news media make to describe our domestic events and international actions. As illustrated throughout this book, "language is not neutral but a highly constructive mediator" (Fowler 1991, 1). The descriptions, in turn, continue the process of image-making by directing attention to events typifying the social construction. News reporting the occurrences completes the circle by legitimating the language use.

As a former enemy, an image of the United States no longer is an integral component of the symbolic universe presented by Russian news media as a depiction of political reality, and, therefore, it cannot be used by Russian citizens as a basis for understanding political and economic events, remote and near. For the Russian public, an image of the United States becomes largely irrelevant to making sense of their daily problem-filled lives. International news generally loses its interest. The Million Man March, which would have given *Vremya* an opportunity to discuss racism in America and arouse indignation among the Russian public, is treated as an event organized by a marginal religious leader with only limited support from African Americans. As such, the item probably is, at most, of passing interest to Russian viewers.

Kompas's coverage of the actions of the United States and Iraq prior to the outbreak of the Gulf War provides an illustration of foreign media construction of U.S. military involvement that does not legitimate the action. United States commercial news media paid great attention to the situation, labeling it a "crisis." This invested events with considerable and immediate importance. In the absence of the American public's belief in the significance of what was happening, the Bush administration would have en-

countered greater resistance to investing major material and symbolic resources and to potentially risking an uncertain number of lives involved
in the direct intervention by the U.S. military. *Kompas's* reports on the
buildup to the conflict attributed less significance to the situation, illustrating, by way of contrast to U.S. news media reports, the constructed nature of *importance* and the ideological role of word choice in describing an
event as a "crisis." Although *The New York Times* may have helped convince its domestic audience to support the U.S. war effort, *Kompas's* pattern of coverage was consistent with the neutral position of the Indonesian
government. By 1990, Indonesia's major newspaper appears to have been
able to resist some of the influence of American media, to which it routinely turned for material, but not the restraint of being part of a developmental press system. Although part of a commercial free-press system, *The
New York Times* operated like *Kompas* in constructing news consistent with
the official position expressed by its nation's government.

A comparison of the coverage by *Kompas* and *The New York Times* also illustrates the role of values in the construction of news. In the United
States, reporters of one nation's violation of the political sovereignty of another establishes the aggressor as a prominent villain on the world scene.
News that a nation violates the human rights of its citizens makes that nation even more reprehensible—potentially one against which the U.S. government ought to apply sanctions of some sort. In Indonesia, due at least
in part to its history with East Timor, reports of the violation of the political sovereignty of one nation by another, and reports of human rights violations appear to be given less attention and to have less serious implications. Even when our news media and the news media of another nation
describe particular actions of some third country in the same way (e.g.,
"This was a violation of national sovereignty"; "The human rights of its
citizens were violated"), the meanings of the characterizations of those actions imposed by the different media are not identical.

Just as there are limits on the ability of our commercial news media to
legitimate the use of American military power to us and to international
audiences (when that is the character of their construction), there also are
limits on their ability to legitimate our policies and practices of international trade. Radio Japan's reporting of U.S.–Japanese trade disputes illustrates the capacity of the media of other nations to construct clear and consistent images of the United States that contrast sharply with those we
routinely encounter in our news stories and accept as unbiased representations of political reality. In a historical period in which trade relations
are among the most important feature of international affairs, Radio Japan's construction of the United States suggests that images of other nations as trading partners also may have become necessary components of
the political cultures of economically powerful nations.

Prior to September 11, 2001, there was mounting evidence that our friends-at-a-distance were becoming increasingly critical of the United States. Long-standing differences on social issues, such as the death penalty, gun control, and access to health care, remained, as did the concern over cultural imperialism, resulting, in part, from the prominence of American products in European film, music, fashion, and even fast-food markets. More-recent dissatisfaction stemmed from the perceived ability of the United States to direct European military affairs through the manipulation of NATO, to use the World Trade Organization as a tool to advance corporate interests, and to set the rules of globalization through influence over the management of the International Monetary Fund (see Daley 2000). Added to this was the lack of support for major international treaties on the environment and on nuclear weapons on the part of George W. Bush's administration.

The preceding suggested that the accumulation of post–Cold War grievances held by our friends-at-a-distance would be reflected in their news stories' becoming increasingly distinct from those constructed by our commercial news organizations. Future differences might have extended beyond reiterating long-heard criticisms of American society, culture, and various political, economic, and military defense policies, and treating U.S. media events as news. Future research might investigate a number of related questions. The questions are deceptively simple and would require the acquisition of vast amounts of data, and content analysis employing a sophisticated research design to provide valid answers.

1. Did the amount of attention devoted to U.S. domestic affairs change significantly between 1990 and 2000?

2. Did the amount of attention devoted to U.S. involvement with particular international issues, such as the role of the U.S. military or U.S. support of various international treaties, change significantly over this ten-year period?

3. Was there any significant change in the various sources cited in items dealing with U.S. domestic affairs (e.g., less reliance on material supplied by the U.S. government and its agencies and greater inclusion of material provided by sources such as U.S. labor, consumer, and environmental organizations)?

4. Was there any significant change in the various sources cited in items dealing with U.S. international affairs (e.g., less reliance on material supplied by the U.S. government and its agencies and greater inclusion of material provided by sources such as U.S. and international social movement organizations, international agencies, and the governments of other nations)?

5. Was there any significant change over the decade in the amount of favorable and unfavorable public sentiment toward the United States around the world reported by the news media of our friends-at-a-distance?

As illustrated by the case study of Russian television news, after 1990, the Cold War frame largely was abandoned by our former enemy. Russian media had become absorbed with its own country's internal problems, and the political utility of talking about us had diminished considerably. Answers to the questions above would indicate if a new, post–Cold War news frame was also being employed by the media of our friends-at-a-distance between 1990 and 2000, and would reveal the qualities assigned to the United States in this frame. Assuming that such a frame were identified, answers to the following questions would suggest whether our friends-at-a-distance now talk about us in yet another way in the context of what CNN has labeled "America's new war." This would also indicate the extent to which reporting of the issues that divided the United States from its long-term allies in the ten-year, post–Cold War era had been overshadowed by reporting of issues associated with our mutual concern with international terrorism.

6. Since the 2001 direct attacks on the United States,

    a. has there been a change in the amount of attention devoted to U.S. domestic affairs (other than those directly linked to the attacks)? If the amount of attention has changed, what issue areas now receive more or less coverage?

    b. has there been a change in the amount of attention devoted to U.S. international affairs (other than those directly linked to the attacks)? If the amount of attention has changed, what actions and policies now receive more or less coverage?

    c. has there been a change in the various sources cited in items dealing with U.S. domestic affairs (other than those directly linked to the attacks)?

    d. has there been a change in the various sources cited in items dealing with U.S. international affairs (other than those directly linked to the attacks)?

    e. has there been a change in the amount of favorable and unfavorable public sentiment toward the United States around the world reported by our friends-at-a-distance?

REVISITING OUR TALK ABOUT OURSELVES

Research reviewed throughout this book has demonstrated that the image of the United States constructed by our commercial news media has been shaped by enduring news values, by historically specific relations between our media and our government, and by the historical context in which the news was produced. It could be informed, as well, by what they have said and are saying about us.

Previous discussions have provided illustrations of the continuing impact of the news values Herbert Gans (1979) identified decades ago. For example, the value of responsible capitalism made it unlikely that *The Cincinnati Enquirer* would not finally apologize formally for its publication of a special section detailing alleged misdeeds of Chiquita Brands International in Costa Rica, Honduras, and Columbia. The amount of control exercised by the Pentagon over media coverage of the Gulf War was far greater than that it exercised over our reporting of the Vietnam War, illustrating changed relations between media and government and a change in their consequences. In the new historical context created by the collapse of the Soviet Union, our media refocused its news to portray America, not so much as a defender of democratic and humanitarian ideals against totalitarian Communism, but as a promoter of globalization and its universal benefits.

Enduring news values and evolving government—media relations can be expected to continue to influence our commercial news media coverage of domestic and international events in the new historical context created on September 11, 2001. Research on news coverage of the wars in Vietnam and the Persian Gulf suggests that news presentations will exhibit considerable ethnocentrism, will rely heavily on materials provided by official government sources, and will offer few discussions of dissenting perspectives on government policy. The amount of media attention devoted to terrorism and efforts to combat terrorism obviously will overshadow discussions of other domestic and international events for some time. However, it seems unlikely that news presentations will locate terrorism in a broad historical context, discuss events in terms of the present structure of the world's political economy, or refer to ideological perspectives that divide the United States, and to a lesser extent other Western nations, from the rest of the world. The vocabulary used to describe events linked to terrorism can be expected to employ typifications (e.g., terrorists, Muslim extremists, terrorism-supporting nations, rogue states) in a newly constructed symbolic universe, which audiences are likely to understand in a commonsense way as a self-evident description of international relations in the context of America's new war.

If the war on terrorism drags on, influential sectors of the American public may become dissatisfied with the commercial news presentations that are obviously dominated by official perspectives. They may turn increasingly to foreign sources of news, such as BBC newscasts now regularly carried on many National Public Radio stations, global satellite telecasts, or on-line British and Canadian newspapers, to help them understand international events. What they say about us may become increasingly important to many of our citizens.

Over time, a high level of elite consensus over the details of government policy is likely to diminish. Such disagreement, coupled with existing dissatisfaction of some significant members of the public with news presentations, would probably prompt representatives of our commercial news media to begin asking more challenging questions of government officials. Hopefully, none would respond, even if only impulsively, "Whose side are you on?"

References

Abshire, David M. *International Broadcasting: A New Dimension of Western Diplomacy.* Beverly Hills, Calif.: Sage, 1976.

Adatto, Kiku. *Picture Perfect: The Art and Artifice of Public Image Making.* New York: Basic Books, 1993.

Adoni, Hanna, and Sherrill Mane. "Media and the Social Construction of Reality: Toward an Integration of Theory and Research." *Communication Research* 2(1987): 323–340.

Alexander, Laurien. *The Voice of America from Detente to the Reagan Doctrine.* Norwood, N.J.: Ablex, 1988.

Alexseev, Mikhail A., and W. Lance Bennett. "For Whom the Gates Open: News Reporting and Government Source Patterns in the United States, Great Britain, and Russia." *Political Communication* 12(4)1995: 395–412.

Almond, Gabriel, and Sidney Verba. *The Civic Culture.* Boston: Little, Brown, 1965.

Altheide, David L. *An Ecology of Communication.* Hawthorne, N.Y.: Aldine de Gruyter, 1995.

Aluetta, Ken. "Raiding the Global Village." In Shanto Iyengar and Richard Reeves, eds. *Do the Media Govern? Politicians, Voters and Reporters in America*, pp. 82–89. Thousand Oaks, Calif.: Sage, 1997.

Andern, Gunnar. "Reliability and Content Analysis." In Karl E. Rosengren, ed. *Advances in Content Analysis*, pp. 43–68. Beverly Hills, Calif.: Sage, 1981.

Ansolabehere, Stephen, Roy Behr, and Shanto Iyengar. *The Media Game: American Politics in the Television Age.* New York: Macmillan, 1993.

Aronson, James. *The Press and the Cold War.* Boston: Beacon Press, 1973.

Bagdikian, Ben H. *The Media Monopoly*, 5th ed. Boston: Beacon Press, 1997.

Balfour, Michael Leonard Graham. *Propaganda in War, 1939–1945: Organizations, Policies and Publics in Britain and Germany.* Boston: Routledge & Kegan Paul, 1979.

Barton, Richard L. "Appropriating the 'Public Mind' of Other Nations in Press—
    Foreign Policy Management: A Case Study from Canadian/American Rela-
    tions." In Abbas Malek, ed. *News Media and Foreign Relations*, pp. 121–139.
    Norwood, N.J.: Ablex, 1997.
Bauder, David. *Campaign Is King on Cable News*. Associated Press Release, March
    2000.
Beckett, Katherine. "Media Depictions of Drug Abuse: The Impact of Official
    Sources." In Philo C. Wasburn, ed. *Research in Political Sociology 7*, pp. 161–
    182. Greenwich, Conn: JAI Press, 1995.
Bellah, Robert N. *The Broken Covenant: American Civil Religion in Time of Trial*. New
    York: Seabury Press, 1975.
Benjamin, Roger W. *The Fairness Debate in U.S.–Japan Economic Relations*. Philadel-
    phia: Temple University Press, 1991.
Bennett, W. Lance. *News: The Politics of Illusion*, 3rd ed. White Plains, N.Y.: Long-
    man, 1996.
———. "Toward a Theory of Press–State Relations in the United States." *Journal of
    Communication* 40(1990): 123–127.
Berelson, Bernard. *Content Analysis in Communication Research*. Glencoe, Ill.: The
    Free Press, 1952.
Berger, Peter, and Thomas Luckmann. *The Social Construction of Reality*. New York:
    Doubleday, 1966.
Berry, Nicholas O. *Foreign Policy and the Press: An Analysis of the New York Times
    Coverage of U.S. Foreign Policy*. Westport, Conn.: Greenwood, 1990.
Bourdieu, Pierre. *On Television*. New York: The Free Press, 1996.
Brown, James, and William P. Snyder. "Introduction: The Three Wars of 1982." In
    James Brown and William P. Snyder, eds. *The Regionalization of Warfare: The
    Falkland/Malvinas Islands, Lebanon and the Iran–Iraq Conflict*, pp. 1–6. New
    Brunswick, N.J.: Transaction Books, 1985.
Browne, Donald R. *International Radio Broadcasting*. New York: Praeger, 1982.
Campbell, Christopher P. *Race, Myth and the News*. Thousand Oaks, Calif.: Sage,
    1995.
Campbell, Karlyn Kohrs, and Kathleen Hall Jamieson. "Inaugurating the Presi-
    dency." In Herbert W. Simons and Aram A. Aghazarian, eds. *Form, Genre,
    and the Study of Political Discourse*, pp. 203–225. Columbia, S.C.: University of
    South Carolina Press, 1986.
Carnegie Endowment Study Group. *Changing U.S.–Japan Relations*. Washington,
    D.C.: Carnegie Endowment for International Peace, 1995.
Cheng, Chu-yuan. *Behind the Tiananmen Massacre: Social, Political and Economic Fer-
    ment in China*. Boulder, Colo.: Westview Press, 1990.
Cherry, Colin. *World Communication: Threat or Promise?* rev. ed. New York: Wiley, 1978.
CNN. "N.Y. Jews' Reactions to Slaying Varied." cnn.com/WORLD/9511/rabin/is-
    rael. November 5, 1995.
Cockburn, Alexander. "The Gulf War and the Media." In David Barsamian, ed. *Ste-
    nographers to Power: Media and Propaganda*, pp. 163–184. Monroe, ME: Com-
    mon Courage Press, 1992.
Cohen, Akiba A., Hanna Adoni, and Hillel Nossek. "Television News and the *Inti-
    fada*: A Comparative Study of Social Conflict." In Akiba Cohen and Gadi

Wolsfeld, eds. *Framing the Intifada: People and Media*, pp. 116–41. Norwood, N.J.: Ablex, 1993.

Cohen, Akiba, Hanna Adoni, and Charles Bantz. *Social Conflict and Television News*. Newbury Park, Calif.: Sage, 1990.

Cohen, Jeff. "The Gulf War as a Case Study in Media Coverage." In David Barsamian, ed. *Stenographers to Power: Media and Propaganda*, pp. 101–112. Monroe, Maine: Common Courage Press, 1992.

Collins, Catherine Anne, and Jeanne E. Clark. "Structuring the *Intifada* in *Al-Fajr Jerusalem* and *The Jersulam Post*." In Akiba A. Cohen and Gadi Wolsfeld, eds. *Framing the Intifada: People and Media*, pp. 192–205. Norwood, N.J.: Albex, 1993.

Combs, James E. *Dimensions of Political Drama*. Santa Monica, Calif.: Goodyear, 1980.

Conteh-Morgan, Earl. *Japan and the United States: Global Dimensions of Economic Power*. New York: Peter Lang, 1992.

Croteau, David, and William Hoynes. *The Business of Media: Corporate Media and the Public Interest*. Thousand Oaks, Calif.: Pine Forge Press, 2001.

———. *By Invitation Only: How the Media Limit Political Debate*. Monroe, Maine: Common Courage Press, 1994.

Cull, Nicholas John. *Selling War: The British Propaganda Campaign against American "Neutrality" in World War II*. New York: Oxford University Press, 1995.

Cumings, Bruce. *War and Television*. London: Verso, 1992.

Dahlgren, Peter. *Television and the Public Sphere: Citizenship, Democracy and the Media*. Thousand Oaks, Calif.: Sage, 1995.

Daley, Suzanne. "More and More, Europeans Find Fault with the U.S.: Wide Range of Events Viewed as Menacing." *The New York Times*, April 9, 2000.

Daniels, Gordon. "Japanese Domestic Radio and Cinema Propaganda, 1937–1945: An Overview." In K. R. M. Short, ed. *Film and Radio Propaganda in World War II*, pp. 293–318. Knoxville: University of Tennessee Press, 1983.

Davis, Dennis K. "News and Politics." In David L. Swanson and Dan Nimmo, eds. *New Directions in Political Communication: A Resource Book*, pp. 147–184. Newbury Park, CA: Sage, 1990.

Dayan, Daniel, and Elihu Katz. *Media Events: The Live Broadcast of History*. Cambridge, Mass.: Harvard University Press, 1992.

Deacon, David, and Peter Golding. *Taxation and Representation*. London: John Libber, 1994.

DeFleur, Melvin, and Sandra Ball-Rokeach. *Theories of Mass Communication*, 5th ed. New York: Longman, 1989.

DeLuca, Kevin Michael. *Image Politics: The New Rhetoric of Environmental Activism*. New York: Guilford Press, 1999.

Department of Information, Republic of Indonesia. *Indonesia: An Official Handbook*. Jakarta: Author, 1988.

Djiwandono, Soedradjat. "Problems of Foreign Trade and the Gulf Crisis." *The Indonesia Quarterly* 19(1991): 74–81.

Downing, John. *Internationalizing Media Theory: Transition, Power, Culture*. Thousand Oaks, Calif.: Sage, 1996.

———. "Trouble in the Backyard." *Journal of Communication* 38(1988): 5–32.

Eberwine, D., E. Manoff, and R. Schiffer. "The End of the Cold War and Opportunities for Journalism." In Everett E. Dennis, George Gerbner, and Yassen N. Zassoursky, eds. *Beyond the Cold War: Soviet and American Media Images*, pp. 126–150. Newbury Park, Calif.: Sage, 1991.

Eckstein, Harry, ed. *Internal War, Problems and Approaches*. New York: Free Press, 1966.

Edelman, Murray. *Constructing the Political Spectacle*. Chicago: University of Chicago Press, 1988.

Elder, Charles D., and Roger W. Cobb. *The Political Use of Symbols*. New York: Longman, 1983.

Entman, Robert M. "Framing: Toward a Clarification of a Fractured Paradigm." *Journal of Communication* 53(1993): 51–58.

———. "Framing U.S. Coverage of International News: Contrasts in Narratives of the KAL and Iran Air Incidents." *Journal of Communication* 41(4)1991: 6–27.

———. *Democracy without Citizens: Media and the Decay of American Politics*. New York: Oxford University Press, 1989.

Epstein, Edward J. *Beyond Fact and Fiction*. New York: Vintage, 1975.

———. *News from Nowhere*. New York: Random House, 1973.

Femenia, Nora. *National Identity in Times of Crisis: The Scripts of the Falklands–Malvinas Wars*. Commack, N.Y.: Nova Science, 1996.

Fialka, John J. *Hotel Warriors: Covering the Gulf War*. Baltimore: Johns Hopkins University Press, 1992.

Fishman, Mark. *Manufacturing the News*. Austin: University of Texas Press, 1980.

Fowler, Roger. *Language in the News: Discourse and Ideology in the Press*. New York: Routledge, 1991.

Fox, Elizabeth, ed. *Media and Politics in Latin America: The Struggle for Democracy*. Newbury Park, Calif.: Sage, 1988.

Frank, Andre Gunder. "A Third-World War: A Political Economy of the Persian Gulf War and the New World Order." In Hamid Mowlana, George Gerbner, and Herbert I. Schiller, eds. *Triumph of the Image: The Media's War in the Persian Gulf—A Global Perspective*, pp. 3–21. Boulder, Colo.: Westview, 1992.

Gamson, William A. *Talking Politics*. New York: Cambridge University Press, 1992.

———. "News as Framing." *American Behavioral Scientist* 33(1989): 157–161.

Gamson, William A., and Kathryn E. Lasch. "The Political Culture of Social Welfare Policy." In Shimon E. Spiro and Ephraim Yuchtman-Yaar, eds. *Evaluating the Welfare State: Social and Political Perspectives*, pp. 397–415. New York: Academic Press, 1983.

Gamson, William A., and Andre Modigliani. "Media Discourse and Public Opinion on Nuclear Power: A Constructionist Approach." *American Journal of Sociology* 95(1989): 1–37.

Ganley, Gladys, and Oswald Granley. *Unexpected War in the Information Age: Communications and Information in the Falklands Conflict*. Cambridge, Mass.: Harvard University Center for Information Policy Research, 1984.

Gans, Herbert J. *Deciding What's News*. New York: Random House, 1979.

Gelman, Andrew, and Gary King. "Why Do Presidential Election Polls Vary So Much When the Vote is Predictable?" Paper presented at Midwest Political

Science Association Meetings, Chicago, 1992. Cited in Ansolabehere, Behr, and Iyengar 1993, p. 161.

Ghorpade, Shailendra. "Source and Access: How Foreign Correspondents Rate Washington, D.C." *Journal of Communication* 34(1984): 32–40.

Giffard, C. Anthony. "Developed and Developing Nation News in U.S. Wire Service Files to Asia." *Journalism Quarterly* 61(1984): 14–19.

Gilboa, Eytan. "American Media, Public Opinion and the *Intifada*: A Comparative Study of Social Conflict." In Akiba Cohen and Gadi Wolsfeld, eds. *Framing the Intifada: People and Media*, pp. 93–115. Norwood, N.J.: Ablex, 1993.

———. *American Public Opinion Toward Israel and the Arab-Israeli Conflict*. Lexington, Mass.: Lexington Books, 1987.

Gitlin, Todd. *The Whole World Is Watching*. Berkeley: University of California Press, 1980.

Glasgow University Media Group (GUMG). *War and Peace News*. Philadelphia: Open University Press, 1985.

———. *More Bad News*. Boston: Routledge & Kegan Paul, 1980.

Graber, Doris A. *Mass Media and American Politics*. Washington, D.C.: CQ Press, 1993.

Grandin, Thomas. *The Political Uses of Radio*. Reprinted 1971. New York: Arno Press, 1939.

Gronbeck, Bruce E. "Popular Culture, Media and Political Communication." In David L. Swanson and Dan D. Nimmo, eds. *New Directions in Political Communication*, pp. 182–222. Newbury Park, Calif.: Sage, 1990.

Gudykunst, William, and Tsukasa Nishida. *Bridging Japanese/North American Differences*. Thousand Oaks: Calif.: Sage, 1994.

Hachten, William A. *The World News Prism: Changing Media of International Communication*, 5th ed. Ames: Iowa State University Press, 1999.

Hale, Julian. *Radio Power: Propaganda and International Broadcasting*. Philadelphia: Temple University Press, 1975.

Hall, Stuart. "The Rediscovery of 'Ideology': Return of the Repressed in Media Studies." In Michael Gurevitch et al., eds. *Culture, Society and the Media*, pp. 56–90. New York: Routledge, 1982.

Hallin, Daniel C. "Sound Bite News: Television Coverage of Elections." *Journal of Communication* 12(1992a): 5–24.

———. "The Passing of 'High Modernism' of American Journalism." *Journal of Communication* 42(1992b): 14–25.

———. "We Keep America on Top of the World." In Todd Gitlin, ed. *Watching Television*, pp. 9–41. New York: Pantheon, 1986.

———. *The "Uncensored War": The Media and Vietnam*. New York: Oxford University Press, 1986.

He, Zhou. *Mass Media and Tiananmen Square*. Commack, N.Y.: Nova Science Publishers, 1996.

Head, Sydney W. *World Broadcasting Systems: A Comparative Analysis*. Belmont, Calif: Wadsworth, 1985.

Hedebro, Goran. *Communication and Social Change in Developing Nations: A Critical View*. Ames: Iowa State University Press, 1982.

Herman, Edward S., and Robert W. McChesney. *The Global Media*. London: Cassell, 1997.

Herman, Edward S., and Noam Chomsky. *Manufacturing Consent: The Political Economy of the Mass Media*. New York: Pantheon Books, 1988.

Hersh, Jacques. *The U.S.A. and the Rise of East Asia since 1945: Dilemmas of the Post-war International Political Economy*. New York: St. Martin's Press, 1993.

Hess, Stephen. *International News and Foreign Correspondents*. Washington, D.C.: The Brookings Institution, 1996.

Higenberg, James F. *From Enemy to Ally: Japan, the American Business Press and the Early Cold War*. Landham, Md.: University Press of America, 1993.

Himmelstein, Hal. *Television Myth and the American Mind*. Westport, Conn.: Praeger, 1994.

Hodge, James. "Foreign News: Who Gives a Damn?" *Columbia Journalism Review* 35(Nov./Dec.1997): 48–52.

Holsti, Ole R. "Sampling Reliability and Validity." In Ole R. Holsti, ed. *Content Analysis for the Social Sciences and Humanities*, pp. 134–140. Reading, Mass.: Addison-Wesley, 1969.

Hourani, Albert. *A History of the Arab Peoples*. Cambridge, Mass.: Harvard University Press, 1991.

Ito, Youichi. "Mass Communication Theories in Japan and the United States." In William B. Gudykunst, ed. *Communication in Japan and the United States*, pp. 249–287. Albany: State University of New York Press, 1993.

Iyengar, Shanto. "Framing Responsibility for Political Issues." *Political Behavior* 12(1990): 19–40.

———. "Television News and Citizen Explanations of National Affairs." *American Political Science Review* 80(1988): 815–831.

Japan Broadcasting Corporation (NHK). "Broadcasting in Japan." In William E. McCavitt, ed. *Broadcasting around the World*, pp. 76–97. Blue Ridge Summit, Pa.: Tab Books, 1981.

———. Program Schedule, April–September, 1995. Tokyo: NHK, 1995.

Jensen, Carl. *Twenty Years of Censored News*. New York: Seven Stories Press, 1997.

Jowett, Garth S., and Victoria O'Donnell. *Propaganda and Persuasion*. Newbury Park, Calif.: Sage, 1986.

Kaplan, Abraham. *The Conduct of Inquiry: Methodology for Behavioral Science*. San Francisco: Chandler, 1964.

Kellner, Douglas. *The Persian Gulf TV War*. Boulder, Colo.: Westview, 1992.

Kracauer, Sigfried. "The Challenge of Content Analysis." *Public Opinion Quarterly* 17(1953): 631–642.

Lederman, Jim. *Battle Lines: The American Media and the Intifada*. New York: Henry Holt, 1992.

Lee, Martin, and Norman Solomon. *Unreliable Sources*. New York: Lyle Stuart, 1991.

Levy, Jack S., and Mike Froelich. "Causes of the Iran–Iraq War." In James Brown and William P. Snyder, eds. *The Regionalization of Warfare: The Falkland/Malvinas Islands, Lebanon and the Iran–Iraq Conflicts*, pp. 127–143. New Brunswick, N.J.: Transaction Books, 1985.

Lindblom, Charles. *Politics and Markets*. New York: Basic Books, 1977.

MacArthur, John R. *Second Front: Censorship and Propaganda in the Gulf War.* New York: Hill and Wang, 1992.

MacDonald, Callum A. "Radio Bari: Italian Wireless Propaganda in the Middle East and British Countermeasures." *Middle East Studies 13*(1977): 195–207.

Mark, Clyde. *Israel: U.S. Foreign Assistance Facts.* Washington, D.C.: Foreign Affairs and National Defense Division, Congressional Research Service, 1991a.

Mark, Stephen. "Observing the Observers at Tiananmen Square: Freedom, Democracy and the News Media in China's Student Movement." In Peter Li, Mark Steven, and Marjorie H. Li, eds. *Culture and Politics in China: An Anatomy of Tiananmen Square*, pp. 259–284. New Brunswick, N.J.: Transaction Books, 1991b.

Masmoudi, Mustapha. "The New World Information Order." Document 21, UNESCO *International Commission for the Study of Social Problems.* Paris: UNESCO, 1978.

McCarthy, John D., Clark McPhail, and Jackie Smith. "Images of Protest: Dimensions of Selection Bias in Media Coverage of Washington Demonstrations, 1982–1991." *American Sociological Review 61*(1996): 478–499.

McNair, Brian. *Images of the Enemy: Reporting the New Cold War.* London: Routledge, 1988.

McNeely, Connie. "The Determination of Statehood in the United Nations." In Philo C. Wasburn, ed. *Research in Political Sociology*, vol. 6, pp. 1–38. Greenwich, Conn.: JAI Press, 1993.

McPhail, Thomas L. 1987. *Electronic Colonialism: The Future of International Broadcasting and Communication.* Beverly Hills, Calif.: Sage, 1981.

McQuail, Dennis. *Mass Communication Theory*, 2nd ed. Newbury Park, Calif.: Sage, 1988.

Mickiewicz, Ellen. *Split Signals: Television and Politics in the Soviet Union.* New York: Oxford University Press, 1988.

——. *Media and the Russian Public.* New York: Praeger, 1981.

Moeller, Susan D. *Compassion Fatigue: How the Media Sell Disease, Famine, War and Death.* New York: Routledge, 1999.

Morley, David. "The Construction of Everyday Life: Political Communication and Domestic Media." In David L. Swanson and Dan Nimmo, eds. *New Directions in Political Communication: A Resource Book*, pp. 123–146. Newbury Park, Calif.: Sage, 1990.

Morrison, David E., and Howard Tumber. *Journalists of War: The Dynamics of News Reporting During the Falklands Conflict.* Newbury Park, Calif.: Sage, 1988.

Negrine, Ralph. *The Communication of Politics.* Thousand Oaks, Calif.: Sage, 1996.

Nester, William R. *American Power: The New World Order and the Japanese Challenge.* New York: St. Martin's Press, 1993.

Neuman, W. Russell, Marion R. Just, and Ann N. Crigler. *Common Knowledge: News and the Construction of Political Meaning.* Chicago: University of Chicago Press, 1992.

Nimmo, Dan D., and James Combs. *Subliminal Politics.* Englewood Cliffs, N.J.: Prentice Hall, 1980.

Nohrstedt, Stif A. "Ruling by Pooling." In Hamid Mowlana, George Gerbner, and Herbert I. Schiller, eds. *Triumph of the Image: The Media's War in the Persian Gulf—A Global Perspective*. Boulder, Colo.: Westview, 1992.

Nordenstreng, Karl. "Bitter Lessons." *Journal of Communication* 34(1984): 141–165.

Norris, Pippa. "The Restless Searchlight: Network News Framing of the Post–Cold War World." *Political Communication* 12(1995): 357–579.

O'Brien, Rita Cruise. "The Political Economy of Information: A North-South Perspective." In Geroge Gerbner and Marsha Siefert, eds. *World Communications: A Handbook*, pp. 37–44. New York: Longman, 1984.

Osborn, Michael. "Rhetorical Depiction." In Herbert W. Simons and Aram A. Aghazarian, eds. *Form, Genre, and the Study of Political Discourse*, pp. 79–107. Columbia, S.C.: University of South Carolina Press, 1986.

Paletz, David L. *The Media in American Politics: Contents and Consequences*. New York: Longman, 1999.

Paletz, David, and Robert M. Entman. *Media Power Politics*. New York: Free Press, 1981.

Parenti, Michael. *Inventing Reality: The Politics of the Mass Media*. New York: St. Martin's Press, 1986/1993.

Pearlstein, Steven. "Debate Goes On, But Terms Change." *The Washington Post*, December 3, 1999.

Pedeltry, Mark. *War Stories: The Culture of Foreign Correspondents*. New York: Routledge, 1995.

Qualter, Terence H. *Advertising and Democracy in the Mass Age*. New York: St. Martin's Press, 1991.

———. *Opinion Control in the Democracies*. New York: St. Martin's Press, 1985.

Radio Nederland Wereldomroep. *Media Wars: Propaganda Past and Present*. Hilversum, the Netherlands: Radio Nederland Transcription Service, 1982.

Real, Michael R. *Super Media: A Cultural Studies Approach*. Newbury Park, Calif.: Sage, 1989.

Remnick, David. *Lenin's Tomb: The Last Days of the Soviet Empire*. New York: Random House, 1993.

Righter, Rosemary. *Whose News? Politics, the Press and the Third World*. New York: Times Books, 1979.

Rosenblume, Mort. "The Western Wire Services and the Third World." In P. C. Horton, ed. *The Third World and Press Freedom*, pp. 104–126. New York: Praeger, 1978.

Sakwa, Richard. *Russian Politics and Society*. New York: Routledge, 1993.

Salisbury, Harrison E. *Without Fear or Favor: The New York Times and Its Times*. New York: Times Books, 1980.

Salwen, Michael, and Frances Matera. "Public Salience of Foreign Nations." *Journalism Quarterly* 69(1992): 623–632.

Sanger, David E. "America Finds It's Lonely at the Top." *The New York Times*, July 28, 1999.

Schiller, Herbert I. "On That Chart." *The Nation* (June 3, 1996): 16–18.

———. *Culture, Inc.* New York: Oxford University Press, 1989.

———. *Communication and Cultural Domination*. White Plains, N.Y.: International Arts and Sciences Press, 1976.

Schudson, Michael. *The Power of News*. Cambridge, Mass.: Harvard University Press, 1995.

———. "Deadlines, Datelines and History." In Karl Manoff and Michael Schudson, eds. *Reading the News*, pp. 79–108. New York: Pantheon Books, 1986.

———. *The News Media and the Democratic Process*. New York: Aspen Institute for Humanistic Studies, 1983.

———. *Discovering the News*. New York: Basic Books, 1978.

Schulman, Holly Cowan. *The Voice of America: Propaganda and Democracy*. Madison: University of Wisconsin Press, 1990.

Schutz, Alfred. *The Phenomenology of the Social World*. Reprinted. Evanston, Ill.: Northwestern University Press, 1932/1967.

Scott, William A. "Reliability of Content Analysis: The Case of Nominal Scale Coding." *Public Opinion Quarterly* 19(1955): 321–325.

Shane, Scott. *Dismantling Utopia: How Information Ended the Soviet Union*. Chicago: Ivan R. Dee, 1994.

Shoemaker, Pamela J., Lucy H. Danielian, and Nancy Brendlinger. "Deviant Acts, Risky Business and U.S. Interests: The Newsworthiness of World Events." *Journalism Quarterly* 68(1991): 781–795.

Shorenstein Center on the Press, Politics and Public Policy. *Turmoil at Tiananmen: A Study of U.S. Press Coverage of the Beijing Spring of 1989*. Cambridge, Mass.: John F. Kennedy School of Government, Harvard University, 1992.

Short, K. R. M. *Film and Radio Propaganda in World War II*. Knoxville: University of Tennessee Press, 1983.

Sigal, Leon V. "Sources Make the News." In Karl Manoff and Michael Schudson, eds. *Reading the News*, pp. 9–37. New York: Pantheon Books, 1986.

———. *Reporters and Officials: The Organization and Politics of Newsmaking*. Lexington, Mass.: D.C. Heath, 1973.

Smith, Anthony. *The Age of Behemoths: The Globalization of Mass Media Firms*. New York: Priority Press, 1991.

———. *The Geopolitics of Information: How Western Culture Dominates the World*. New York: Oxford University Press, 1980.

———. *The Shadow in the Cave: The Broadcaster, His Audience and the State*. Urbana: University of Illinois Press, 1973.

Smith, Larry David, and Dan Nimmo. *Cordial Concurrence: Orchestrating National Party Conventions in the Telepolitical Age*. New York: Praeger, 1991.

Soley, Lawrence C. *The News Shapers*. New York: Praeger, 1992.

Speier, Hans, and Margaret Otis. "German Radio Propaganda to France during the Battle of France." In Paul Lazarsfeld and Frank Stanton, eds. *Radio Research: 1942–1943*, pp. 208–247. Reprinted 1979. New York: Arno Press, 1944.

Sproule, J. Michael. *Propaganda and Democracy: The American Experience of Media and Mass Persuasion*. New York: Cambridge University Press, 1997.

Sutopo, Ishad. *Development News in Indonesian Dailies*. Singapore: AMIC, 1983.

Thelen, David. *Becoming Citizens in the Age of Television*. Chicago: University of Chicago Press, 1996.

Times Mirror (now Pew) Center for the People and the Press. "A Content Analysis: International News Coverage Fits Public's Ameri-Centric Mood" (undated news release on polls conducted from March 1 through June 30, 1995): 1–2. Cited in Paletz 1999: 321.

Tuchman, Gaye. *Making News: A Study in the Construction of Reality*. New York: Free Press, 1978.

Tunstall, Jeremy. *The Media are American*. London: Constable, 1977.

Turpin, Jennifer. *Reinvesting the Soviet Self: Media and Social Change in the Former Soviet Union*. Westport, Conn.: Praeger, 1995.

Utagawa, Reizo. "Prospects and Complementaries in U.S.–Japan Economic Relations." In Richard L. Grant, ed. *Strengthening the U.S.–Japan Partnership in the 1990s*, pp. 18–39. Washington, DC: The Center for Strategic and International Studies, 1992.

van Ginneken, Jaap. *Understanding Global News*. Thousand Oaks, Calif.: Sage, 1998.

Vatikioitis, Michael. "Saddam or Satan." *Far East Economic Review*. (September 20, 1990): 20.

Wallis, Roger, and Stanley Baran. *The Known World of Broadcast News*. New York: Routledge, 1990.

Wasburn, Philo C. *Broadcasting Propaganda: International Radio Broadcasting and the Construction of Political Reality*. Westport, Conn.: Praeger, 1992.

Wolfsfeld, Gadi. *Media and Politics Conflict: News from the Middle East*. New York: Cambridge University Press, 1997.

Woodward, Gary. *Perspectives on American Political Media*. Boston: Allyn & Bacon, 1997.

Wu, H. Denis. "Systematic Determinants of International News Coverage: A Comparison of 38 Countries." *Journal of Communication* 50(2)2000: 110–130.

Zassoursky, Yassen. "Changing Images of the United States and the Soviet Union." In Everett Dennis, George Gerbner, and Yassen Zassoursky, eds. *Beyond the Cold War: Soviet and American Images*, pp. 151–168. Newbury Park, Calif.: Sage, 1991.

Zeman, Zbynek A. *Nazi Propaganda*. London: Oxford University Press, 1964.

Author Index

Subject Index

About the Author

Philo C. Wasburn is Professor of Sociology at Purdue University. He is the author of *Political Sociology: Approaches, Concepts, Hypotheses* and *Broadcast Propaganda: Radio Broadcasting and the Construction of Political Reality* (Praeger, 1992).